30.99

FAILED CRUSADE

STEPHEN F. COHEN

FAILED CRUSADE

AMERICA AND THE TRAGEDY
OF POST-COMMUNIST RUSSIA

W · W · NORTON & COMPANY

NEW YORK   LONDON

For information about permission to reproduce selections from this book, write to Permissions, W. W. Norton & Company, Inc., 500 Fifth Avenue, New York, NY 10110

The text of this book is composed in M Walbaum
with the display set in Beach Savage
Composition by Gina Webster
Manufacturing by The Haddon Craftsmen, Inc.
Book design by Margaret M. Wagner

Library of Congress Cataloging-in-Publication Data
Cohen, Stephen F.
    Failed crusade : America and the tragedy of post-Communist Russia / Stephen F. Cohen.
        p. cm.
    Includes index.
    ISBN 0-393-04964-7
    1. United States—Foreign relations—Russia (Federation) 2. Russia (Federation)—Foreign relations—United States. 3. United States—Foreign relations—1989–1993. 4. United States—Foreign relations—1993– I. Title.
E183.8.R9 C56 2000
327.73047—dc21 00-035501

W. W. Norton & Company, Inc., 500 Fifth Avenue, New York, N.Y. 10110
www.wwnorton.com

W. W. Norton & Company Ltd., 10 Coptic Street, London WC1A 1PU

1 2 3 4 5 6 7 8 9 0

For Katrina

With Love and Gratitude

CONTENTS

INTRODUCTION

Russia is a country that no matter
what you say about it, it's true.
Will Rogers

Will Rogers was right, but it's no longer a joke. What
influential Americans have believed and said about
post-Communist Russia under Boris Yeltsin and Vladimir
Putin, and acted upon, has contributed to a world of
unprecedented danger.

It is not the first time that Americans have sought
and found in that remote and different civilization primarily "the kind of Russia we want." In the twentieth
century alone, there was the Red Menace of the 1920s
and the Stalinist future that purportedly worked of the
Depression-era 1930s; the populist ally of the war
against Nazi Germany and the immutable "evil empire"
of the early 1980s; the technological "colossus" that put
the first satellite in space in 1957 and the economic
"basket case" of the late 1980s.

Some of those perceptions had serious consequences, but none so perilous as the official U.S. view, widely shared by journalists, scholars, and others, that since the end of the Soviet Union in 1991, Russia has been a nation ready, willing, and able to be transformed into some replica of America. It has contributed to a human tragedy on a massive scale and, for the first time in history, the destabilization of a fully nuclearized country.

Failed Crusade can be read as contemporary political history, a warning, and an urgent call for a different American relationship with post-Communist Russia. Part I is an indictment, though I hope a civil one, of the U.S. professions that most engaged (actually misengaged) Russia in the 1990s, including my own colleagues in academic life. Part II is my dissenting account of Russian developments and American-Russian relations since 1992. Though the essays in that section were written as events unfolded, I have updated them here in postscripts. Part III proposes a fundamentally new U.S. policy toward our former superpower rival.

This critical book may not be well received by my fellow academics or by journalists, but readers should not mistake my criticism of the media for ivory-tower contempt. Ever since I had to decline a New York newspaper's offer to become its Moscow correspondent in the late 1970s, journalism has been my avocation. In the 1980s, I even wrote a syndicated column ("Sovieticus") for *The Nation* magazine. And in addition to commenting on Russian affairs on other network broadcasts, I have been a CBS News analyst for more than a decade.

In short, no professional antipathies underlie this book, only alarm over what has happened in Russia, my own country's complicity, and the dangers we now face. During many years of visiting and living in Russia, I have often heard its fervent patriots say, "The West doesn't need the truth about Russia." But we do, now more than ever.

I have several important debts to acknowledge. Despite disagreeing with most of its contents, Professor George Breslauer allowed me to rehearse an early fragment of Part I in the valuable journal he edits, *Post-Soviet Affairs*. Marina Spivak helped me prepare the book in essential ways, both by assisting with the research and by putting my old-fashioned manuscript on the now necessary disc. James Mairs, my longtime friend and editor at W. W. Norton, coped with my missed deadlines and supported me in related crises, as he always has.

Above all, there are my wife, Katrina vanden Heuvel, to whom the book is lovingly dedicated, and our nine-year-old daughter, Nika. As a Russia specialist herself and the editor of *The Nation*, Katrina has her own informed and strongly held views on the subjects treated in *Failed Crusade*. I am greatly indebted to her for many matters of substance and style, and especially for ridding my drafts of mistakes and misjudgments. Any that remain are my own stubborn doing.

It may seem odd to thank a child for anything more than forgiving an author's parental absence, but it is different with Nika. She has been with us during every stay in Russia, more than twenty, since her birth in 1991, just before the starting point of this book. Through her fresh eyes and innocent questions about life there, I have seen and thought about things I would otherwise have missed. For that, and for accepting Russia in her own life, I am also lovingly beholden.

S.F.C.

New York City
June 2000

Note on Transliteration

There are various ways of spelling Russian names in English. In the text, I have used the form most familiar or accessible to general readers. In the notes, wherever Russian-language sources are cited, I have used the Library of Congress system of transliteration (though without soft or hard signs) so that specialists will easily recognize them.

PART 1

RUSSIA-WATCHING

WITHOUT RUSSIA

The Russian prospect over the coming years and decades is more promising than ever before in its history.
David Remnick, journalist, 1997

The guarded optimism of the economists . . . seems justified; the "holistic" transformation of Russia will continue.
Richard Ericson, economist, 1998

Optimism prevails universally among those who are familiar with what is going on in Russia.
U.S. Vice President Al Gore, 1998

Russia looks terrific to me, compared to the way it looked in the 1970s, 1980s, or in 1992.
Robert Kaiser, journalist, 1999

Russia is a radically different place today than it was ten years ago. . . . And just seven years into this transition, basic arrows on all the big issues are pointing in the right direction.
Michael McFaul, political scientist, 1999

Only a few years from now . . . what will be left standing is the towering edifice of Yeltsin's achievement.
Leon Aron, biographer, 2000

We want to remind the world that transition can kill.
Head of the Red Cross in former Soviet Georgia, 1996

Russia is a zone of economic catastrophe.
N. Petrakov and V. Perlamutrov,
Russian economists, 1997

It is obvious that today Russia is in the deepest
crisis of its entire history.
Aleksei Podbereskin,
Russian nationalist leader, 1999

A human crisis of monumental proportions is
emerging in the former Soviet Union.
U.N. Development Program, 1999

Russians are deeply pessimistic about the
direction of their country: 78 percent believe
Russia is heading in the wrong direction; only
7 percent believe the country is heading in
the right direction.
Anti-Defamation League Survey, 1999

As a result of the Yeltsin era, all the fundamental
sectors of our state, economic, cultural, and moral
life have been destroyed or looted. We live literal-
ly amid ruins, but we pretend to have a normal
life. . . . We heard that great reforms were being
carried out in our country. They were false
reforms because they left more than half of our
country's people in poverty. . . . What does it
mean to continue these reforms? Will we continue
looting and destroying Russia until nothing is left?
. . . God forbid these reforms should continue.
Alexandr Solzhenitsyn, 2000

America's Russia-watchers, with only a few exceptions, committed malpractice throughout the 1990s. The results have undermined our values and jeopardized our nation's security.

When the Soviet Union ended in 1991, four American professions laid claim to special expertise on post-Communist Russia: government policymakers, economic and financial advisers, journalists, and scholars. Mainstays of what was known as the "Washington Consensus," Russia specialists in all those occupations professed to know the cure for what ailed their subject, gave regular assurances about the ongoing treatment, and, while noting occasional relapses, predicted a full recovery. In reality, their prescriptions, reports, and prognoses were fundamentally and predictably wrong.

A full inventory of the failures of U.S. policymakers, particularly during the years of the Clinton administration, belongs to the final section of this book. We need to recall here, however, that their grand policy was nothing less than missionary—a virtual crusade to transform post-Communist Russia into some facsimile of the American democratic and capitalist system.

Moreover, it was not only an official project; it captivated investors, journalists, and scholars as well.

The Crusade for the "Russia We Want"

The idea that the United States might one day remake Russia in its own image, or at least "do their thinking for them," originated after World War II among extreme advocates of the forty-year Cold War.[2] By 1992, the first post-Soviet year and last year of the Bush administration, it had reemerged in the American mainstream. In April, for instance, a special gathering of government, business, media, and academic representatives recommended that the United States and its allies "deeply and swiftly engage themselves in the process of transforming the political and economic orders of these former Soviet republics." A policymaker-turned-academic was more specific: "The West should create an elite corps of experts to live in the former Soviet Union and help officials there run government and business."[3]

But it was the Clinton administration that turned the missionary impulse into an official crusade—though, it should be emphasized, with enthusiastic bipartisan support in Congress. Almost immediately after President Bill Clinton's inauguration in January 1993, his experts were privately discussing "how best to reform Russia" and formulating a policy of American tutelage. The "whole policy" that emerged, as a State Department official later explained, was "aimed at the domestic transformation of Russia."[4] In effect, the United States was to teach ex-Communist Russia how to become a capitalist and democratic country and oversee the process of conversion known as a "transition." Certainly, Russia was not to be trusted to find its own kinds of change, lest it wander off, as a media enthusiast of the crusade warned, on "a strange, ambivalent path of its own confused devising."[5]

The lessons to be taught were simple but stern. Economic reform meant "shock therapy" and tight-fisted monetarism, especially severe budgetary austerity, an end to Soviet-era consumer and welfare subsidies, wholesale privatization of Russian state enterprises and other assets, opening the country's markets to foreign producers, and a minimal role for the government. Political reform came to mean little more than fulsome support for President Boris Yeltsin because, top Clinton officials explained, "Yeltsin represents the direction toward the kind of Russia we want."[6] In addition to free instructions, which meant "dictating national economic policy," the administration promised to help finance the transition, primarily through loans by the International Monetary Fund (IMF), unless Russia "fails to meet our conditions."[7]

In that spirit, legions of American political missionaries and evangelists, usually called "advisers," spread across Russia in the early and mid-1990s.[8] Funded by the U.S. government, ideological organizations, foundations, and educational institutions, they encamped wherever the "Russia we want" might be proselytized, from political movements, trade unions, media, and schools to Moscow offices of the Russian government itself.

Among other missionary deeds, U.S. citizens gave money to favored Russian politicians, instructed ministers, drafted legislation and presidential decrees, underwrote textbooks, and served at Yeltsin's reelection headquarters in 1996.[9]

For the sake of appearances, all of this had to be done, of course, with some diplomacy. Rarely if ever was the Clinton administration as bluntly missionary as the former national security adviser who announced that Russia's "economic and even political destiny . . . is now increasingly passing into de facto Western receivership." Or as categorical as the anonymous programmatic letter that circulated in Washington in 1993: "The key to [Russia's] democratic recovery is no longer in its hand. It is in ours."[10] Instead, Clinton officials periodically made a special point of declaring (usually when the crusade was going badly), "Russians themselves have to decide. We can't do it for them."

But that was not how the administration really thought or made policy, as evidenced, to take only a few random examples, by its unrelenting insistence on "our conditions"; by the U.S. ambassador's boast in 1996 that "without our leadership . . . we would see a considerably different Russia today"; and by the testimony of a diplomatic insider that Vice President Al Gore, who played a leading role in the policy, "undertook to reinvent Russia." Indeed, as late as 1999, one of the crusade's chief architects was still extolling it: "Our policy toward Russia must be that of a lighthouse. . . . They can locate themselves against this light."[11]

By then, the crusade had long since crashed on the rocks of Russian reality. (One direct result was more anti-Americanism than I had personally ever observed in forty years of studying and visiting Soviet and post-Soviet Russia.) How badly the Clinton policy failed may be a matter of opinion, and we will return to it in the final part of this book. My own view, as readers will understand later on, is that it was the worst American foreign policy disaster since Vietnam, and its consequences more long-term and perilous.

But we can judge the failure by exact criteria. After the breakup of the Soviet Union in 1991, the foremost goal of U.S. policymakers should have been a Russia in full control of its enormous quantities of nuclear weapons and other devices of mass destruction, and therefore one that was prospering, politically stable, at peace, and fully cooperating with the United States on the most threatening international problems. As the twenty-first century began, neither Russia nor Russian-American relations looked much like that.

American financial specialists on post-Communist Russia also failed spectacularly, and for related reasons. They bought zealously into the great crusade, which for them meant "Russia's emerging market." They too set out to build a neo-America on the Moscow River by using the "best minds that Wall Street and Washington could muster." Among them was the billionaire financier and philanthropist George Soros, who personally pledged "to direct the means for solving today's pressing problems in the Russian economy."[12]

U.S. investors were as missionary in their way as the Clinton administration. "Prominent U.S. investment advisers packaged most of the Russian bond offerings," a former *Wall Street Journal* correspondent reminds us, and "American stock-brokers wrote the book on Russia's supposed industrial recovery." Solicitations they sent to potential clients could have come from an American businessman already in Moscow: "This is entrepreneur's heaven. There's no telling how quickly this country . . . could look like the United States." And so legions of Western profit seekers also invaded Russia "with American investors leading the charge."[13]

The failure of these Russia-watchers can be quantified, at least approximately. Western bankers and investors were reported to have suffered their biggest single loss in history, potentially $80 billion to $100 billion, in Russia's financial collapse in August 1998. (Soros' Quantum Fund alone lost $2 billion, and several small funds were bankrupted.) American financial specialists on post-Communist Russia also failed in another way. They entered the twenty-first century mired in charges that their ventures had resulted in huge money-laundering schemes and other dubious transactions.[14]

Nor can most American journalists who wrote about Russia in the 1990s look back with pride. Still worse, they had long been forewarned. At the birth of Communist Russia, Walter Lippmann and Charles Merz published an analysis of U.S. press coverage of the 1917 Revolution and ensuing civil war between Reds and Whites that became a celebrated textbook case study of journalistic malpractice. Lippmann and Merz found that in terms of professional standards the reporting was "nothing short of a disaster" and that the "net effect was almost always misleading." The main reason, they concluded, was that American correspondents and editors had believed fervently in their government's anti-Red crusade and had thus seen "not what was, but what men wished to see."[15]

Eight decades later, it happened again. Most journalists writing for influential American newspapers and news magazines believed in the Clinton administration's crusade to remake post-Communist Russia. Like a *Washington Post* columnist, they quickly "converted to Yeltsin's side." Like *Business Week*'s Moscow correspondent, they "hoped for the liberal alternative" and believed in the "job that Yeltsin and his liberal reformers had begun." Like the *New York Times* foreign affairs columnist, they were certain Russia needed the "same basic model" that America had. And with that newspaper's correspondent, they worried constantly that Russia might opt instead for a "path of its own confused devising." Some were even more embattled. For a longtime *Washington Post* correspondent, the post-Communist crusade was another chapter in a "Cold War . . . not yet really over."[16]

Leaving aside a plethora of factual errors, the first casualty, as Lippmann and Merz had warned, was professional objectivity. Moscow correspondents, according to a 1996 survey, tended to look at events there "through the prism of their own expectations and beliefs." Three years later, a reviewer of a book by a former correspondent concluded that her "spectacularly wrong projections" arose out of her personal hopes for Russia, "which prompted her to accept appearances for reality and desire for fact."[17]

Such hopes and fears produced a U.S. media narrative of post-Communist Russia that was Manichaean, at best one-dimensional, and based largely on accounts propounded by U.S. officials. (As a *Washington Post* correspondent explained approvingly, a determining feature of the saga was "IMF standards for becoming a normal market economy.")[18] On the side of good were President Yeltsin and his succession of crusading "young reformers," sometimes called "liberal democratic giants"—notably, Yegor Gaidar, Anatoly Chubais, Boris Nemtsov, and Sergei Kirienko. On the side of darkness was the always antireform horde of Communist, nationalist, and other political dragons ensconced in its malevolent parliamentary cave. Chapter by chapter, the story was reported over and again for nearly a decade, always from the perspective of the "reformers" and their Western supporters (the "smartest Russia-watchers") who were invariably also its sources. It was, a leading Russian journalist thought, a "deception."[19]

Yeltsin and his team were, it seemed, the only worthy political figures in all the vastness of Russia. Most Russians saw his shock therapy and other measures as extremist, but for the U.S. press Yeltsin was the sole bulwark against "extremists of both the left and the right."[20] There was little if any room for non-Yeltsin reformers. When one, Grigory Yavlinsky, ran against Yeltsin in the 1996 presidential campaign, he was pilloried in American dispatches and editorials: "History will remember who was the spoiler if things go bad for democracy." On the other hand, whoever Yeltsin appointed, however unsavory his political biography, invariably turned out to have "clean hands" and be "one of the democrats" and a "real reformer," including Yelstin's designated successor, Vladimir Putin, a career KGB officer.[21]

Sustaining such a Manichaean narrative in the face of so many conflicting realities turned American journalists into boosters for U.S. policy and cheerleaders for Yeltsin's Kremlin. As early as 1993, even a pro-American Russian thought the U.S. coverage of his country was "media propaganda." A New York press critic made a similar point in 1996, complaining that newspaper reporting was a "mirror of State Department doublethink." For a senior American scholar, the media's pro-Yeltsinism even "recalls the pro-Communist fellow-travelling of the 1930s," though the "ideological positions are reversed."[22]

American journalists created, for example, cults of those Russian politicians whom the U.S. government had chosen to embody its policy. The extraordinary Yeltsin cult of the early 1990s—"as Yeltsin goes, so goes the nation"—was eventually eroded by his policy failures and personal behavior. But as late as 1999 he remained, according to the *New York Times*, the "key defender of Russia's hard-won democratic reforms" and "an enormous asset for the U.S."[23]

As for Yeltsin's "young reformers," no matter how failed their policies or dubious their conduct, their reputations hardly suffered at all, at least not for long. Consider Chubais, whom U.S. officials regarded as a "demi-god" and head of an "economic dream team."[24] Even after he was widely suspected of having ordered a cover-up of a Kremlin crime by his aides (later confirmed), a *New York Times* correspondent informed readers that "Chubais is plotting how to carry out the next

stage of Russia's democratic revolution." And long after
he was known to have personally profited from the privatization programs he administered, in part by rigging
market transactions, he remained, according to another
Times correspondent, a "free-market crusader," indeed
the "Eliot Ness of free-market reform."[25] Nor was the
Times alone in such reporting. A 1999 study by two
American journalists concluded that the *Wall Street Journal*'s Moscow bureau had been "little more than a PR
conduit for a corrupt regime."[26]

There were even worse malpractices at the expense
of American values. In 1993, U.S. columnists and editorialists almost in unison followed the Clinton administration in loudly encouraging Yeltsin's unconstitutional
shutdown of Russia's Parliament and then cheering his
armed assault on that elected body. The reasons given
were uninformed and ethically specious. Insisting that
"it would be not just expedient but right to support
undemocratic measures," journalists even rehabilitated
the ends-justify-the-means apologia long associated with
and thoroughly discredited by Soviet Communists
themselves: "One can't make an omelette without
breaking eggs."[27] Even the next Parliament, the Duma,
elected under Yeltsin's own constitution, became a target of U.S. media abuse, as though Russia would be
more democratic without a legislature, with only the
president and his appointees.[28]

One other example should be given because it under-
lines the irrelevance, even cold indifference, of much
U.S. reporting on post-Communist Russia, where (even
according to a semi-official Moscow newspaper) most
people were "being exploited" and impoverished in

unprecedented ways. Discussing the brutal impact of economic shock therapy on ordinary citizens, another pro-Western Russian complained that American correspondents had "no desire to look Russia's tragic reality straight in the eye." A Reuters journalist later made the same observation: "The pain is edited out."[29]

Poverty and health problems were, of course, reported, but usually as sidebars to the main story of Russia's transition and as legacies of the Communist past. Virtually all American correspondents and editorial writers were contemptuous of any Russian proposals for a gradual, "somehow less painful reform," whether by Yeltsin's vice president in 1993 or Prime Minister Evgeny Primakov in 1998 and 1999. Indeed, they seemed to think, following U.S. and Russian economists whose policies had already failed disastrously, that more shock therapy was needed, as in eliminating the housing and utilities subsidies that sustained tens of millions of impoverished families, perhaps half the nation or more. In May 2000, a *New York Times* editorial even urged Russia's newly elected president, Vladimir Putin, to abandon progressive taxation—a fixture of democratic capitalist systems—for a plan that could only benefit the well-off and further victimize ordinary citizens.[30]

Like old-time Soviet journalists, American correspondents pardoned present deprivations in the name of future benefits that never materialized. As the country sank ever deeper into economic depression and poverty, they continued to parrot Kremlin and Washington assurances that the economic stability and takeoff, which still have not come, were just around the corner. (Vice President Gore is quoted as having said in March

1998, "Optimism prevails universally among those who are familiar with what is going on in Russia.")[31] On the eve of its 1998 financial meltdown (and even after, as we will see later on), they still found ways to assure readers that Russia was "a remarkable success story." Not even Putin's subsequent admission that "poverty exists on an unusually large-scale in the country" made it a focus of U.S. reporting.[32]

Many American correspondents clearly did not like "doom and gloom" stories about unpaid wages and pensions, malnutrition, and decaying provinces, where, a Russian journalist tells us, "desperation touches everyone." (*Newsweek*'s correspondent advised the poor to continue living on bread: "They could do worse.")[33] Nor did they report more than a very few of the desperate acts of protest taking place around the country, and virtually none of the ways the "reform" government deprived workers of whatever rights and protection they had had in the Soviet system. American journalists found instead preferable "metaphors for Russia's metamorphosis"[34]—usually in the tiny segment of Moscow society that had prospered, from financial oligarchs to yuppies spawned by the temporary proliferation of Western enterprises.

Thus, for a *Washington Post* columnist who had recently been a correspondent, an especially successful insider beneficiary of state assets was a progressive "baby billionaire" and, for the *Wall Street Journal,* a "Russian Bill Gates."[35] For many others, like a *New York Times* editorial writer and also former Moscow correspondent, "One of the best seats for observing the new Russia is on the terrace outside the cavernous McDonald's [that] serves as a mecca for affluent young Muscovites. They arrive in Jeep Cherokees and Toyota Land Cruisers, cell phones in hand."[36] In the new Russia at that time, the average monthly wage, when actually paid, was about sixty dollars, and falling.

No wonder few readers of the American press were prepared for Russia's economic collapse and financial scandals of the late 1990s. Those who relied on the *New York Times*, for example, must have been startled to learn—from an investigative reporter, not a Russia-watcher—that contrary to its prior reporting and editorials, "The whole political struggle in Russia between 1992 and 1998 was between different groups trying to take control of state assets. It was not about democracy or market reforms."[37]

To be charitable, we might find partial excuses for the failures of all these Russia-watchers. Policymakers may have been misled by politics, investors by profit seeking, journalists by deadlines and their editors' expectations. Moreover, Russia was not the primary profession of most of them, who actually knew little about the country, not even its language. (The latter factor no doubt accounts for the striking absence of references to the local press by most American correspondents in Moscow.)

But how to explain the equally large failure of scholars, at universities and think tanks, whose careers were devoted to the study of Russia and who were supposed to be exempt from those financial and political considerations? Begin by putting aside two misconceptions: that academics could not make elementary errors of fact or judgment; and that they rarely engaged in public affairs.

Consider two disparate examples of error. In their eagerness to denigrate the anti-Yeltsin Parliament of 1993, two senior professors writing in the *New York Times* apparently mistook that legislature, which had been freely elected in the Russian Republic of the Soviet Union in 1990, for the Soviet Parliament elected less democratically in 1989. And in 1999, when commercial misrepresentations in Moscow were commonly known, Harvard's Russian center wildly overpaid for what it thought would be the first U.S. copies of Soviet-era archive documents but which had been at another American research institution for years. Said the associate director, "Oh, brother. That's embarrassing."[38]

Political engagement was also a tradition in Russian studies. During the Cold War 1960s, 1970s, and 1980s, scholars played a prominent role in congressional and media policy debates, for example, over détente and Gorbachev's initiatives. Several university professors even served in the White House and State Department in Democratic and Republican administrations.[39] And Russia scholars influenced American perceptions still more broadly through close relations with influential journalists. Moscow correspondents frequently prepared for the assignment by studying with academics, read their books, and later solicited their comments for dispatches and analysis.

However, whereas previously there had been a fair number on both sides of issues, in the 1990s the overwhelming majority of scholars commenting on contemporary Russian affairs shared the U.S. government and media outlook on post-Communist Russia. Not surprisingly, they were strongly favored by the most influential newspapers and news magazines for opinion-page articles, quotations, and book reviews. Nor were they only "missionaries from neoconservative think-tanks," as a British scholar thought; they came from across the mainstream political spectrum. Meanwhile, the handful of Russia scholars who strongly dissented from "Yeltsin's American apologists" went largely unneeded, unheard, and unheeded.[40]

As a result, most of the media commentary by Russia scholars, and by their colleagues in related academic fields, hardly differed in substance or tone from that of journalists. Sometimes it was even more missionary and partisan. Scholars also believed in the need for a "Western economic strategy for Russia," for a "massive Western presence" there, and for the United States "to provide the leadership." One no doubt spoke for others in arguing that America should seize "this opportunity to change the traditional pattern of Russian history."[41]

And like U.S. officials and journalists, most scholars enthusiastically embraced Yeltsin as the "guarantor of reform" in Russia, one Berkeley historian putting him at once in the tradition of Peter the Great, Locke, and Jefferson.[42] They too provided regular assurances of post-Communist Russia's ongoing "success story" and dismissed even non-Communist Yeltsin opponents as "go-slow reformers," "old-reform economists," "spoilers," and "frustrated rabble-rousers."[43]

When the ethical test came in 1993, university professors also failed. Believing that action was "long-overdue," they urged Yeltsin to ignore "political propriety" and carry out a "coup" against the elected Parliament—or as a Harvard historian recommended, "resort

to methods that in the West would be unacceptable."
Lest anyone think Yeltsin lacked sufficient legitimacy,
a Yale constitutional scholar compared him favorably to
George Washington.[44]

It was a shameful episode in the history of Russian
studies but not the field's main contribution to the collective American folly of the 1990s. The contribution
that mattered most, and carried over into the new century, was to provide pseudo-substance and legitimacy
for the basic assumption underpinning the entire U.S.
crusade—the idea that Russia was in transition to
American-style capitalism and democracy. The "transition" rationalized U.S. policy, was made the ongoing
narrative of media coverage, and gave scholars a new
paradigm for research, funding, and promotion.

Transitionology

American scholars of Russia generally prefer consensus,
even orthodoxy, to controversy, probably in reaction to
political winds that have periodically chilled the field
since the McCarthy era. From the late 1940s to the
1970s, the orthodoxy was known as the totalitarianism
model. Its adherents, who dominated teaching and
research, maintained that it explained the entire course
of Soviet history, the full nature of the system that
emerged, and the impossibility of any fundamental
change in it.

During the Cold War, using the totalitarianism
approach was an ideologically satisfying way of con-

demning the Soviet Union—"pinning a 'boo' label on a 'boo' system," one critic remarked. But like most ortho-doxies, it obscured more reality than it revealed. Even before Gorbachev's reforms of the 1980s confounded the axiom that the Soviet system was immutable, research by a new generation of American scholars had already undermined the totalitarianism school both as historical interpretation and as political analysis.[45]

The end of the Soviet Union required a different con-sensus, and it quickly emerged. Since the early 1990s, American scholars of post-Communist Russia have enthusiastically embraced a new guiding concept. Some-times known as "transitology," it should be called "transitionology" in order to underline all its assump-tions and implications.

Not all scholars adopted the new approach; as in jour-nalism, there have been important exceptions whose work is admirably different. But in terms of the profes-sion's main developments, transitionology has become a near-orthodoxy—as its proponents tell us, the "standard fare," the prevailing "organizing theme," the "way of posing questions." For decades, the word *totalitarian* was ubiquitous in titles of articles and books; now it is *transition.*[46]

The basic premise of transitionology is that since 1991, however "rocky" the road, Russia has been in a reform process of "transition from Communism to free-market capitalism and democracy." Underlying that premise is another: Russia's "transition," no matter how painful and costly, is good, progressive, and necessary. That is why scholars, along with U.S. officials and journalists, frequently characterize it as "historic" and "great."[47]

Practitioners of transitionology have little use for traditional ways of studying Russia that involve history, culture, popular attitudes, and extensive empirical research, which they dismiss as mere area study. (Many of them like to say that Sovietologists "lost their subject," but as we shall see, it was they who lost sight of Russia.) They argue that their "theoretical" approach is far superior for two reasons. It is devoutly comparative—that is, it always examines Russia's "transition" in the context of the same or similar transformations in other times and places, mostly in the West—and thereby transcends area study. And, according to these scholars, because they use purportedly universalistic concepts, methods, and theories taken from comparative social sciences, particularly political science and economics, their work is truly scientific.[48]

Their claims have given rise to two misperceptions. One is that thanks to transitionology, the 1990s were an especially fruitful or "fecund period in Russian studies." The other is that the new approach is the product of young scholars, a kind of academic "young Turkism."[49] In fact, transitionology in Russian studies was launched by senior scholars at major universities, who have recruited, trained, and promoted its young cohort. Therein lies the full dimension of the problem. Most of the field—its senior, middle, and young generation—has succumbed to a concept that has already misled and devalued the profession even more than did the totalitarianism orthodoxy.

Indeed, the defects of transitionology are remarkably similar to those of its predecessor, with certain pluses and minuses reversed. Like the totalitarianism school,

the new one is inherently ideological, and it too professes to explain Russia's past, present, and future. Like
the old model, transitionology has a singular idea about
causal factors and outcomes. In the totalitarianism interpretation, it was omnipotent state power and the impossibility of change for the better; for its successor, it is
"civil society" and the near certainty of such change. As
a result, transitionology, like its predecessor, is an elliptical or blinkered approach, highly selective in what it
chooses to study and emphasize and thus in what it
ignores, obscures, or minimizes.

These defects, which appear also in the thinking of
U.S. policymakers and journalists, need to be examined
more closely. The problem begins with the ideological
premise of Russia's "transition." Even leaving aside the
misnomer "free-market capitalism," which does not
correctly characterize modern capitalist systems, why
should anyone assume that Russia's future must look so
much like America's present? There are other kinds of
market economy and democracy. At bottom, the assumption is merely a political conceit. Arrogant and teleolog-
ical, it is an academic expression of America's
post-Soviet triumphalism, a pseudo-scientific version of
Francis Fukuyama's "End of History" thesis, which
along with most of the "Washington Consensus" did
not survive the twentieth century.[50]

Not much more can be said on behalf of the new
school's understanding of Russia's past. Here too the
flaw is in the basic premise. Why date "Russia's transition from Communism" from 1991? "Communism," as
that system was long defined in the West, barely existed in the Soviet Union in 1991. It had already been

largely dismantled by Gorbachev's reforms. And yet, the Gorbachev years are routinely dropped from the standard narrative—if not blamed for bad developments—partly because commentators are reluctant to credit anything Soviet but also because of two other assumptions: his reforms "failed," the Soviet system having proved to be unreformable; and having proved to be unsustainable in transition, the Soviet Union "collapsed."

This is not the place for a historical digression, but readers should know that neither generalization is adequately supported by the evidence. During Gorbachev's years in office, despite policy failures, the Soviet system turned out to be remarkably reformable—certainly far more so than most Western experts had ever imagined. The record also shows that the Union did not so much "collapse" as it was disassembled by a small group of ranking Soviet officials, Yeltsin foremost among them, in a struggle over power and property.

However historians eventually answer these large and complex questions, they are crucial for understanding developments after 1991—the first essential reference point for any serious analysis of what has happened in post-Communist Russia and why. But here too transitionology shuns fundamental questions, as did the previous orthodoxy, for the sake of dogma (and perhaps political correctness).

Dating Russia's "transition" from the end of the Soviet Union led many scholars to another unfortunate premise. They took for granted that Yeltsin's U.S.-backed policies, which got under way at the same time, were the only meaningful kind of reform (usually called "radical reform") for Russia, particularly the shock-therapy and monetarist measures, and their attendant politics, that so profoundly affected the country after 1991. Equating "real reform" with Yeltsinism, as Russians sometimes categorize his leadership and policies in the 1990s, has had unseemly consequences, especially for scholars who should know better.

On the elementary level of fact, the equation is either false or inappropriately subjective. Since the early 1990s, a number of different programs for Russia's marketization and democratization have been put forward by non-Communists as well as by Communists.[51] Some of those alternative policies are at least as reformist as were Yeltsin's and conceivably would have been more effective. Certainly, they would have caused less suffering. Nonetheless, they have been dismissed, even vilified, in the standard narrative by both scholars and journalists.

In some instances, the result is an odd American mind-set. According to prevailing conceptions of "transition," Franklin Roosevelt's New Deal, for example, would not qualify as authentic reform, if only because it did not practice shock therapy or monetarism. During Evgeny Primakov's brief tenure as Russian prime minister in 1998 and 1999, he appealed to the Clinton administration for support by likening his own policies to FDR's. Not surprisingly, he was met with undisguised suspicion by U.S. officials, journalists, and scholars.

Equating Yeltsinism with the desired "radical reform" also has had moral consequences, even apart from the incongruity that Americans do not themselves usually favor anything radical. In political history and philosophy, as in dictionaries, the word *reform* has a normative content that means improving people's lives. Long before Russia's financial collapse in 1998, it had been amply clear that Yeltsin's policies were substantially worsening the living standards of the great majority of Russian citizens. Why scholars, or anyone else, would persist in calling them reforms is an ethical puzzle.

Some scholars stumbled into a deeper moral swamp, again along with U.S. officials and journalists. Proponents of "radical reform" for Russia understand that it results in "suffering on a large scale," which they too excuse in the name of the future. Instead of identifying the victims by class or occupation—middle-class families, unpaid workers, or laid-off women, for example—they classify them by generation. The "transition," they explain, "is unfair. It discriminates by age. The old do worse than the young."[52]

They reason, of course, that the young, who are presumed to be much more democratic and entrepreneurial, can adapt while the Soviet-reared old cannot.[53] In the exceedingly unlikely event that most young Russians actually favor "free-market capitalism," this may seem a small price to pay. But since non-young in these arguments usually means everyone over thirty-nine, even over thirty, transitionologists in effect endorse sacrificing Russia's middle-age and elderly citizens—in plain language, parents and grandparents—and even looking forward to their premature deaths.[54] Need it be said that no American scholar, politician, or journalist would support such policies for his or her own country?

As those ethical lapses suggest, scholars too were carried away by the great crusade, as they above all should not have been. Smitten with the Yeltsin government's "reforms," some became not merely its boosters but, with U.S. government and foundation support, its employees or "advisers." (Some of them seemed ready to play the same role for the "reformer Putin.") Here we find yet another curious reenactment of the old totalitarianism school. Many of its adherents related their scholarship to the perceived Cold War interests of the U.S. government. Transitionologists seem to have related theirs to the present-day interests of both the U.S. and the Russian governments. However sincere their intentions, no such relationship with official policy on either side is good for scholarship.

But these shortcomings are far from the full story of the failure of transitionology. As the 1990s unfolded into the twenty-first century, it was clear that its practitioners had overlooked Russia itself.

Russian Studies Without Russia

Language is the basis of discourse, including scholarly analysis and press coverage. If the language is false, so too is the discourse, as George Orwell went to lengths to warn. By trying to squeeze Russia's post-Communist realities into American and other "comparative" preconceptions, by giving things names they do not warrant, scholars and journalists have debased the vocabulary of their professions.

Here, at the expense of some repetition, is a partial inventory:

- Since 1991, Russia's realities have included the worst peacetime industrial depression of the twentieth century; the degradation of agriculture and livestock herds even worse in some respects than occurred during Stalin's catastrophic collectivization of the peasantry in the early 1930s; unprecedented dependence on imported goods (foremost food and medicine); the promotion of one or two Potemkin cities amid the impoverishment or near-impoverishment of some 75 percent or more of the nation; more new orphans than resulted from Russia's almost 30 million casualties in World War II; and the transformation of a superpower into a beggar state existing on foreign loans and plagued, according to the local press, by "hunger, cold, and poverty" and whose remote regions "await the approaching winter with horror."[55] All this, scholars and journalists have called *reform, remarkable progress,* and a *success story.*
- By any meaningful criterion, Russia's was the worst-performing modern economy of the 1990s, and yet it was anointed the *best-performing emerging market.* That market, whose large transactions have been shaped less by competition than by presidential decrees and other administrative measures, and which features contract killing as the supreme form of litigation, has been called a *free market*—even though one of its most ardent proponents concedes that the "fundamentals of a market economy— remain unknown in Russian commercial life."[56]

- An economic system that lacks any real national treasury or property laws and every year abets incalculably more capital flight abroad than capital investment in domestic production, and which regularly ranks near the top of international lists of corrupt systems, is called *capitalism*. Insider beneficiaries of state property fire sales and asset strippers—"looters," many citizens charge—are called *robber barons*, as though they are Russian Rockefellers and Carnegies laying the nation's foundations. Institutions that launder money, have few if any small depositors, and make no loans to productive business or homeowners are called *banks*, and enterprises feeding off the state and subject to its whims are termed *privatized*. (In April 2000, Putin's soon-to-be prime minister finally acknowledged that most "have never been banks in the real sense.") [57]
- Proclaimed a *great achievement* of reform, *privatization* requires a short digression. While small businesses struggle desperately to survive in a hostile state and economic environment—as late as 2000, they employed only 870,000 people—thousands of large privatized enterprises are said to represent the new capitalist economy. In the mid-1990s, scholars and journalists assured readers that the "Russian Privatization Center . . . helps turn state enterprises into private, profitable businesses." At the end of the 1990s, we learned that these industrial enterprises were only half as productive as when they belonged to the Soviet state, in no small measure because privatizing often meant asset stripping.[58]

Nor does *private* in Russia necessarily mean nonstatist or autonomous. The founder of one of the largest banks, for example, referred to the prime minister as "my boss" and only half jokingly remarked, "I don't own anything. I rent it." A Russian scholar explains, "Financial groups today are dependent in the most direct way on state preferences and budgetary resources." As an authoritative insider tells us, "The Government, if it wanted, could always have destroyed the oligarchs in a minute." Thus, even the biggest "private" owners, or perhaps especially they, have always been prepared to leave the country on short notice in case the state decides to terminate their leases. No wonder an economics scholar concluded in 2000 "that privatization in Russia was largely a formality rather than a true reform."[59]

- Specifying other *reform achievements* has been more bizarre. Until mid-1998, the government's nonpayment of wages, pensions, and other obligations, along with a massive pyramid of short-term debt sometimes at triple-digit rates, was said to be a *victory over inflation*. (Work without pay could have been called by its original name, slavery, or, as it was known in tsarist Russia, serfdom.)[60] A ruble artificially maintained at a fourth or less of its actual value, until 1998, largely by infusions of billions of IMF dollars, was called a *stable currency*.[61] Without the slightest irony, the barterization, or demonetarization, of some 50 percent or more of all economic transactions was termed *monetarism*. And the ongoing destabilization of a nuclear country was called *macrostabilization*.

- Post-Communist society has also been fictionalized. The large, highly educated, and potentially entrepreneurial Soviet middle classes were decimated by shock therapy in the early 1990s. Then there emerged a tiny, yuppie-like strata paid relatively well to serve as an island of prosperity sustained temporarily by foreign firms mostly in Moscow, but a group that owned little property and excluded most doctors, teachers, scientists, nuclear specialists, and other professionals. It was nearly wiped out by the financial meltdown of August–September 1998. This has been called the *creation of a middle class.*[62]

In the same vein, the tiny percentage of citizens who have profited from Yeltsinism and exhibited American-like ideas and behavior are designated *civil society*—an essentially ideological (not sociological) concept, even a "polemical" one, that can be made to include or exclude almost anything—while the rest of the nation is deplored for having failed to attain that exalted status.[63] The poor, whom a leading Russian economist and even President Putin call the country's "No. 1 social problem," are rarely mentioned. That is why the often cited *well-stocked stores* usually resemble "museums, where people come to look but not to buy."[64]

• Presiding over all this in the 1990s and into the twenty-first century was a barely disguised form of Russian authoritarianism that was called *political reform* and *democratization.* It featured a monarch-like president who ruled mostly by decree in defiance of a Parliament existing anxiously in the shadow of its recently destroyed predecessor, but who was himself so fearful that he relied increasingly on security officers as his prime ministers. In the end, he resigned only after having been guaranteed immunity from prosecution and having made the head of the former KGB his successor. The arrangement was termed *constitutional democracy*, even though political outcomes were so uncertain that a previous internal security minister did not rule out the possibility of a bloody "Indonesian or even Albanian variant."[65] (Forgotten, it seems, was Russian political history, which witnessed many constitutions but very little constitutionalism.)

The president was supported or not, depending on oligarchical interests, by a largely controlled, bought, or otherwise manipulated media said to be a *free press*. (Yeltsin, according to a Russian scholar, referring to oligarchical control of the media, was "not so much the *guarantor of democracy* as the guarantor of the oligarchy.") Beyond the capital, the Kremlin's relations with feudal-like baronies that in the 1990s periodically ignored the constitution, refused to pay taxes, forbade essential products from leaving their territories, and threatened to print their own currencies have been called *federalism*. Its Potemkin-village nature was demonstrated in 2000 when many previously "independent" governors, confronted with the prospect of a strong leader in Putin and his steps to reduce their power and reimpose Moscow's traditional control over the provinces, initially capitulated before beginning to resist.[66]

• To conclude this inventory with an even larger example, anti-Western sentiment had never been as strong or widespread in modern-day Russia as it was at the end of the twentieth century. In 1998, the U.S.

Chamber of Commerce in Moscow warned Americans to conceal their nationality during protest demonstrations. Leaders said to personify U.S. goals in Russia, notably Yeltsin and his "young reformers," were among the most despised in the country. And 96 percent of Russians surveyed—including purportedly pro-American young people—thought the U.S.-led NATO bombing of Yugoslavia in 1999 was a "crime against humanity." By 2000, some 81 percent believed U.S. policy in general was anti-Russian and even pro-Western Russians thought a "reverse iron curtain" was being imposed on the country's borders. And yet, Russia's entire "transition" was supposed to be synonymous with *Westernization* and *joining the West.*[67]

A profound irony leaps out of all these misnomers and obscurations: In many respects, academic study and media coverage of Russia since 1991 have been Orwellian. If nothing else, they found mainly the "Russia we want." Even when harsh realities were taken into account, scholars and journalists saw promise above all else in them. An Ivy League professor concluded, "The guarded optimism of the economists . . . seems justified." An influential, prizewinning journalist went further: "While it is undoubtably true that daily life in Russia today suffers from a painful economic, political, and social transition, the Russian prospect over the coming years and decades is more promising than ever before in its history."[68]

Sustaining so many detachments from reality meant that the narrative of post-Communist Russia had to be selective. Like journalists, scholars relied heavily on a narrow range of sources, primarily fellow transitionologists and official data. The significance of some developments had to be inflated—for example, prosperity inside the Moscow beltway—and that of others minimized, as was corrosive poverty in the provinces and even in the capital, where half the city's citizens were officially poor by 2000. Some had to be virtually omitted. Since 1991, Russia has suffered a terrible economic depression, but in the 1990s the word rarely appeared in scholarly or media accounts, still less any description or analysis of its consequences.

As paradoxical as it may seem, American scholars and journalists have told us considerably less that is truly essential about Russia after Communism than they did when it was part of the censorious Soviet system. What, then, have been the actual main developments in Russia since 1991? There have been several, but two must be emphasized, neither of which conforms to the still prevailing notion of a Russian "transition" or to any reasonable meaning of "reform."

Though it is no longer fashionable to say so in the social sciences, and journalists by nature pay little attention, political, economic, and social realities are shaped by a historical process. Imagine very briefly Russia's history since 1991 as experienced by Russians themselves. It was punctuated by an extraordinary series of traumatic shocks *(shok)* without therapy inflicted on society from above.

- In December 1991, Yeltsin and a small band of associates suddenly, without any legal or practical preparation, abolished the Soviet Union. For most Russians, it terminated the only citizenship they had ever known. For their economy, which had for decades been an integral part of the Soviet economy composed of fifteen republics, the cost was the loss of many vital suppliers, consumers, and other markets.

- In 1992 and 1993, hyperinflation generated by economic shock therapy and the abrupt decontrol of prices wiped out the life savings of most Russians, including the middle classes. Private pyramid schemes tolerated by the government and a 1994 currency collapse then took much of what was left, while the false promises of "democratic" voucher privatization gave most people nothing in return.

- In October 1993, Yeltsin used tank cannons to destroy not only the elected Parliament that had brought him to power and defended him during the attempted coup of August 1991 but the entire political, constitutional order of Russia's post-Communist republic. Along with much else, including a good deal of popular idealism—for most Russians, their first experience with democracy had been voting for parliaments in 1989 and 1990, including the one now destroyed—the country lost four years of progress, begun under Gorbachev in 1989, toward its first truly empowered legislature in modern times.

- In December 1994, Yeltsin precipitately launched a war against the tiny breakaway republic of Chechnya. By the time it ended in a temporary truce in 1996, the war had killed tens of thousands of civilians, many of them ethnic Russians in the capital city Grozny; eviscerated and alienated the army; blown an even larger deficit in the federal budget; made a mockery of constitutional federalism; and, barely noted, earned the horrendous distinction of being the first civil war ever to occur in a nuclearized country.

- In August 1998, following a number of financial dealings that victimized or failed to benefit most Russians, the government, after pledging not to do so, suddenly devalued the ruble, defaulted on its debts, and froze bank accounts. In effect, people's savings were again expropriated, this time decimating even the post-1991 middle class.

- And in the fall of 1999, bombs were mysteriously exploded in apartment buildings in Moscow and other cities, killing nearly three hundred people and spreading panic throughout urban Russia. Playing upon public fears, Yeltsin's government, now headed by the former secret police chief who was soon to succeed him, launched a new all-out war against what remained of Chechnya. By the spring of 2000, the result was thousands more deaths, hundreds of thousands of refugees, the literal razing of Grozny, and nuclear threats on both sides. It has been said that Russia's twentieth century actually began with its entry into World War I and the Communist Revolution that followed. Its twenty-first century began with a new kind of savage war with no end in sight.

The first point to be made about this nine-year history of shock politics and economics is that such measures were always deplored by U.S. policymakers, journalists, and scholars when they were inflicted by the Soviet government. The second point is that the history unfolded in accord with a certain internal logic, or dynamic, each event reducing alternatives and paving the way to the next. In particular, each further undermined aspects of the seventy-year-old Soviet order—institutional, economic, human—that could have been building blocks of a reformed Russia but were instead destroyed.

This post-Communist history of needless, counterproductive destruction was actually encouraged and applauded by American scholars and journalists on the basis of an astonishing theory. It too must be noted because it reminds us again that the U.S. crusade and its missionaries can be coldly indifferent to the human consequences for Russia.

According to the theory's many proponents, Russia's "transition . . . requires the razing of the entire edifice" of the pre-1992 order or, as another political scientist put it, the "demolition of the Soviet ancien regime." It was "desirable," a Harvard historian wrote, "for Russia to keep on disintegrating until nothing remains of its institutional structures." The greater the "rubble," a word regularly used, the better. An economist explained, "A successful reform program must be trenchantly negative. . . . It must aim at destroying institutions." Given such exalted scholarly authority, no wonder a correspondent could report admiringly on "Yeltsin's many acts of necessary destruction."[69]

When it came to Russia, or possibly any country except their own, academic economists were especially nihilistic: "Any reform must be disruptive on a historically unprecedented scale. An entire world must be discarded, including all of its economic and most of its social and political institutions, and concluding with the physical structure of production, capital, and technology." Unfortunately, such nihilism was not confined to Ivy League classrooms. As a World Bank official later regretted, "Some economic cold-warriors seem to have seen themselves on a mission to level the 'evil' institutions of communism and to socially engineer in their place . . . the new, clean, and pure 'textbook institutions' of a private property market economy."[70]

Readers will intuitively understand that behind all these condemned abstract "institutions" were Soviet-era programs and enterprises essential to the well-being of tens of millions of ordinary Russians—from health care provisions and pharmaceutical industries to food-processing plants. They were to be "razed" in the name of a privatized "free market" that almost a decade later has yet to replace them. One result has been a Russian demographic catastrophe unprecedented in peacetime.[71]

Transitionologists blame it and almost everything else on a "Soviet system that imploded into rubble," but in truth most of those essentials were still intact in 1991. As a Russian scholar points out, "The real destruction took place . . . in the period from 1992 to 1998." Contrary to American scholars and journalists, there were non-Communist alternatives. A reformer opposed to Yeltsin and to the Communist Party protested, "I think that to build, it is not necessary to destroy everything first."[72] That so many Americans shared the nihilistic zealotry of the Kremlin can be explained only by a crusade blinded by ideology.

Whatever the explanation, the history of post-Communist Russia hardly fits the imagery of a country "in

transit" to a progressive political and economic destina-
tion. Indeed, it does not look like any kind of forward
"transition" in Russia's development. The disdain for
gradualism and penchant for extremist measures, the
imposing of Western ideas of change from above, the
destruction of a parliament, the overweening role of a
supreme leader and bureaucratic decrees, the government's use of force against its own people—all this had
been seen before in Russian history, before and after
1917. If it looks like regression, again, why call it
"reform" or "progress"?[73]

Is it really possible that such a historical process leads
directly to stable democracy and a civilized market
economy, as was the mantra of the 1990s? Focus on just
one post-Communist Russian reality: An impoverished
people who have been deprived of their hard-earned
wages and hard-won welfare entitlements, and whose
savings have been confiscated more than once—all to
the apparent benefit of a tiny, ostentatiously rich segment of society. It alone is enough to inspire ominous
regressions in Russia's development.

In the mid-1990s, to take an example familiar to historians of Russia, that nation's old "accursed" question
"Who is to blame?," which so often had led to pogroms
and blood purges, began to be heard again across the
land. And once again, the Moscow establishment began
to fear the *narod,* the people. No real student of Russia
could have been surprised when Yeltsin and his family
desperately sought ways to avoid possible prosecution,
or persecution, as the end of his constitutional term in
office grew near. Or that so many members of the political and financial elite had sent their children to edu-

cational sanctuaries abroad, along with their wealth.

If there has been no "transition" in Russia since 1991—or only one in directions unforeseen and unexplained by its theorists—what has been the main development? Evaluating the economic and social consequences of "reform" in the 1990s, Russia's own scholars reach for analogies. One points to the devastation of World War II, another speaks of "genocide," still another compares them to the estimated destruction of a "medium-level nuclear attack." In my own experience, the words *collapse, disintegration, tragedy* come more readily to the minds of most Russians than does *transition*, unless it means "from a state of crisis to a state of catastrophe."[74] For them, the image of their country is not of a train making its way on rails, however roundabout, from one station to another, but of an out-of-control express that has plunged off the edge of a cliff. But what more specifically has happened?

The answer begins with Russia's post-Communist economic depression—"The Great Transition Depression"—one considerably greater and more protracted than America's of the 1930s. Even before the financial collapse in August–September 1998—contrary to prevailing opinion, its primary cause was not the "Asian flu" but Russia's own underlying economic malignancies—GDP was barely half what it had been in the early 1990s, meat and dairy herds about a fourth, and real wages less than half. (For comparison, during the American Depression, output fell 27 percent.)[75]

By the end of the 1990s, even a relatively prosperous Muscovite could see the "pitiful ruins of the Russian economy stuck out on the bared sandbars as if after a shipwreck."[76] The storm may not be over. Despite a small and probably temporary economic upturn in 1999 and 2000 largely because of higher world prices for Russia's oil and the ruble's collapse, which favored domestic goods over expensive imports, the "pitiful ruins" remain unrepaired, real wages continue to fall and unemployment grow, and new investment is minimal.

If capital investment is the lifeblood of an economy, Russia's was dying throughout the 1990s. In 2000, investment was 20 percent what it had been a decade earlier. It means that Yeltsin's Russia was living off the historical product of the much maligned Soviet economy, from its capital stock to its educational system, while "reforms" confiscated, redistributed, and stripped its property and other assets. A provincial governor explained, "Since 1991, we've survived six, seven years on the previous regime. As of today, those reserves are 100 percent exhausted."[77] Having produced almost nothing new and consumed most of what was readily at hand, the "reforms" collapsed.

But something even more catastrophic has been happening in Russia since the early 1990s. To anticipate a theme that appears later in this book, the nation's economic and social disintegration has been so great that it has led to the unprecedented demodernization of a twentieth-century country. The process has gone virtually unnoticed in the United States, but even a pro-Yeltsin Russian newspaper finally had to acknowledge it: "Russia has dropped out of the community of developed nations." A Russian scholar made the point in human terms, emphasizing that the 1990s had resulted in "the collapse of modern life."[78]

The statistical and observed evidence speaks for itself. For example, essential infrastructures of modern life have lost decades of development, from science and production to health care and heating. (A specialist speaks of the "disappearance of the national R&D base.") Most people work without regular pay, have few if any welfare benefits or savings, and live in or near poverty. Three of every four of them grow their own food to survive, though Russia is predominantly urban. Barter is often used instead of money. "Russia's health profile," an expert tells us, "no longer remotely resembles that of a developed country." Epidemics of typhus, typhoid, cholera, and other diseases have reemerged. Most children, millions of whom no longer attend school, suffer from malnutrition, and male life expectancy has plunged to less than sixty years, about what it was at the end of the nineteenth century.[79]

The worst of this "transition" back to a premodern age is unfolding in the remote provinces, where a "steady retreat of civilization" is under way. An American Peace Corps volunteer reported on one provincial town:

> It's decaying and dying. . . . There is no work at all. . . . Some people are eating dogs, others are giving their last kopecks to buy a loaf of bread. . . . There is no phone service in parts of the town because thieves stole the phone cables. . . . There is no police force to stop them. Apartments have broken toilets, no gas, running water only in the kitchen, certainly no hot water ever. . . . In fact, these people are actually better off than people in Siberia. Out there some of them don't have heat or food at all.[80]

The "reform" plague has even reached Russia's agricultural heartland, where proximity to food normally cushions life in bad times. In January 2000, a Canadian journalist set out to discover the fruits of his country's U.S.-style crusade to transform Russia's large collective farms into small family homesteads. He found this:

> The Canadians are long gone. So are the cattle, the fields of grain, the tractors, and even the roofs and walls of the cow barns. The buildings are gutted and looted. . . . Most of the farms are dead or dying. . . . The fields are full of weeds and bushes. There has not been a harvest for two years.

When asked about her hopes for the new millennium, a seventeen-year-old girl in another provincial town spoke for tens of millions of Russians: "The twenty-first century? It's difficult to talk about the twenty-first century when you're sitting here reading by candlelight. The twenty-first century does not matter. It's the nineteenth century here."[81]

There is something both old and new in this tragedy of post-Communist Russia. Yeltsin's "young reformers" claimed to be pursuing the "historic modernization" of Russia. In this respect, they were following an old tradition. From tsars to commissars, Russian governments had tried repeatedly to enact modernization, or "catching up with the West," from above. Sometimes the attempt had been relatively painless, sometimes "modernization through catastrophe."[82] But never before had the outcome been an actual loss of modernity.

For American scholars, Russia's tragedy has meant another profound irony. Concepts and theories of modernization have been a major part of academic Russian studies for many decades. In this respect, they too were following an old tradition.[83] For all its new language and social science pretense, transitionology is little more than a latter-day version of those old approaches in the field, now equating Russia's modernization with a transition to American-style democracy and capitalism.

And yet, the transitionologists, scholars and journalists alike, missed the most important development in Russia since 1991, the exact reverse of the process they purported to study and report, the country's year-by-year demodernization. In the end, the result was Russian studies and media coverage without Russia.

What Is to Be Done?

Russians believe that their politics is cursed by two perennial questions—"Who is to blame?," as already noted, and "What is to be done?" By the end of the 1990s, American politicians and pundits were accusing each other of complicity in their own version of the first question, "Who lost Russia?" But hardly anyone was interested in asking what should be done to end the malpractice by Russia-watchers that contributed so greatly to the debacle.

The general answer is simple. Journalists and scholars, whose work is supposed to be grounded in fact, have to stop producing virtual accounts of a "Russia we want." They have done it before, as I pointed out in the introduction, indeed repeatedly in the twentieth century.[84] This time, however, the result has been much worse—widely believed misperceptions and false analyses of a country laden with nuclear and every other device of mass destruction.

At least three steps are needed to dispel these exceedingly dangerous beliefs. The first is for journalists and scholars to distance themselves from U.S. policy and whatever larger consensus on Russia may exist at the time. Cooks have to produce for popular tastes and approving consumers, but in a democratic culture, scholars and journalists are supposed to be indifferent to prevailing appetites. In the 1990s, many of them abdicated their true mission to become missionaries.[85]

The second step is for journalists and scholars to liberate themselves from pseudo-experts, particularly ones who think Russia is just like any other country, regardless of its history, merely a "laboratory" for their theories.[86] (Surely there is something special about a nation in which both Communism and capitalism have been popularly discredited in barely eighty years.) Two kinds of self-professed experts played large detrimental roles in the 1990s: theoretical economists and financial investors. Both were like all those weapons specialists of another era who because the Soviet Union had weapons were considered "Soviet experts."

Globe-traveling economic shock therapists, from universities, think tanks, and official agencies, were particularly influential in shaping media opinion about post-Communist Russia. Unfortunately, most of them knew little about the country (except that it had an economy) and did not care, seemingly in a Marxist-like belief that their laws and prescriptions applied equally to all societies. (Some were so little informed that their own undertakings in Moscow ended up mired in scandal.)[87] To be fair to that profession, many of their fellow economists strongly disagreed with their theories, and for good reason. Economic shock therapists turned out to be stupendously wrong about Russia.

Scholars and journalists were swayed by missionary economists bearing prestigious Ph.D.'s, but why did they think financial investors were authoritative "information providers"? The reason, we are told, is that those profit seekers had invested so heavily in Russia.[88] The flaw in this reasoning—we already know what happened to their investments—is explained by two dissenting American journalists: "Any good business reporter knows that few stock analysts or brokers in emerging markets will go on the record as saying anything negative about their host country's economies—because if they do, no one will buy into its market."[89]

Investors, economists, and U.S. officials were designated experts on post-Communist Russia, even ranked among the "smartest Russia-watchers," because they were leading actors in the missionary narrative. On the other hand, people who had real knowledge of Russia, or a different story to tell—many of them disdained as "sages of Sovietology" and relegated to the "ashbin of history"—were usually shunned.[90]

Two victims of the Communist system, the Russian literary artists Andrei Sinyavsky and Aleksandr Solzhenitsyn, to take examples known to some readers, had for many years been cited approvingly by American specialists for their anti-Soviet writings. But when they protested what was happening in their country after 1991, they were ignored or derided. According to an American journalistic expert on Russia, Sinyavsky's "understanding of the Russian transition" was "analysis based on emotion, conspicuous omission, disorientation, and anecdote." Once lauded for his insights, Sinyavsky was now castigated for "deeply flawed judgments based on surprisingly erratic observation." As for Solzhenitsyn, even his formerly admiring biographer, an Ivy League professor, now dismissed him as an "irrelevant political dinosaur."[91]

Instead of trendy experts for the political season, real Russia-watchers have to find their own answers and, equally important, their own questions, even if they are not in fashion. The place to begin, which is the third step toward understanding post-Communist Russia, is with history. Journalists and scholars of contemporary affairs do not have to become historians, but they do need some general knowledge about what happened before 1991. Judging from generalizations made by young transitionologists and factual errors by journalists, neither know very much.[92]

If they did, they would understand that Russia, as a Soviet reformer once remarked, can't leap out of its long history any more than we can jump out of our skin.[93] They would know that many measures adopted by Yeltsin, whose admiration for Peter the Great is well-established, had less to do with democracy or capitalism than with recurring Russian leadership practices. They would worry that shock therapy and other U.S.-sponsored policies are reinforcing some of Russia's worst political traditions. And they would not perfunctorily rule out alternative ways of reforming Russia today, some "third way" between orthodox Soviet Communism and the dogmas of the American crusade. Looking back, they would even have to ask if more productive and less costly possibilities had been abandoned in 1991 with the Soviet Union.

One alternative from the past is already on the present and future agendas of post-Communist Russia. U.S. crusaders insist on the need for a fully privatized "free market" system, but it is in conflict with Russia's tradition. Before and after 1917, except for the aberrant Stalinist command system of 1929–86, the country has always had what Russians call a "mixed economy"— one featuring both state and private sectors in a market setting over which the government has substantial influence but not control.

Ever since Russians were first asked in the late 1980s, large majorities have repeatedly expressed their preference for a "mixed economy."[94] Today it means one that would combine freedom of private market enterprise with characteristic features of the latter-day Soviet system, including job guarantees, some regulated or subsidized consumer prices, extensive welfare provisions, and state ownership of most essential industries. Those latter features largely explain why 75 to 85 percent of Russians surveyed in 1999 regretted the breakup of the Soviet Union, and a large majority of them in 2000 look back on the Brezhnev 1970s and early 1980s, before the onset of Gorbachev's reforms, as "a golden era."[95]

What most Russians want, in other words, is similar

to European social democracy but contrary to the program (or "conditions") of the American crusade. Any other kind of economy will have to be imposed on them, as was tried in the 1990s, to the detriment of democracy. Indeed, the "free market" disaster of that decade has only increased popular support for a "mixed economy," which is now promised by almost every significant party in Russia.

Thus does a bit of historical knowledge focus attention on contemporary realities instead of myths, which is, of course, the most important step toward understanding what has really happened in Russia since 1991. Russia has to be brought back into Russian studies and coverage, especially its people, whose fate U.S. politicians, journalists, and academics so lamented when they were the Soviet people. Books will eventually be written about all the developments omitted or obscured by American specialists in the 1990s, but let two examples represent the others.

When Moscow's U.S.-backed "reformers" of the 1990s leave the scene, as they soon will one way or another, their primary legacy will be, in addition to millions of premature deaths, "social problem number one"—the impoverishment of their country. At the onset of the new millennium, some 50 percent of Russians live below the official poverty line of $30 to $35 a month and probably another 25 to 30 percent very near to it. (The tragedy is not only Russian: the number of people living in poverty in the former Soviet republics rose from 14 million in 1989 to 147 million even prior to the 1998 crash.)[96] In modern peacetime, never have so many fallen so far.

It is the only truly significant human "transition" that has occurred in post-Communist Russia. Poverty existed in Soviet Russia, as the crusade's apologists always remind us, but in modern times never anywhere near as broadly, deeply, and desperately—and, of enormous political importance, never amid such ostentatious official corruption and ill-gained private wealth. This catastrophic reality is now the essential context for any truth-telling journalism, meaningful scholarly analysis, and humane policy-making, Russian or American.

And yet, despite one authoritative report after another detailing the extent of Russia's impoverishment and its terrible human consequences, most U.S. officials, pundits, and Russia-watchers still either do not see it or do not care.[97] When the spell of "Yeltsin's reforms" began to burst in the United States at the end of the 1990s, it was due not to the suffering of the Russian people but to the Kremlin's default on Western credits and news reports that its officials and oligarchs had used U.S. banks to launder billions of dollars. In most of the hand-wringing over "Who lost Russia?," the lost lives of perhaps 100 million Russians seem not to matter, only American investments, loans, and reputations.[98]

Even when Russia's hard times are acknowledged, they are still justified by the myth that the country's young people nonetheless support U.S.-sponsored reforms and are, or will be, their "winners."[99] People under forty, particularly under thirty, have favored those policies more than have their elders. But to inflate this marginal statistic into a generalization about young Russians, or even a majority of them, is to assume, against all evidence and common sense, that young coal miners, factory workers, soldiers, teachers, students, fathers, and mothers have not been "losers"—and that they are indifferent to the fate of their own parents and grandparents.

In truth, extensive studies show that as the "transition" continues, the "outlook is bleak for millions of young Russians." Younger workers, for example, are becoming poorer than older ones. As for children, asked by specialists to draw their expectations of the future, six-year-olds to fifteen-year-olds portray it in "dark, depressive tones."

It is not hard to understand why. Many parental and institutional structures that sustain a child's health and education are disintegrating. Even leaving aside millions of orphaned, homeless, and more severely malnourished ones, 50 to 80 percent of all school-age Russian children are classified as having a physical or mental defect. It even turns out that in the purported transit to a better life, "children are more likely than adults to be impoverished."[100] In short, a great many young Russians may not be healthy enough, educated enough, or live long enough to be "winners."

No wonder an eminent Russian economist—he too was once admired in the West but no longer—warns that his country has become a "zone of catastrophe," and even a moderate nationalist believes that "Russia is in the greatest crisis of its entire history."[101] In light of all this, can any American doubt that it is long past time for the United States to call off the crusade, stop demanding that Russia "stay the course," and begin to think how we can really help that tormented nation and thus ourselves?

For that to happen, at least some of the architects and promoters of the crusade have to acknowledge its intrinsic fallacies and colossal failures—not for the sake of *mea culpa* but because a consequential rethinking process has to include mainstream Russia-watchers in the various professions. Even now, however, there are few signs that any of them are ready to do so. Since Moscow's pseudo-financial system collapsed in 1998, there have been two general American reactions to the disaster in Russia and in U.S.-Russian relations. One denies there has been a disaster; the other denies any responsibility for it.

The Clinton administration's fawning endorsement of Vladimir Putin demonstrated that the official sponsor of the American crusade intended to retire in January 2001 still proclaiming success. Russians with long-standing democratic credentials warned that the little-known Putin's sudden ascension to the presidency was more akin to a Kremlin "coup d'etat" or uncontested Soviet balloting than a real election and might bring the former KGB back to power. The administration, however, quickly proclaimed Putin "one of the leading reformers" with whom "the United States can do business," forgave his destruction of Grozny as a campaign to "liberate" the city, and hailed his March 2000 election as "a genuine democratic transition."[102] To justify its failed policies of the 1990s, the Clinton administration had to make Putin its Yeltsin of the twenty-first century.

The tenacity of other American crusaders is more remarkable. We expect journalists and scholars to respond to facts. But "Russia looks terrific" to a *Washington Post* correspondent, and another still extols the "great Russian transition," marveling that "Russians have accomplished much of what we asked." With the Clinton administration, journalists reported that Putin occupied the Kremlin as the result of a "free transfer of power" and hoped he would now "drive home democratic and market reforms that Yeltsin was unable to realize." According to the *New York Times* Moscow correspondents, the former KGB chief "clearly has an intellectual grasp of democracy" and, despite some lamentable "populist comments," could push through the "most radical reforms."[103]

Indeed, with the help of newly bullish investors, the entire standard media narrative of "Russia's transition" has been refurbished. The country's economic boom is again said to be just around the corner, if not already under way, and its market the "best performing" one around. "Russians still have faith in a free-market system." Chubais, though scandal-ridden and accused at home of behaving like a war criminal and "Stalinist" during the new Chechen war of 1999–2000, remains a liberal hero in the U.S. press, even godfathering a new cadre of "Russia's best and brightest economists" for Putin. According to journalists, foreign investors are particularly optimistic about the new president because he has a "passion for order" and "a little authoritarianism might be just what Russia needs."[104]

Scholars have also turned out to be resistant to Russia's realities. Economic specialists tell us that a "lot more has been accomplished than virtually anyone would have predicted." A think-tank analyst eulogizes the "immensity of Yeltsin's achievement," which is certain "to fulfill most Russians' hopes." A leading politi-

cal scientist, a historian, and an economist come forth
to report more "good news." Putin came to power
through Russia's "first ever democratic transition" and
shows a "keen understanding of the historical moment,"
and thus "prospects for meaningful reform in Russia
are now excellent." *Reform* still means, of course, "radical reform," or Chubais's U.S.-backed program, which
"most of us in the West would support."[105]

Nor has reality extinguished belief in the necessity or
righteousness of the American crusade. According to an
editor of the *New York Times Book Review,* which strongly influences how books on Russia policy are received,
"Few in Western Europe and the United States doubt
the desirability of remaking the former Soviet Union in
a Western image." The only "problem," he adds, "is
how to get there from here." The same paper's foreign
affairs columnist knows how. He proposes a more determined U.S. wager on "young Russians" with Americans
"laying out a clear, strategic pathway for them."[106]

Charitable readers might feel some sympathy or even
admiration for these true believers whose ideological faith
defies mountains of refutation. Perhaps they are quintes-
sential Americans, Gatsby-like policy dreamers believing
"in the green light, the orgiastic future that year by year
recedes before us," and so they "beat on, boats against the
current." Or perhaps they are hapless Don Quixotes
unaware that the Russian windmill they are storming is
full of historical demons and nuclear devices.

Then there are all the lapsed true believers since
1998 who have turned Hank Williams's confessional
into an oxymoron: I was never blind, but now I see the
light. (Or is it, as a Russian observer remarked, "a col-

lective recovery of sight"?)[107] As happened when the U.S. war in Vietnam ended in disaster, so many pundits, scholars, politicians, and former officials now criticize the results of the crusade to remake Russia, it appears that hardly anyone was ever part of the "Washington Consensus" behind it.

Thus, the Clinton administration's missionary approach long had considerable bipartisan support in Congress—Yeltsin was given the rare honor of addressing it in joint session even before President Clinton was elected—but Republican committee chairs later hold hearings demanding to know, "Who lost Russia?" In the 2000 presidential primary campaign, all Republican candidates insisted it wasn't them. Their tongues untied, ranking Clinton officials come in out of the cold to say they had known about the policy failures all along. An international affairs columnist concludes that Yeltsin's Russia is "lost to constructive engagement with Washington," leaving us to wonder why he had earlier "converted" to Yeltsin. Newspapers and magazines editorialize similarly, also without noting that their opinions have changed.[108]

There are many such cases. An influential newspaper itemizes "lost illusions about Russia," but not its own. A former Moscow correspondent exposes the "myth" created about American shock therapists and Russian "radical reformers" without mentioning that he had been their enthusiastic proponent. Known for his upbeat analyses, another former correspondent complains about "wishful thinking." Yet another correspondent abruptly reverses his positive interpretation of Yeltsin's economic policies and is awarded a Pulitzer Prize for the revised rendition. A World Bank economist, also no longer tongue-tied in public, denounces the Russia policies of the IMF and his own institution.[109]

Scholars too suffer from amnesia. A Columbia University economics professor bemoans the unproductivity of Russia's "real economy," which earlier he had advised be destroyed, and then, also without any acknowledgment of his turnabout, challenges the entire "assumption of 'transition'" he had previously espoused. A senior Berkeley historian informs readers that "Russia's liberal experiment has now collapsed in a spectacular and completely unexpected fashion" without telling them he had been among its most zealous exponents or that the outcome had not been "unexpected" for some of us. A Stanford and Carnegie political scientist asks, "What went wrong, so quickly?," neglecting to point out that his own long-standing analysis had also gone wrong.[110]

Indeed, what went wrong—that is, the underlying cause of the disastrous failure of U.S. policy toward post-Communist Russia—still is not generally understood or acknowledged. All the postmortems and finger-pointing notwithstanding, there has been almost no public recognition that the American crusade itself, along with its missionary economic "conditions," was ill-conceived and doomed from the outset. The crusade has failed, but there is, alas, no reason to conclude, as does a prominent policy intellectual, "that the attempt to transform Russia into a liberal democracy is over."[111]

Instead, American policy elites and pundits continue to believe that the United States has "an absolute responsibility to make sure the Russian experiment with democracy comes out the right way" and that "dictating national economic policy" is the way to do it.[112] Most of them look forward to another opportunity, as we have seen, for "re-making the former Soviet Union" with the same but "much more radical reforms," the "most stringent possible conditions," and a Russia that will "stay the course." Thus, with Putin's election in March 2000, IMF and other missionaries resumed their treks to Moscow in expectation of a "second beginning."[113]

But if the "point is not that we've misengaged Russia," as a leading academic specialist insists,[114] how are the failures of U.S. policy explained? One way has been to adopt a new mantra: "Russia was never ours to lose." Though completely true, it is, of course, a much belated afterthought: the underlying premise of the crusade has always been that Russia is ours to remake and keep from a "path of its own confused devising."

The main way of explaining the failures of Russia policy, however, is to blame everything (and everyone) else. Some current and lapsed missionaries blame the Clinton administration or IMF for implementing the policy badly; some charge Yeltsin and his ministers with having lacked resolve; others indict the Russian Parliament; and still others blame ordinary Russians, who "don't get it." (An expert elaborates, "The Russians are such a calamitous nation that even when they undertake something sane and banal, like voting and making money, they make a total hash of it.")[115] Overwhelmingly, though, the "legacy of 70 years of Communist rule" is blamed, as though Russia's prior history was not known in 1992 or can be used indefinitely to excuse every U.S. policy failure.[116]

Not only is the missionary venture not blamed; officials, scholars, and journalists closely associated with it
are honored and promoted even as the disaster continues to unfold. In 1999, for instance, the deputy head of
the U.S. Treasury Department who oversaw economic
policy toward Russia was given the top position, while
his former boss, on whose watch tens of millions of Russians were impoverished, entered the private sector guaranteed at least $30 million for his first two years in his
new position. A Harvard shock therapist under U.S. federal investigation for financial dealings in Moscow was
awarded the "most prestigious prize in economics short
of the Nobel." A journalist who misreported the story
won a Pulitzer Prize. Even a former Yeltsin prime minister accused of corruption, Viktor Chernomyrdin, was
still being honored in the United States.[117]

Why are the "most fundamental, starting-point questions," as a critic of U.S. policy asks, avoided?[118] The
puzzle is greater because some were raised, however
fleetingly, in influential circles. In 1997, Alan Greenspan,
chairman of the Federal Reserve Board, questioned
another missionary premise, doubting it was possible to
"automatically establish a free-market entrepreneurial
system" in post-Communist Russia. In the immediate
aftermath of the 1998 financial meltdown, the *Washington Post,* a longtime supporter of the crusade, suddenly admitted, "We thought we knew how a
Communist country could transform itself into a capitalist one. . . . A lot of rethinking needs to be done."
The head of the U.S. Chamber of Commerce in Moscow
had a similar reaction: "We, all of us, believed in the
reform process. And now it turns out we were wrong."[119]

Why did doubts stop there and no influential rethinking actually ensue? A former top Russian official in several Yeltsin cabinets has a cynical explanation: "The IMF was pretending that it was seeing a lot of reforms [while] Russia was pretending to conduct reforms."[120] His answer may reveal a good deal about his own conduct, but most American crusaders were true believers. The critic of U.S. policy quoted just above thinks the answer may be a "lack of intellectual honesty,"[121] but this too requires explanation.

Part of it may be a generic memory of McCarthyism. (How else to explain U.S. cover story titles like "Red Alert" and "Red Scare" when it seemed that the Communist presidential candidate might defeat Yeltsin in 1996, or a young American scholar's need to characterize him as "the odious Communist candidate"?)[122] Throughout the 1990s, the American crusade and its all-out support for Yeltsinism were seen, or presented, as the only alternative to the "threat of a Communist comeback" in Russia. No other non-Communist possibility, a former insider testifies, was "even considered."[123] Nor have most Russia-watchers been able to imagine another alternative. When some of them were asked in late 1998 by the White House and IMF if they had any new proposals for Russia, "none did." And in 2000, anti-Communism was given by U.S. officials, journalists, and academics alike as a primary reason for now supporting the former KGB officer Putin.[124]

Many Russia-watchers may therefore worry that criticizing the basic premise of American policy will be labeled pro-Communist or, in today's code expression, "nostalgia for the Soviet Union." Readers may be surprised, but it does still happen. In recent years, I have witnessed this obscene political practice in my own profession, journalists in theirs, and even the former chief economist of the World Bank in his, "From this cold-war perspective, those who showed any sympathy to transitional forms that had evolved out of the Communist past and still bore traces of that evolution must themselves be guilty of 'Communist sympathies.'"[125]

On the other hand, this factor should not be exaggerated, especially in light of the heretical questions posed in the *New York Times Magazine* in 1999 by a once pro-Yeltsin journalist, albeit a British one: "Has the President we in the West supported, feted, lauded become worse than the Communists we helped him to overcome? Have the market reforms that we promoted and helped pay for been so counterproductive that we have helped create a Frankenstein's monster of a state, which lost its way out of the gradualist reformism in the 1980s into a shock no society could bear?"[126] The writer, a person of impeccable standing in high political and financial circles, backs away from an answer. But if his question marks are deleted, the passage reads like an epitaph for the American crusade, even a rehabilitation of Gorbachev's much maligned Soviet reforms.

We need, then, a larger or additional explanation for the failed crusade's near immunity from fundamental criticism, at least on the American side. It is probably to be found in the nature of those professions that do most of the Russia-watching. None of them are inherently self-critical. U.S. politicians and officials, as we know, are allergic to self-criticism, as evidenced by the near absence of a modern-day American history of resignation from government on matters of principle. They even shun lesser degrees of nonconformity. "Washington policymakers," according to a Beltway insider, "almost *never* speak their mind in ways that will offend people."[127]

Mainstream journalists and scholars also have strong conformist conventions. Much as Russia scholars prefer consensus, even orthodoxy, to dissent, most journalists, one of them tells us, are "devoted to group-think" and "see the world through a set of standard templates."[128] For many decades—we need only recall the findings of Lippmann and Merz in 1920—both professions have usually taken their "templates" on Russia, for better or worse, from U.S. policy. They did so during the long Cold War with Soviet Russia and now again during the decade-long crusade to transform post-Soviet Russia.

For them to break with "standard templates" requires not only introspection but retrospection, which also is not a characteristic of either profession. In the practice of journalism, acknowledging basic misjudgments of reporting, news analysis, or editorial opinion is rare; as an eminent columnist laments, "There is not much of a place for looking back."[129] Scholars sometimes do look back on their work, but not often or very critically in the politically thin-skinned field of Russian studies.

At the end of the 1990s, a few journalists and scholars did begin to rethink their assumptions about U.S. policy and post-Communist Russia. A *Washington Post* columnist characterized the crusade's policies as a "reform-to-ruins process," though he still believed in "helping the Russians get it right." His counterpart at

the *New York Times* took the next step: "We should butt
out of their politics. We have done more harm than good
to genuine reform."[130] A few scholars also began to
reassess their thinking. One admitted, "We were wrong,"
and another tried to explain why: "Since 1991, we have
viewed Russian reality through the lens of ideology." A
young scholar even acknowledged, "We gravely misun-
derstood the patient."[131]

But these remain exceptions and well short of the
essential truth behind the failed crusade: The United
States does not have the right, wisdom, or power to
intrude so deeply into Russia's internal affairs—indeed,
into its destiny. Any attempt to do so will be dangerously counterproductive, as happened with such dire
consequences in the 1990s. We have survived a decade
of a recklessly misconceived American policy toward
the first nuclearized country in history to have fallen
into a state of political, economic, and social instability, but time for a fundamental change of course is run-
ning out.

Escaping a calamitous political dead end requires acts
of what Russians call "civic courage." In this case, to
reemphasize the point, it requires the architects of the
U.S. crusade and its leading missionaries to acknowledge they were wrong, and why. In democratic America, the political price of such courage is cheap, whereas
in Communist Russia it was very high but many people were willing to pay it.[132]

The contrast is still valid. As the question "Who is to
blame?" becomes a clamor for blood retribution, the
cost of civic courage in Russia is again escalating. Some
Russians, unlike their American counterparts, again

seem willing to risk it. The makers, practitioners, and defenders of U.S. policy toward post-Communist Russia in the 1990s should consider the desperate plea of a young Russian politician. Not long ago, he and his party stood with Yeltsin and his U.S.-sponsored "radical reforms." Now he "delivers an indictment of all the heroes of this era, including ourselves." He continues,

> The names of people on the right and on the left will forever be among the names of the architects of the ruins to which Russia has been reduced. Today, we still have a chance to admit our mistakes, to draw genuine lessons from what happened to our country. If we don't do it, the people will; if the people don't do it, history will; if history doesn't do it, God will.[133]

PART II

THE AMERICAN CRUSADE
AND POST-COMMUNIST
RUSSIA: FOLLY AND
TRAGEDY, 1992–2000

For fools rush in where angels fear to tread.
Alexander Pope

Washington and other capitals have an enormous stake in the writing of the history of the Yeltsin era that has begun in Moscow.
Jim Hoagland, in the Washington Post[1]

Journalists like to say that their work is "a first rough draft of history." American press coverage of Russia in the 1990s, as we have seen, failed to serve that purpose. This section of the book is an alternative draft of that history—nine articles and an interview I published in a weekly magazine and two newspapers in the years from 1992 to 1999. Of varying length, two originated as congressional testimony, the others in response to events.[2] Arranged by year, they form an analytical chronicle of post-Communist Russia and U.S. policy.

The articles and interview appear here as they were originally published, except for postscripts appended at the end of each, an expanding of the last piece to June 2000, and some small alterations. In one case, I have restored the original text abridged by editors and in another added several lines from an article written at about the same time but not included here.[3] I have deleted a few brief digressions on matters no longer of interest and inserted an occasional word or date to clarify the time frame. Most of the articles were written three weeks before the publication date given at the end of each of them.

This section of the book has an additional purpose. American scholars and other commentators who were wrong about post-Communist developments in the 1990s usually excuse their failure by maintaining, as has a prominent historian, that "no one . . . anticipated anything quite like such an impasse" in Russia today. Looking back on the "transition" and resorting to primitive labels, the leading missionary economist, to take another example, claims that "Russia has perplexed us all. . . . Optimists and pessimists can find evidence to support their past predictions, but both have been surprised in one way or another." Or as a journalist succinctly misstates the matter, "Everyone was wrong."[4]

Such assertions are not only untrue—they detract from a full discussion of what went wrong in Russia and in U.S. policy. If nothing else, they disregard and thus exclude from consideration arguments made by the few scholars, myself included, who dissented from American policy and the standard narrative of the 1990s, and who warned of dire consequences, as did a number of economists who were not Russian specialists.[5] (For the record, it should be noted that a handful of political figures and non-academic commentators also criticized the Clinton administration's policy before it became customary to do so, most of them, for whatever political or intellectual reason, conservatives.)[6]

More important, to claim that no one understood post-Communist Russia is to revert to an old and now more dangerous notion that Russia, whether Communist or not, is by nature too aberrant to be understood.

It is to leap from the crusading arrogance of the early 1990s that knew everything about Russia to a contemptuous unwillingness to learn anything about it. In policy-making, it is to relegate the world's largest territorial country, and a fully nuclear one, to some perverse realm that can only be isolated and contained.

Hence the revival of Winston Churchill's unfortunate aphorism that Russia is "a riddle wrapped in a mystery inside an enigma," and the widespread blaming of that "calamitous nation" for America's failed policies and expectations. Thus, for what is thought to be an exceptionally sophisticated Western magazine, Russia has become "a strange country, perhaps a uniquely strange country." Even the Clinton administration, in complete incongruity with its missionary assumptions, adopted a version of this nonsense, the banal malarkey of a nineteenth-century poet favored by maudlin Russian intellectuals and their Western devotees, "Russia is understood not by the mind. . . . In Russia one can only believe."[7] It too is not only untrue—it is a reckless abdication of reason in a world made ever more perilous by Russia's ongoing disintegration.

The publications that follow, along with the writings of some of my colleagues, are, I believe, evidence that Russia can be understood and therefore wisely engaged. No special brainpower, methodology, or theory is required, only a willingness to set aside preconceptions and learn as much as possible about Russia's past and present. To the extent that I have succeeded and my warnings been confirmed by events, I wish I had been wrong.

What's Really Happening In Russia? (March 1992)

Q: *The long-standing discrepancy between American media perceptions and Soviet realities was a constant concern in your column, "Sovieticus," in* The Nation *in the 1980s. You have recently returned from a visit to post-Communist Russia. Given all the changes in the former Soviet Union, and the end of Russian censorship, is there no longer a discrepancy?*

SFC: We have much more information about Soviet, and particularly Russian, affairs than we had before Mikhail Gorbachev came to power in 1985, and American reporting from the scene is better—less simplistic and more detailed. But new stereotypes, myths, and misconceptions have emerged in our mass media—especially in what passes for commentary—and in our political discourse. And though they are the opposite of Cold War misperceptions, they too obscure much more than they reveal. Indeed, I worry that it may become just as difficult to have an informed, dispassionate discussion of Russia in the United States today as it was during the Cold War years.

The basic problem, as always, is the American habit of interpreting Russia through the prism of our own ideology—of finding there only what we seek, and seeking only what we find comforting. For decades, it was an alien "Communism" and "totalitarianism." Now it's an American-style "free-market democracy" and "civil society." Many commentators, and some correspondents, are functioning less as journalists than as cheerleaders for "free-market capitalism," which they can't distinguish from corrupt black marketeering.

Some base their accounts on self-described Moscow democrats, who aren't always objective sources and whose radical views may be no less self-destructive than those of Russia's pre-Soviet intelligentsia. Even eminent professors have entered the fray. A Berkeley historian tells us in the *New Republic* that we shouldn't hold Boris Yeltsin to high democratic standards, because of the good things he is trying to achieve. Yeltsin deserves our support, but didn't American apologists for the Bolsheviks, and even for Stalin, offer the same excuses?

Each of us has the right to hope that Russia will become what we think it should be. But the ideological perspectives of the American right and left can't make analytical sense of that country's defiantly complex history and politics. As always, they only distort our political discourse and policies toward Russia.

Q: *You speak of new myths about Russia. Give us an example.*
SFC: Myths may not be entirely false. Usually, they inflate a partial truth into an overwhelming one that obscures other truths. Take, for example, the current notion that a "civil society," eager for a democratic market system, has emerged as the driving force in Russian political life, even defeating the attempted coup against Gorbachev in August 1991. For many observers of Russia who consider themselves to be right-minded—scholars, journalists, and democratic activists alike—this has become a new orthodoxy. Everything used to be attributed to a "totalitarian Kremlin." Now we have another extreme of simplistic analysis.

"Civil society" isn't even a very meaningful or useful concept in this context. Borrowed from the history of Western democratic theory, it's another attempt to squeeze Russia's traditions and realities into our ideological constructs. Indeed, the idea of a civil society is more philosophical than sociological because it is assumed to be democratic by nature. If so, how to explain Nazi Germany, which had some kind of civil society? Nor is it a valid empirical generalization about Russia's 150 million people. Opinion polls tell us that a great many of them don't understand or don't want markets or democracy. Some Russian sociologists worry that much of their country is more akin to a "lumpen society," the opposite of civil society. Anyway, to explain everything in terms of a surging civil society is bad analysis and history. Several hundred thousand Russians may have actively opposed the August 1991 coup; the rest were passive or silent.

Myths popularized by the failed coup, which remains a mystery in important respects, would matter less if they did not focus on partial truths. A struggle for markets and democracy is part of the Russian political story today, though that saga began under Gorbachev, not under Yeltsin after the coup. But consider two other large developments.

In most of the former Soviet republics, notably in Russia itself, leaders are calling for radical political and economic reform in the name of society. Even leaving aside how much of this may be designed to win American support, most of these leaders were Communist Party functionaries in the Soviet system—members of Soviet elites that fragmented during the Gorbachev years—now engaged in a zealous struggle over vast property and power formerly controlled by the Soviet state: factories, banks, land, shops, television networks, publishing houses, apartments, transportation, and, of course, military property. Like yesterday's Marxists, today's anti-Communists understand that property is power, so the struggle is raging everywhere, from the capitals to the provinces. Some of these people, perhaps many of them, are sincere converts to marketization and democratization. But it is foolish to ignore the politics of confiscation unfolding since late 1991 and its dangerous echoes of politically motivated expropriations earlier in Soviet history. It helps to explain the revival of some authoritarian traditions around governments in the former republics professing to be democratic, including Yeltsin's.

The second development is related. Our attention is riveted on Yeltsin's government in Moscow. But in Russia and several other former Soviet republics, considerable real power has migrated from the capital to the provinces. The process began under Gorbachev as central political authority weakened and elections made provincial officials more dependent on local constituencies. But it's now being driven and intensified by the economic situation. The scarcity of goods and the breakdown of distribution have put enormous power in the hands of producers. That means the country's large state factories and farms are still run by the old elites and *nomenklatura* and are located mainly in the provinces. Neither Yeltsin nor any other Moscow leader can govern, much less reform, Russia today without at least the tacit support of these powerful provincial elites. Real power—to produce and deliver goods—is in their hands. They could, for example, starve the large cities, the bastions of whatever democracy now exists, while bartering among themselves. Many of these economic elites want to take more direct control of their enterprises by "privatizing" them, but is that real marketization? Most of them now profess to be anti-Communists, but does that make them democrats? And what about their close ties to provincial military commanders? Whatever the case, while our diplomats and journalists seek Russia's destiny in Moscow, it is being determined largely in the vast and remote provinces.

Q: *For someone who always argued that fundamental change was possible in the Soviet system, you don't seem to be impressed by the dramatic changes that have occurred.*

SFC: Despite prevailing scholarly and media views to the contrary in the 1970s and early 1980s, it was easy to understand that significant changes would eventually come in the Soviet system. Nothing in history or politics is immutable, and factors favoring reform were already observable. It is much harder today to be certain about what has actually changed irrevocably and what has not, and to weigh what has passed against what remains. Take, for example, the prevailing conclusion, which has become so axiomatic that hardly anyone disputes it: "The Soviet system has collapsed."

Certainly, this is so in important ways, but also not so in important ways. It's a mistake to equate the Soviet system over the years so completely with the Communist Party—or Communism with what we might call "Sovietism." The party was a very important part of it, but far from all of it. For example, the party controlled the state, but the state—the "administrative-command system," as it became known—primarily controlled society, at least the economy. So what happened? The Communist Party actually lost its monopoly on politics as early as 1989—in that fundamental respect, the Leninist system was already disintegrating as a result of Gorbachev's reforms—but the state administration continued to function. After the 1991 coup attempt, the party collapsed, but has the Soviet state system? We shouldn't be misled by surface changes, however dramatic. Many links in the system have been ruptured, especially between Russia and the former republics and in economic distribution. The names of lots of cities, institutions, and streets have been changed.

But consider some fundamental continuities in Russia itself. The economy—at least 95 percent of it—remains in the hands of the state. No new elites, as I said before, have emerged. At the regional and local levels, the old authorities are largely still in place, having fled from the party to other power structures. And class relations are as they were. A new class of entrepreneurs is emerging, but it remains tiny and weak. Many popular attitudes do not seem to have changed greatly. Most citizens still expect the kind of cradle-to-grave welfare state that was a defining component of latter-day Soviet Communism.

In all these fundamental respects, no new revolution has occurred in Russia, although it is fashionable to speak of one. And if we ask more correctly about the prospects of further reforms in the system, the towering question that faced and undermined Gorbachev also remains: How do you actually implement marketization and democratization in a system where large segments of local officialdom—which evolved over decades into an entrenched caste of political, economic, and military power holders—and of the populace are opposed? It can be done, I think, but not easily or quickly.

There's an even larger interpretive question here. Was Communism or Sovietism really something entirely alien to and imposed upon Russia, as many Western and Russian commentators now insist? If so, we could imagine a quick escape from the past. We could believe Yeltsin when he tells us he is president of "another country." But if to a significant degree Soviet Communism grew out of and perpetuated Russia's authoritarian traditions, as I think was the case, we need a different perspective. Despite the modernizing and Westernizing changes that have occurred over the years, Russia cannot jump out of its skin—certainly not into ours.

I even have some doubts about another prevailing certainty in the media—that we've seen the last of something like the Soviet Union. The Union has collapsed politically. All fifteen former republics say they are fully independent states. Some have gained diplomatic recognition, and some are moving toward separate militaries and currencies. But here too we have to think about continuities and factors that may favor some kind of new union of several or most of the former republics.

Think of these pro-union factors as grids that stretch across and bind the entire territory. There is, of course, a single energy and economic grid. Few essential industrial enterprises can produce without components made in other republics. There is a single military grid. For all the rival claims to military property, the Soviet army is still garrisoned in most of the republics and largely under Moscow's command. And there is a human grid—75 million former Soviet citizens who live outside their ethnic territories, including 25 million Russians; millions of ethnic intermarriages; millions of non-Russians who speak only Russian and Russians who live elsewhere but can't speak the native language. Not surprisingly, in a recent referendum, in March 1991, some 77 percent voted for preserving the Soviet Union.

These ties that bind now seem less important than nationalist politics in the newly proclaimed states, but here we have to think further. Most nationalist leaders are ex-Communists engaged in political struggles at home. If their conversion to nationalism is less than sincere or complete, how long and fully will they play the nationalist card on territorial space that has been dominated by Russia's size and power for centuries? Meanwhile, Yeltsin insists that the imperial "center" ended with the Soviet government. But Russia, or Moscow, was the center of the Soviet Union. And though Yeltsin has renamed those Soviet ministries "Russian," they still exist. Some are being reduced, but others are being consolidated, including the security ministries. Moreover, Russian nationalism, the strongest ideological force in Moscow today, won't disregard its 25 million compatriots living elsewhere, or easily concede the Soviet Union's former economic and military property, as we see in the dispute over armed forces in Ukraine.

I'm not predicting a new Soviet Union, only arguing that here too there are more good questions than

answers. One is whether Gorbachev was right in insisting that marketization and democratization stood a better chance in a reformed Soviet Union rather than
without a union.

Q: *So you don't put much credence in the Commonwealth of*
Independent States, which was created in December 1991 by
abolishing the Soviet Union and Gorbachev's government?
SFC: We should wish it well, because it's a fine idea.
But it's a paper idea unlikely to withstand all the factors I've already mentioned, from the struggle over
property to the enduring union grids. In fact, republic
leaders who joined the commonwealth had conflicting
reasons for doing so. Some hoped it would become a
reformed union along the lines proposed by Gorbachev;
others, a way station to total independence. Not surprisingly, there's been more conflict than consensus ever
since the documents were signed. Moreover, it's not possible to create a new state or commonwealth overnight,
just by declaring it. Even the best such political intentions require decades, and not all the intentions leading
to the commonwealth were of the highest political
order. Much of the process was based on a chain of
political betrayal. Gorbachev's own ministers—by the
way, they were chiefly men of the state, not the
party—betrayed him by staging the August 1991 coup.
Gorbachev returned to Moscow and reached a series of
political arrangements with Yeltsin, who then betrayed
him and all the leaders of the non-Slav republics by
going to Belarus with the Ukrainian leader Leonid
Kravchuk in December to abolish the Soviet Union.
Kravchuk then betrayed Yeltsin and the Russian Par-

liament by reneging on several military and financial agreements. And so it goes. How much that is good or durable can be built on the politics of betrayal?

Q: *Most of the changes we now see are results of Gorbachev's almost seven years in power. As one of the few American scholars who argued from the beginning that he was an authentic reformer, can you now evaluate his years as a leader?*

SFC: It's not a simple matter. Political obituaries published since Gorbachev left office differ greatly. Western commentators tend to agree, and rightly, that his role in international affairs has earned him a great and positive place in history. More than anyone else, he deserves credit for ending the Cold War, liberating Eastern Europe, reuniting Germany, and ending Russia's long isolation from the West. On the other hand, many people, particularly in Russia, insist that no leader who presided over the disintegration of his own country, the crisis of its economy, and the collapse of his own party can be called successful. Others try to strike a balance: Gorbachev brought freedom but eliminated sausage.

So, many complex factors and outcomes have to be taken into account. A full scholarly evaluation of Gorbachev's leadership won't be possible for many years, for several reasons. First, Sovietologists who denied for decades that change was possible in the system now lack useful concepts for even defining the success or failure of such reforms. Second, Gorbachev attempted something unprecedented in history: simultaneous transformations to democracy, a market economy, and real federalism. Comparisons with lesser reforms in other societies are therefore partial or seriously misleading. Third, we still do not know how much freedom of decision-making Gorbachev had during his years in power, and thus how many unwise decisions were actually of his own making. For this, we need memoirs and archives. Fourth, it's not impossible that Gorbachev will have some kind of political afterlife that will alter our judgment.

But mainly, much depends on how the great transformations he set into motion turn out in the years and decades ahead. If Russia becomes a predominantly democratic state with a flourishing market economy coexisting benignly with the former Soviet republics, historians may conclude that Gorbachev was the twentieth century's greatest leader, having launched the transformation of its largest country. But if Russia plunges into a new despotism, with a rapacious state economy and imperialism, he's more likely to be viewed as another tragic leader in Russia's long history of failed reform.

Q: *Fair enough. But surely you can make a tentative evaluation today.*

SCF: On an interim basis, I would rank Gorbachev among this century's greatest reformers and as the greatest reformer in Russian history. Setting himself against centuries of Russian and Soviet experience, he consciously set out to liberate his society from the state's political and economic domination, and he succeeded far beyond what anyone could have imagined. Incidentally, many of the people who today criticize Gorbachev's domestic reforms as inadequate are those same people who previously said he would change nothing. Moreover, along the way, Gorbachev led Russia closer to a real democratic process than it ever had been before. He persuaded even the country's conservative elites of the need for substantial marketization and privatization. And the dogma of a monopolistic state economy was only one of the orthodoxies he shattered, a feat that bequeathed political capital to new reformers for years to come. Still more, unlike any previous tsarist or Soviet leader, Gorbachev offered to negotiate Russia's empire with its constituent nations. And in doing all this, he caused remarkably little bloodshed, which is a great tribute to his belief that radical purposes had to rely on centrist tactics and consensual approaches. Finally, Gorbachev achieved all this despite far greater opposition than is generally known. Pop analysts fault him for not moving more quickly and taking even bolder steps. But leaders must be judged in light of the obstacles they face. And there is plenty of evidence that Gorbachev's reforms—from overhauling the political and economic system to negotiating with the United States and withdrawing from Afghanistan—were actively opposed, even sabotaged, by political forces at high levels in the party and the state.

Q: *You credit Gorbachev with moving the Soviet Union toward democracy and suggest that Russia's future political development will strongly influence the fate of the other republics. What are the prospects for democracy in Russia?*

SFC: Democracy may still have its best chance ever in Russia, but it's a slim chance for the near future. The mythology of the failed coup in August 1991 generated the illusion that big obstacles to democratic development had been swept away. Some antidemocratic institutions were crushed or weakened, but many authoritarian obstacles remain, as I've already pointed out. Nor is it true that all the anti-Communists who call themselves democrats are actually democratic, as I know from firsthand observations. In addition, Russia still lacks many aspects of a functioning democracy, even leaving aside the absence of markets and a consensual democratic culture. It's a long list: a parliament and judiciary comparable to the traditions of executive power, a multiparty system, regularly scheduled elections, a nationwide and self-sustaining free press, and more. Russia doesn't even have a real constitution yet.

Still worse, antidemocratic developments have grown stronger and more numerous since the failed coup. These include not just the deteriorating economic situation—scarcity, rampant inflation, and unemployment have never fostered democracy—but other, less noted factors. The military has been politicized in unprecedented ways. It began in 1989 when Gorbachev had to allow active officers to stand for the new Soviet Parliament. During their final showdown in 1991, both Gorbachev and Yeltsin had to plead openly for the military's support. Yeltsin won because he could make budgetary promises, though dubious ones. Since then, the military has been drawn even more deeply and clamorously into politics, as its top leaders protest the country's disintegration and the efforts in several former republics to defy their authority and seize their property. They've marched onto the political stage, as we saw in January 1992 when a large assembly of wrathful officers convened in the Kremlin. They are only a step from center stage. Wildcat acts by district commanders may be no less a threat—in the Baltics, for example, where large Russian garrisons are feeling increasingly disfranchised; in the Transcaucasus, where civil wars could incite them; or in the Russian provinces, where garrison elites are part of the military-industrial-agricultural complex. Even if traditional generals have no stomach for taking power, don't overlook colonels and captains, who are closer to the woeful economic plight of junior officers.

We ought to take notice of other antidemocratic factors as well. Before the coup, a progressive conservatism was emerging in Soviet political debates. It was discredited by the coup, unfairly I think, and the result is even greater polarization between self-professed radical democrats and militant reactionaries, who have found new adherents among disemployed Communist officials and disadvantaged workers. Add here increasingly assertive "national-patriotic" movements, one of the strongest of which is indignantly called "Ours." Russian nationalism may turn out to be liberal and democratic, but it's hard to see how, in present circumstances. It is already menacing the Chechens, Tatars, and other large non-Russian minorities that want more independence within the Russian Federation. And a retrograde nationalism, yet another legacy of both tsarism and Stalinism, is also likely to be fed by an indignant backlash against Westernization, which is becoming excessive and primitive. Have a look at all the Western advisers swarming over Russia and at the amount of

imported rock videos and soft porn on government-run
television.

Q: *Are you saying that Russia has not moved closer to democracy since the failed coup and the disintegration of the Soviet Union?*

SFC: It depends on your understanding of democracy.
Russia has a popularly elected president and Parliament. That's very important. But as a process, there
may be less democracy now than before. Yeltsin is ruling primarily by decree, an old Russian tradition, rather
than through constitutional process or parliamentary
legislation. Some of his decrees are of dubious legality.
Banning a political party and confiscating property, even
the Communist Party [which was banned from August
1991 to November 1992] and Soviet property, doesn't set
democratic precedents. More generally, there's Yeltsin's
campaign to build "presidential power," which already
involved postponing regional elections in December 1991
and establishing an apparatus of personal envoys to
oversee provincial officials. Real Russian democratization must move toward political decentralization and
representative government at all levels. Yeltsin's campaign seems to be relying on the tsarist and Soviet tradition of centralizing authority in Moscow and
imposing it on the rest of the country.

To be fair, a case might be made that these measures
are necessary to cope with an emergency situation and
to implement reforms. In fact, Yeltsin's people are saying that some of them are only temporary. But it's a
mistake to pretend they are democratic; that will only
distort or discredit the democratic idea in Russia. And

don't forget that temporary emergency measures have a habit of becoming permanent in Russia.

On the other hand, I don't share the widely held view, which began in Moscow and has spread to the American media, that the only choice now is between democracy and fascism. Both possibilities exist, but there's a large spectrum of authoritarian outcomes in between them that seem more likely. Nor do I share the widespread notion, which also originated in Moscow, that a popular upheaval from below is lurking in the wings. It's a very remote possibility exaggerated by the lingering spell of 1917. Russia is no longer the country it was in 1917.

Q: *Speaking of the political class, you spoke earlier of its growing polarization. Is there no consensus about the country's future?*

SFC: Russian politics has often revolved around two questions: What is to be done, and who is to blame? Part of the problem today is that because so many people don't know what to do, they demand to know who's to blame. Therein lies the danger of another political witch-hunt, actually encouraged by Westerners who advise putting former Communist officials on trial in a country that had 20 million party members.

I don't think Russia can move toward a stable system, much less a democratic one, until the political class openly discusses and resolves on some consensual basis three fundamental questions. First, should everything created during the Soviet period be rejected as criminal or unworthy, and everything built from scratch? Or should important aspects of the existing system be retained? Second, what kind of system is best for Russia: one that tries to imitate a Western model or one that borrows from Western experiences but is equally reliant on Russian traditions and circumstances? And third, how fast should the country move toward a new system? In a leap through "shock therapy" or gradually and incrementally? (In thinking about such questions, it's important to understand that Russia's need in the foreseeable future is not to produce an American-style excess of goods but to eliminate scarcity of those goods necessary for a comfortable life.) Gorbachev generally preached moderate answers to these questions. The danger inherent in a very radical approach, which may now be ascendant, is that it could plunge Russia into another Bolshevik-like experiment, further polarize the country, and produce a system that is neither stable nor democratic.

Q: *Now that Yeltsin has launched his own economic program by liberalizing prices, which approach has he embraced?*
SFC: In economic policy, the conflict is between those who want to dismantle the state economy and build on a "free market" and those who want to combine large parts of the state sector with a market economy—to walk on both legs, so to speak. Yeltsin's government includes advocates of both approaches. His present economic team, headed by Yegor Gaidar, is preaching radical abolitionism and market "shock therapy," while his vice president, Aleksandr Rutskoi, advocates policies similar to Gorbachev's. Rutskoi, a relatively young and very substantial political figure, is increasingly nationalistic and critical of the Gaidar team for practicing

"economic genocide." He has been excluded from Yeltsin's inner circle but hardly from the political scene.

Yeltsin has espoused both views. Politically, he has rejected virtually the entire Soviet experience and suggested the need for a Western-style system. But economically, he is promising to retain large parts of the state and welfare system, which were the bedrock of Soviet "socialism." Having risen to power by assailing Communism, Yeltsin may now be finding that there are few social constituencies and circumstances favoring its opposite, capitalism. If so, he'll probably have to act even less democratically and make more inflationary concessions to public opinion in order to maintain stability. Eventually he may have to form a coalition with the Rutskoi forces.

It's not clear what Yeltsin really hopes to achieve by letting prices soar, as was done in Poland two years ago with very mixed results. Yeltsin says it will cause hard times but also generate many more goods and trigger extensive marketization. He says prices, and the general economic situation, will stabilize by the end of 1992. Let's hope so. But Russia is not Poland, a small homogeneous country where private farming and a rudimentary market infrastructure already existed. No substantial demonopolization, denationalization, or privatization of Russian industry, agriculture, or even trade has yet taken place. The process is scheduled to begin this year, but first and primarily in the areas of shops and housing, not the productive sectors. And no one knows if newly adopted land reform legislation will actually create a sizable number of productive private farmers.

Yeltsin may also have less-publicized reasons for liberalizing prices so soon. One could be to skim off the
excessive rubles in consumer hands, the "ruble over-
hang" that economists complain is inflationary but that
represents people's life savings. Another could be to
reduce the state's enormous budget deficit by sharply
cutting subsidies for essential consumer goods. And yet
another, to entice more foreign aid by convincing Western governments and banks that Yeltsin is acting on
their advice. But it is hard to imagine anything except
an even deeper economic and political crisis, perhaps as
early as April, if people have been deprived—some say
"robbed"—of their everyday necessities, savings, and
possibly jobs. At worst, such policies could vaporize
already weak constituencies for reform and bring reactionary forces to power in Moscow or in the provinces.
At best, they would create a situation compelling
Yeltsin, or another leader, to try to revive a gradual
incremental approach, if it's not too late.

Q: *What should or could the United States do about all these
changes and dangers in the former Soviet Union? Has the
Bush administration adopted the right policies toward Russia?*
SFC: What policies? There are no clear ones except for
desperately trying to safeguard Soviet nuclear weapons
and hoping for good political outcomes in the fifteen
former republics. We claim to be leading an international economic assistance program, but we've given less
than 7 percent of the total, mainly in credits to buy our
agricultural surplus and that must be repaid, while
Europeans have contributed more than 75 percent. We

promised to help Russia and the others through a potentially destabilizing winter but held a midwinter conference on the problem, and none of the food aid promised in November 1991 had reached Soviet territory by early February 1992. We are giving lots of "technical advice," but much of it is dubious. Meanwhile, we rushed to recognize the independence of several republics on the assumption that the proclaimed Commonwealth of Independent States was a divorce, when actually it was only a separation. Now they're fighting over a final settlement, and we've squandered diplomatic influence.

To be fair, these are complex questions without easy answers. The Bush administration has good intentions, but will it act on them? After all, it never came to Gorbachev's financial aid in ways that might have prevented the August coup. There may also be some bad intentions in or close to the administration. One occasionally hears triumphalist suggestions that the United States should exploit Russia's weakness to prevent it from becoming such a great power again—by preventing Russia from regaining strong influence over the former republics, as Henry Kissinger seems to be urging, or by imposing a unilateral disarmament on it. Great powers don't disappear and great countries don't stay in crisis forever. If we act on these unwise and dangerous proposals, what kind of Russia will then confront us?

But I'm even more worried about the consensus emerging among people inside and outside the administration, conservatives and liberals alike. It assumes that U.S. aid should be conditioned on Russia's following our economic and political advice, which means replicating our system and having a large American presence in Russia: economic advisers to the government, business advisers to enterprises, political advisers to parties, guardians against black-market corruption, inspectors to gather and dismantle their weapons, and more. In short, a great crusade to convert Russia to our way of life.

Almost everything is wrong with this kind of missionary and exceedingly intrusive American policy. It presumes that a political-economic-social system can be artificially and firmly implanted in a different, much older civilization, that we can intervene wisely in a seething cauldron of rival Russian ideas and movements, and that in the end Russia will be grateful. In reality, it means blatantly allying ourselves with one extreme program, "free-market shock therapy," and with the enormous social pain it will cause. And remember, political pendulums always swing. Anti-Westernism remains a powerful Russian tradition. When the natural backlash against excessive Westernization comes, hordes of Americans perceived to be engineering everyday pain, Klondike capitalism, and the exploitation of the country can only make it worse and direct it against us. Similarly, the Bush administration's plan to import Russian nuclear scientists may be a virtuous effort to prevent proliferation, but how will Russians eventually react to this Alaska-like purchase of their best and brightest?

Many well-intentioned Russians want this kind of American policy, but we lack the wisdom, power, and right to intervene so directly and deeply. Post-Communist Russia must find its own, native future, or it will never be stable. Why presume there can be no good third—or fourth and fifth—way? The West began with markets and moved toward state regulation and welfare. Russia begins instead with a statist system. Let it resolve the duality in its own way. Where is our fabled open mind and pluralism?

Q: *Are you saying that the United States should do nothing? Have a policy of benign neglect toward Russia?*
SFC: I want a much more generous American policy of helping Russia reform, but a far less smug, conditional, and intrusive one. Most Russian elites and movements now accept the need for marketization and privatization. They disagree over how much, how fast, and how to do it. So long as the general direction is toward reform, under Yeltsin or other leaders, let us give generously from afar and let them decide. Plenty of Russian economists understand the problems and possibilities better than do itinerant ones from Harvard, Hoover, Heritage, the IMF, and other international institutions who know little or nothing about Russia.

The United States ought to mobilize economic assistance comparable to the Marshall Plan, but, alas, that isn't going to happen. Given our own economic problems and presidential-year politics in 1992, there's no sufficient constituency or leadership, and won't be. But at a minimum, we must do several large things immediately, without any more excuses about aid going into "black holes" and black markets, for the sake of our national security and national honor.

Massive humanitarian relief has to be given, not for one winter but several, to those citizens most imperiled by marketization—the very young and very old. Why are none of our vaunted elder statesmen leading a supplementary private aid mission, as Herbert Hoover did in the early 1920s? A very large, long-term, low-interest credit program is needed so Russia can import essential goods and technology. Similarly, existing debt has to be restructured and interest considerably deferred or even forgiven. If Western private capital is really a large part of the solution, a stabilization fund, as was done for the Polish zloty, is required to make the ruble convertible. And surely it's time to abolish U.S. Cold War laws and regulations discriminating against the Russian economy.

All this is a bare minimum, but far more than we're now doing. It's said we can't afford even the few billion dollars a year that would be the U.S. contribution to such an international effort. Of course we could, simply by reducing defense spending in degrees truly responsive to cuts now under way in Russia.

Clearly, a larger problem is at work: Four decades of Cold War have so militarized our thinking that we can't think politically about our real national interests at home or abroad. For example, the post–Cold War world may be even more dangerous than the Cold War era if only because thousands of Soviet nuclear weapons, particularly battlefield ones, are scattered across that enormous, unstable territory. Only political solutions can bring security, but the only one proposed is to convert fifteen independent states, most of them with barely any democratic experience, into replicas of America. It's a conceit, not a policy. As for Russia itself, a Eurasian country, perhaps Europeans should bear the brunt of economic assistance. But if a reformed Russia moves closer to Europe—to Germany, for example—than to us, will we accept that natural political development?

What's needed is new political thinking about ourselves and the world, not the new weapons we continue to develop. Indeed, future historians of the late twentieth century may wonder why so many unorthodox political ideas germinated in the old authoritarian Soviet system and so few in democratic America.

[*The Nation*, March 2, 1992]

POSTSCRIPT

At the beginning of the interview, readers may have detected a moment of unwarranted optimism. The "less simplistic and more detailed" American reporting that I noted in early 1992 quickly gave way, as we saw in the preceding section, to the "new stereotypes, myths, and misconceptions" that I also noted. Indeed, despite the much greater information and access, reporting from post-Communist Russia, for reasons we have already examined, turned out to be less objective, balanced, thorough, and generally reliable than it had been from the Soviet Union during the heavily censored Cold War 1970s and early 1980s.[8]

Four other matters touched on in this interview, given less than two months after the end of the Soviet Union, are worth updating here, even though they reappear in the pages ahead.

As I suggested, when "privatization" of large-scale state property began in 1993–94, members of the for-

mer Soviet elite, or *nomenklatura,* were its main beneficiaries. A new Soviet Union has not appeared, but
Russian popular nostalgia for the old one has grown
almost yearly since 1992. (The following saying has
become popular among Russian politicians, "Anyone
who does not regret the breakup of the Soviet Union
has no heart. Anyone who wants to re-create it as it was
has no head.") Partly in response to those sentiments,
in December 1999, President Yeltsin of Russia and
President Aleksandr Lukashenko of Belarus, another
former Soviet republic, signed a new "Union Treaty,"
which was quickly ratified by both parliaments. In January 2000, Lukashenko became the formal head of the
new Union, and in April the body established to be its
government met for the first time. What will actually
come of the Union, and whether or not other former
republics will join, may not be known for years, but the
new Russian president, Vladimir Putin, has strongly
supported it.

Nor has the Russian military left the political stage.
Though shrunken, weakened, and demoralized by large
budget cuts and loss of a consistent mission, elements of
the armed forces have been repeatedly drawn into
domestic conflicts. By 2000, the army was again playing a major role in the country's political life in connection with the Chechen war and Putin's rise to power.
Finally, the "indignant backlash" against Western
influence in Russia that I foresaw did indeed develop,
becoming another major factor in politics in the late
twentieth and early twenty-first centuries.

A Cold Peace? (November 1992)

For the first time in at least fifty years, in 1992 Russia was not an issue in an American presidential campaign—indeed, it was rarely even mentioned. Given the corrupting influences of Cold War politics over the years, the omission should be good news. Unfortunately, it was based on a misconceived and potentially dangerous assumption: that with the end of the Soviet Union in 1991, Russia and the United States left behind all their decades-long conflicts and entered, as Presidents Boris Yeltsin and George Bush proclaimed at their summit meeting in June, "a new era of friendship and partnership."

In reality, no such "era" is under way, and its proclamation at the highest political levels and in the media may well turn out to be another of the ideological myths that have prevented stable relations between the two nuclear-laden giants for so many years. Serious conflicts in U.S.-Russian relations are already on the political horizon, with important implications for domestic policy. None of the presidential candidates, including President-elect Bill Clinton, even hinted how they might react, or noted the impact such tensions would have on their campaign promises.

The current image of post-Communist Russia as America's new best friend and like-minded partner rests on many misconceptions, if not a general myopia, about post-Soviet developments. In most accounts, the image assumes Russian policies at home and abroad that are inspired and endorsed by the United States, or at least faithfully pro-American. It assumes, above all, that Russia is embracing Western-style democracy and capitalism, eschewing imperial behavior toward the other former Soviet republics, and entering a de facto alliance with the United States in world affairs, including in the realm of nuclear weapons. All these areas of Russian decision-making today are characterized by complexities, contradictions, and uncertain outcomes, but in none of them do recent trends fit prevailing American notions of what Russian policy is or ought to be. Consider the following:

• The process of Russian democratization begun under former Soviet President Mikhail Gorbachev has progressed very little, if at all, since the collapse of the Communist Party and abolition of the Soviet Union last year. It may have even regressed, due in no small part to President Yeltsin's expansive practice of ruling by decree and his campaign to re-create "strong executive power" at the expense of parliamentary and local government. Meanwhile, elites with little interest in further democratization have gained new power in the post-Communist political system and around Yeltsin himself, notably directors of monopolistic state economic enterprises and military-security officials.

At best, it might be said that democratization has been frozen for almost a year, not a good omen in a country with only fragmentary and fragile aspects of a real democratic process. Even leaving aside persistent authoritarian strains in elite and popular attitudes, Russia still lacks an authentic constitution, consensual separation of powers (or even tolerance) between the executive and legislative branches, an independent judiciary, regularly scheduled elections, a multiparty system, habits of civil political discourse, and a free press capable of operating without state subsidies. Contrary to the views of American enthusiasts, few of Russia's committed democrats any longer call the post-Communist order democratic. And even some of Yeltsin's Russian supporters now deny that the democratic movement ever came to power under the Russian president.

• In Russian economic life, the process of marketization is moving forward, however fitfully and painfully, but it hardly seems headed toward the "free-market capitalism" endorsed by Western cheerleaders. The leap-to-capitalism shock therapy inflicted on Russian society this year by Yeltsin and his chief minister, Yegor Gaidar, at the urging of Western governments and banks and spearheaded by the International Monetary Fund, has predictably failed to fulfill any of its reassuring promises. Instead, it has brought skyrocketing consumer prices, a further collapse of the ruble, impoverishment of most Russian families, plummeting industrial production, and a continuing decline in popular support for liberal economic and political reform and for Yeltsin himself, the nation's first and only popularly elected leader. (Several opinion polls give him barely 30 percent positive ratings, below those of his vice president, General Aleksandr Rutskoi, who has opposed shock-therapy policies from the start.)

Indeed, while Yeltsin continues to speak in a pro-

capitalist idiom to his Western boosters, at home he
is moving steadily away from Gaidarism and toward
the very different program of its most formidable
opponents, a coalition of state industrial and agricultural managers, nationalistic military officers, former
Communist Party reformers, and lapsed radicals who
have formed a political organization known as Civic
Union. That program calls for a specifically Russian
"mixed economy" and "regulated market," looks
admiringly upon the "Chinese model" of gradual,
state-guided economic reform, and speaks contemptuously of the IMF and the West's other would-be
architects of Russia's future. With more than 90 percent of the economy still in state hands, Civic Union's
policies would be progress in Russia, but not the kind
insisted upon and expected in the United States.

• Russia's relations with the other former Soviet republics,
inside or outside the successor way station known as the
Commonwealth of Independent States, are not likely
to resemble U.S.-Canadian relations anytime soon, if
ever. Despite raucous political disunion since 1991,
powerful factors still bind many of the fourteen other
former republics to Russia—particularly, essential
economic ties, inescapable military realities, and
inalienable human bonds in the form of large ethnic
diasporas and intermarriages. Not surprisingly, opinion polls show growing Russian nostalgia for the old
union, while leaders of some of the non-Russian
republics increasingly call for a new one. If these
trends continue, the not unreasonable charge by
opponents of the breakup that the Soviet Union did
not in fact "collapse" in December 1991 but was con-

spiratorially abolished by Yeltsin and his allies in Ukraine and Belarus is likely to become a compelling issue in Russian politics.

No less important is the combustible combination of 25 million Russians living in former Soviet republics outside of Russia and a Russian army still encamped throughout those territories. In one way or another, that army has already been involved in at least four civil wars outside of Russia—in Moldova, Georgia, Tajikistan, and the Armenian enclave of Nagorno-Karabakh in Azerbaijan. If the number and intensity of civil wars in the former republics grow, as seems likely, so will the imperial role of the Russian army and thus the potential for renewed Russian hegemony. (Inexplicably, former Soviet Foreign Minister and current Georgian leader Eduard Shevardnadze's charge in October 1992, "a war between Russia and Georgia in essence . . . is already under way," was scarcely reported in the U.S. media.) Elsewhere, elements of the Russian military in Estonia and Latvia, where large Russian minorities have been disfranchised, are itching for a fight; and on October 29, Yeltsin ordered a suspension of Russian troop withdrawals from the Baltics. Meanwhile, none of the potentially explosive conflicts between Russia and Ukraine, the second-largest former republic, have yet been resolved or even defused.

American pundits and policymakers attribute these examples of Soviet-like behavior to Russian "hardliners," but such policies are supported in various ways by Russian leaders with some democratic credentials who are associated with Yeltsin. Vice President Rutskoi may be the government's most vocal defender of the army's role outside Russia, but even the head of Parliament's foreign affairs committee, Yevgeny Ambartsumov, a radical democrat who earlier broke with Gorbachev in favor of Yeltsin, now calls for a "Monroe Doctrine" that will give Russia hegemony over the entire former Soviet territory. That aspiration is growing among many leading Russians we call democrats, but would the United States accept its own historical relationship with Latin America as the model for post-Communist Russia's relations with its neighbors?

- Finally, there is the preposterous notion that post-Communist Russia will now follow an Americanized policy in world affairs, as though only Marxist-Leninists could think up conflicts with the United States. In fact, Yeltsin's policies under Foreign Minister Andrei Kozyrev have been angrily criticized in many political quarters in Russia precisely because until recently they gave the appearance of being made-in-America. Again, U.S. commentators point to ex-Communists—who in power in Russia today is not one?—and other "hard-liners," but the most telling critics have been leaders we identify as democrats, including Ambartsumov, the radical anti-Communist parliamentarian Oleg Rumyantsev, Yeltsin's high-level aide Sergei Stankevich, and his impeccably democratic ambassador to Washington, Vladimir Lukin, who recently protested "infantile pro-Americanism" in Russian foreign policy.

As in domestic affairs, a struggle is under way over Russian foreign policy, but it is hard to imagine specific or general outcomes like those expected by American politicians and commentators. Despite President Bush's campaign boasts, none of the nuclear-weapons problems once associated with the "Soviet threat" have actually been eliminated; they've only been papered over. The START II agreements, which if signed promise substantial reductions but require three former republics with strategic nuclear weapons to hand them over to Russia, will face a struggle for ratification in the Russian Parliament, and they are already the subject of profound second thoughts by the leadership of Ukraine, the most powerful of those republics. If the likelihood of ill-attended reactors and fugitive tactical weapons on former Soviet territories is added to this de facto proliferation, the nuclear danger is greater today than it was under the Soviet regime.

Is an anti-Communist government in Moscow enough to assuage American fears about that threat, once it becomes known? The U.S. media amply reported and disapproved of Russia's recent sale of strategic technology and weapons to China, Iran, and India, but missed a more startling revelation, in September, by Russian Marshal Yevgeny Shaposhnikov. It turns out that Russia's intercontinental missiles, which Yeltsin said he ordered retargeted away from the United States early this year, have not been retargeted, partly because, Shaposhnikov explained, the United States has not reciprocated. That position might be understandable, but it is not the reaction of a "friend and partner." Nor was the warning in October by Yeltsin's defense minister, General Pavel Grachev, that Russia might resume nuclear testing in mid-1993 unless the United States adopts its own permanent test ban.

As for the larger international rivalry that divided the United States and the Soviet Union for so long, Russia will continue to pursue good relations with the Western powers, but will that be enough to satisfy American ideological expectations? If post–Cold War divisions emerge between the United States and its NATO allies in Western Europe, Russia will have significant diplomatic and economic opportunities. It might find closer friends and better partners on its own continent. Nor should the symbolism of another recent development be overlooked. Yeltsin abruptly canceled his much-touted trip to pro-Western Japan in September, but he will visit the last great Communist power, neighboring China, in December.

None of these "un-American " trends in Russian policy at home and abroad portend a renewal of the Cold War, which was the product of historical factors that have largely passed. They do mean, however, that a U.S.-Russian relationship based on "friendship and partnership," on the same national values and interests, is an exceedingly unlikely prospect. What is the alternative? Much depends, as before, on our own perceptions and reactions, and therein also lies a great danger.

Most American thinking about Russia today, across the political spectrum, is based on a missionary premise that the United States can and should help convert that historically very different society into a replica of America. Of all Russia's future possibilities, Americanization is not one of them. Recent developments there are the result not primarily of nefarious political intentions, poor understanding of markets and democracy, or baneful hard-line influences but of deeply rooted traditions and intractable circumstances. One of those traditions, belief in the nation's special destiny, is already inspiring a predictable political backlash against the West's sponsorship of Yeltsin's traumatic economic policies and the legions of American and other foreign "advisers" now swarming across Russia.

But what will be the reaction of our own opinion shapers and policymakers when Russian realities explode the prevailing myths about America's post-Communist friend and partner, as they soon will? If missionary dogmas persist, the American backlash is easy to foresee—at best, cynicism and indifference to Russia's plight; at worst, a sense of betrayal and a revival of reflexive Cold War attitudes. In either case, the first victim will be prospects for substantial reductions in U.S. defense spending, the post–Cold War "peace dividend."

The necessary alternative is the kind of common sense and plain talk that was so lacking in the presidential campaign. A reforming, stable Russia at peace with its neighbors is a crucial American interest, but such a Russia can find its way only within the limits of its own traditions and possibilities, not ours. Such a reformation does not need our political tutelage, but it is equally worthy of our financial support.

If the United States cannot accept this first principle of post-Communism everywhere, the sequel to the Cold War is likely to be a very cold peace.

[*The Nation*, November 23, 1992]

POSTSCRIPT

I do not claim a patent on the term *cold peace,* and am not even certain I was the first to use it in this context, but it subsequently began to appear frequently in the U.S. and Russian press—and remarkably even in a statement by President Boris Yeltsin. (My article was published in Moscow, in Russian, under a similar title.) On December 5, 1994, protesting the Clinton administration's plans to expand NATO eastward, Yeltsin warned, "Europe is in danger of plunging into a cold peace."[9] (I take no pleasure from the expression's subsequent currency or relevance.)

Several other updates are in order. Civic Union soon collapsed, as did most of its "centrist" successor movements until the late 1990s, when they gained support, but its "mixed economy" program grew steadily in elite and popular appeal. The Russian army is no longer encamped in all the former Soviet republics, notably the Baltics and Ukraine, but it remains in several of them, along with the reality or potential of civil wars. During the Chechen war of 1999–2000, for example, Russia's military relations with Georgia, which borders Chechnya, became even more acute than usual.

In January 1996, Yeltsin replaced the demonstratively pro-American and unpopular Andrei Kozyrev as foreign minister with Evgeny Primakov. Oleg Rumyantsev ceased to be a "radical anti-Communist" in October 1993, for reasons readers will soon understand. Yeltsin's onetime aide Sergei Stankevich was later charged with taking bribes and fled to Poland. (The charges were dropped in 1999.) And Ambassador Lukin soon returned to Moscow to become the second-ranking leader, after Grigory Yavlinsky, of the democratic reform party Yabloko.

The three former Soviet republics with strategic nuclear weapons—Ukraine, Kazakhstan, and Belarus—did turn them over to Russia. But it was not until 2000 that START II, which was signed in 1993, was finally ratified by a Russian parliament, and the new Union Treaty between Russia and Belarus suggests that nuclear weapons might one day be returned to that westernmost former republic. Missiles on both sides were eventually retargeted, but it was a merely symbolic act since reverting to previous targets can be done in seconds. A truly significant step would be to take all the missiles on both sides off hair-trigger status.

As for divisions between the United States and its NATO allies leading to closer Russian-European relations, such a possibility has been forestalled by NATO's 1998 expansion, its 1999 war against Yugoslavia, and Russia's renewed war in Chechnya in 1999–2000. It cannot, however, be ruled out for the future, as I will argue more fully later in this book.

Can America Convert Russia? (*March 1993*)

Events in recent years have brought us to a fateful moment in the history of American-Russian relations. There is the possibility of a fundamentally new, demilitarized, and truly cooperative relationship between these

longtime superpower rivals, but also of a perilous collision between post-Communist Russia's complex realities
and post–Cold War America's simplistic expectations.
That danger has been exemplified by the Clinton
administration's unwise interventions in Russian domestic politics and support for Boris Yeltsin's threat to
resort to dictatorial "special powers." Yeltsin has
stepped back for now, but such measures could terminate Russia's historic and exceedingly fragile democratization experiment.

Whatever direction the relationship takes, Russia will
be the United States' largest foreign policy concern for
many years to come. That country's development—
because of its history, size, economic potential, and
unprecedented capacity for nuclear mishap—will profoundly affect international security in much of the
world. Yet Russia's ongoing collapse—its political, economic, social, and even psychological crisis—is far from
over, as events of past days remind us.

Within Russia, meanwhile, the missionary and intrusive nature of U.S. policy since 1991 has contributed
specifically to the growing anti-American backlash. The
problem is not primarily xenophobic nationalists who
see the Yeltsin government as a U.S.-sponsored "occupation regime," but a more general backlash against
"Yankee-ization" that has spread across the Russian
political spectrum. Thus, pro-market Russian economists once admired in the West, such as Nikolai
Petrakov, have objected to U.S. economic advisers in
Yeltsin's government because the monetarist, shock-
therapy policies they demand are "fundamentally unacceptable to Russia." And the Russian ambassador to the

United States, Vladimir Lukin, a man well known for his pro-Western views, continues to protest an "infantile pro-Americanism" in his country's foreign policy.

Russian politicians and editorialists tolerated U.S. missionary rhetoric in the beginning because it included promises of very large U.S. aid and investment. Neither has arrived, and neither is in sight, despite President Clinton's statements. The result is another kind of backlash: a growing conviction that the United States will never put its money where its mouth has been ever since the Gorbachev years and is interested only in exploiting Russia's natural resources, not in helping to rebuild its economy.

Even more objectionable to many Russians have been the many U.S. intrusions into the cauldron of Russian politics. From the beginning, the U.S. government has focused almost all of its relations and good will exclusively on Yeltsin and his handpicked team, while virtually ostracizing other elected institutions and leaders, particularly the Russian Parliament and its speaker, Ruslan Khasbulatov—not to mention the country's vice president, Aleksandr Rutskoi. The forty-five-year-old Rutskoi, who has considerable elite and popular backing, is certain to play a major role in the future, as indeed he is in the present crisis.

The Clinton administration steadily escalated this kind of interventionism—first by contriving the planned April 1993, Vancouver summit as an attempt to "help Yeltsin" in his ongoing confrontation with the Russian Parliament, next by publicly hinting support for the Russian president's threats to disband the legislature, and then by endorsing Yeltsin's suspended effort to seize "special powers" from virtually all of Russia's other new democratic institutions. The Clinton administration even suggested that Clinton might go instead to Moscow for a solidarity summit with Yeltsin.

The result was to put the U.S. government in bad institutional company: Yeltsin's move was opposed not only by the Russian Parliament but by the Constitutional Court, procurator, justice minister, vice president, most local legislatures, and large segments of the democratic-minded press. Supporting or leaning toward Yeltsin's strategy were heads of the Russian military, former KGB, militia—and the Clinton administration. Indeed, Clinton and Yeltsin have been egged on by a plethora of U.S. congressional leaders and columnists, who maintain that Yeltsin's professed democratic goals justify his means.

Surely, twentieth-century history, and especially Russia's history, teaches the lethal folly of that premise. Even if Yeltsin's gambit succeeds, it risks destroying what little rule-of-law government Russia now has and putting the country's political fate in the hands of the military and other security forces.

American officials may accept Yeltsin's assertion that the Parliament's majority is insufficiently reformist. But let us remember that this "reactionary" Russian Parliament, as it is now dubbed in U.S. press and government accounts, was greatly admired not long ago for its heroic pro-Yeltsin resistance, in its tank-encircled Moscow "White House," to the August 1991 coup.

Moreover, there can be no democracy in Russia, whose history is full of overweening executive power and abolished legislatures, without a parliament. Nor can there be any ratified arms treaties without one. Indeed, perceived U.S. contempt for the Russian Parliament and its leadership has already made ratification of the START II agreements more difficult. And last week, not surprisingly, the Parliament passed a special resolution condemning the West's "crude interference in the internal affairs of Russia."

U.S. policy and behavior have been even more intrusive at lower political levels. American economists, notably the Harvard team headed by Professor Jeffrey Sachs, sit as official advisers to the Russian government. U.S. political organizations, some with federal funds, reward favored political factions. The AFL-CIO is deeply involved in Russian trade union politics. Proposals are even afloat to put a resident corps of Western "experts" in Russia's governing bureaucracies, to assign NATO advisers the job of reshaping Russia's armed forces, and to make the dollar an official Russian currency. Americans need only imagine their own reaction if Russians were playing such roles in our government and political life.

Not surprisingly, the anti-American backlash is also gathering force below. As a result of the U.S.-backed "shock therapy," millions of Russian families have lost their life savings and fallen below the poverty line. To many of those citizens, their misery seems to be "made in the U.S.A." It is not true, but given U.S. rhetoric why would they think otherwise?

Recall how this situation came about. The breakup of the Soviet Union in 1991 generated both alarm and euphoria in U.S. policy circles—alarm over the disposition of Soviet "loose nukes," euphoria over the pro-

American possibilities thought to be inherent in post-Communist Russia. Accordingly, the Bush administration pursued a twofold policy, which remains in place under President Clinton. The administration negotiated, and offered to subsidize, a substantial abolition of Soviet-built strategic nuclear weapons, and it urged a fast Russian transition to democracy and capitalism, for which it promised to mobilize large financial support. Some progress was made toward the "new era of friendship and partnership," as proclaimed by Presidents Bush and Yeltsin at their summit meetings, but most of it was, and remains, rhetorical.

Clearly, the United States needs a serious reexamination of its post–Cold War thinking. It must begin with ourselves: We lacked the right, wisdom, and power to convert Russia into an American replica. Wise policies require realistic perceptions, not missionary assumptions, about what has been happening in post-Communist Russia:

• Important changes have taken place since 1991, but they remain an embryonic alternative system within the old Soviet system, which is still responsible for people's essential needs—housing, employment, food and other basic supplies, welfare provisions, public order, and more. Russia's journey to stable markets and democracy, if there is to be one, will therefore be long and jagged.

• There is no real evidence that popular anti-Communist activities in 1991 constituted a national referendum in favor of democratic "free-market capitalism" as we understand it. Opinion polls have already shown, for example, a steady rise in public support for new authoritarian leadership, and considerably more popular esteem for the army and the Orthodox Church than for the new democratic institutions. Not surprisingly, the Parliament responded by deposing the "shock-therapist" prime minister, Yegor Gaidar, and Yeltsin's own popular rating fell from about 80 percent in autumn 1991 to about 30 percent a year later, somewhat less than that of Vice President Rutskoi.

U.S. policymakers have assumed that Russia's struggles over democracy and markets are the primary ones. In reality, they have been dwarfed and distorted by other towering conflicts—in particular a bitter dispute about the desired national identity of post-Communist Russia. Should Russia be part of the West or apart from the West? Should Russia be greater territorially ("imperial") or lesser? Should the nation's own vastness be governed chiefly by a dominant Moscow state or locally? No consensus, to say the least, exists on any of these fundamental questions.

A parallel conflict continues to rage over all the enormous property formerly monopolized by the Soviet state: natural resources, banks, factories, communication facilities, buildings, transport, even military equipment. Though this struggle is often waged under the banner of "privatization," much of it is corrupt even by Soviet standards. And yet another confrontation pits central authorities in Moscow against local authorities in the vast provinces, where much real economic and political power has migrated in recent years. This epic struggle is exacerbated by the presence of non-Russian majorities in several of those internal administrative regions.

Thus it is exceedingly difficult to identify all the "good" and "bad" actors in Russian political life today, especially if the role of easily recognized extremists is discounted. What are we to make of a political arena where, for example, leaders we call "conservatives and reactionaries" defend the idea and institution of parliament against "democrats"; and those we disdain as "centrists" hold the balance of power? Where we see constant menace in "ex-Communists," but where almost all leaders on all sides, including Yeltsin, are former Communist Party members? If even well-informed Russians cannot decide which leaders and policies to favor from month to month, or in the present crisis, how can we?

In fact, whatever the full nature of Russia's political and economic future, it will not be a replica of America's present or the Soviet past. It will be, as is said increasingly in Moscow, some "third way." Here is what President Yeltsin himself told the nation in October 1992: "We are not leading Russia to any kind of capitalism. Russia is simply not suited for this, Russia is a unique country. It will not be socialist or capitalist." We may believe it or not, but most Russians evidently do.

We also need realistic thinking, not fairy-tale expectations, about U.S.-Russian relations in the larger context of world affairs. Russian policy must be made and sustained politically in Moscow, not Washington. Having a very different geopolitical relationship with China, a close cultural one with Serbia, and a divorced family's relations with other former Soviet republics, Russia is certain to adopt policies unlike ours toward most of those countries—and even toward Europe. None of this is reason for a new Cold War or for refusing to help Russia's reforms, only for more realistic expectations about U.S.-Russian relations. Indeed, even America's "best hope," as the Clinton administration characterizes Yeltsin, has objected to "a U.S. tendency to dictate its terms," adding, "No other state can command such a great nation as Russia."

Finally, post-Communist Russia's relationship with many if not all of the other former Soviet republics is far from being resolved. The United States evidently assumes that all of them will remain fully independent states, but many powerful factors continue to generate proposals, in Russia and several other former republics, for a new and voluntary federal or confederal state that would naturally revolve around Russia. One school of U.S. thinking, represented by Henry Kissinger, insists that any political regrouping around Russia must be opposed as resurgent Russian "imperialism." But a number of factors continue to work in its favor.

U.S. policymakers have given this fateful problem little serious thought, though even some Russian democrats have been calling for a Russian "sphere of influence" throughout the former Soviet Union, a demand now echoed in Yeltsin's own assertion that Russia should have "special powers as guarantor of peace of stability in regions of the former U.S.S.R."

Russia is not, of course, ours to win or lose, but our national security and much else is at stake there. It is

time to help Russia's reforms in ways that are generous and functional, not illusory and counterproductive. The United States cannot do everything, but if
it really aspires to international leadership, it must
provide it.

Solutions to the several kinds of nuclear threats on former Soviet territory cannot wait. Any lopsided inequities
in the hastily drafted strategic-weapons agreements that
might prevent Russian ratification should be rectified.
Russian tactical (battlefield) nuclear weapons, which
are particularly dangerous given ongoing civil conflict in former Soviet republics, should be reduced
drastically, along with our own. Programs to safeguard Soviet-built reactors, some as catastrophe prone
as the one that exploded at Chernobyl in 1986, and
already the target of terrorist threats, must be imple-
mented.

Russia's traumatic "transition" to a market system
still cries out for massive, multiyear humanitarian
relief, especially essential nutrients and medicines for
the growing number of very young and old victims of
the process. The nation's crushing $84 billion foreign
debt, which continues to grow, must be restructured—
quickly, fully, and generously. And new credits and
loans, less burdensome and less conditional, must be
provided. Special funds are needed to subsidize benefits
for Russia's growing unemployed and start-up capital
for small entrepreneurs, but nonintrusive ones administered by Russians and in rubles. The U.S. government
should move at last to guarantee mutually beneficial
U.S. private investment in Russia—for example, in its
lagging energy sectors. And something should be done

to help the nearly destitute educational centers of Russia's professional and other middle classes, which were the original social basis for reform in the 1980s but now are its victims.

Having spent trillions of dollars over forty-five years trying to force Soviet Russia to give up its bad ways, the U.S. government will be judged harshly by future citizens and historians alike if it does not generously help Russia change now that the moment has come. Or if it risks being remembered for having supported measures that destroyed another nascent Russian experiment with parliamentary democracy and plunged the country back into its despotic traditions. Nor will Russia, when it reemerges in its predestined role as a very great power, as it certainly will, forget how other powers treated it during its present time of troubles. What we do now, or fail to do now, will shape our children's and grandchildren's relations with Russia as well.

[*Washington Post*, March 28, 1993]

POSTSCRIPT

This entire book is an answer to the rhetorical question posed by the title of this article. Many Russians have expressed their own postmortem on the American crusade as one of those bitter witticisms that were a hallmark of Soviet political humor: "We thought the Communists were lying to us about socialism and capitalism, but it turns out they were lying only about socialism."

"Parliament Is Burning!" (October 1993)

As the possibility of dictatorship looms yet again over Russia, the Yeltsin government is relentlessly imposing an epic spin on last week's carnage in Moscow. Russia's political winners have usually enforced their might-makes-right version of events as the nation's official history, but this is the first time it has ever been echoed and endorsed by an American government.

According to President Boris Yeltsin, he had to order special military forces to attack the nation's Parliament with tank fire and arrest his two leading political rivals, Vice President Aleksandr Rutskoi and Speaker Ruslan Khasbulatov, because they had launched a "criminal mutiny" against Russia's democracy. President Clinton says approvingly that "if such a thing happened in the United States," he too would have taken "tough action." But who actually began that "mutiny"?

In fact, on September 21, 1993, Yeltsin dealt a wounding, possibly fatal, blow to Russia's historic and exceedingly fragile democratization experiment by terminating Parliament and all other elements of rule-of-law government in Moscow. He had tried but failed to do exactly the same thing on March 20. In the intervening months, respected Russian political observers, including members of his own entourage, warned that such a step would certainly lead to substantial violence, if only because many parliamentary deputies believed in their own democratic legitimacy and would resist. Knowing all this, Yeltsin nonetheless struck again, with the predictable outcome we have witnessed.

The Clinton administration, Yeltsin's leading cheer-leader in the West, therefore committed a grave misdeed by supporting Yeltsin's actions so fully from the outset and justifying their fateful consequences now.

Russia's democratization was begun by Mikhail Gorbachev, then Soviet leader, in the late 1980s, and grew into the first sustained attempt in the nation's centuries-old history. By 1991, it led to the creation of fragmentary but essential components of a democratic system—a popularly elected parliament, president, and vice president, an independent constitutional court and procurator, substantially free national media, and elected local legislatures.

By September 21, Yeltsin had banned or suspended that Parliament, vice president, court, and procurator; shut down parliamentary publications; imposed self-serving censorship on nationwide television channels; threatened to disband local assemblies that did not fall in line; and brought armed security forces onto political center stage. In short, well before the Parliament's infuriated defenders recklessly tried to capture the television headquarters by force on October 3, there was no longer democracy in Moscow, and it was in grave danger of crumbling elsewhere in the country in the aftermath.

Yeltsin justified all this, and won enthusiastic support from both the Clinton administration and virtually all of the U.S. media, by insisting that his coup against opponents would lead to greater democracy in Russia. Defending Yeltsin, two prominent American journalists, one a specialist on Russia, even tried to rehabilitate the infamous Stalinist adage "You can't make an omelette without breaking eggs." But as needs to be emphasized again and again, it seems, if twentieth-century history, and especially Russia's experience, teaches any lesson, surely it is that even a professed democratic end never justifies bad means, which produce only masses of broken eggs in the form of crushed hopes and lives.

Nor is it possible to be confident about Yeltsin's promise of fair parliamentary and presidential elections in the near future. They would require, at the very least, that Yeltsin

- retract his accusation that all of the Parliament's deputies who did not defect to him during the crisis were part of a "bloodthirsty Communist-Fascist" conspiracy, an ominous echo of the trumped-up "Right-Trotskyist conspiracy" that fueled Stalin's terror of the 1930s;
- release his political opponents from prison;
- rescind his ban on opposition movements, including the Communists, the largest party in Russia;
- stop other reprisals against his many adversaries and even mere critics across the country;
- completely and unconditionally end the new media bans he has imposed;
- give challengers fair access to national television, where nearly 90 percent of Russian voters get their information (something he refused to do in his April 1993 referendum campaign and in the confrontation with Parliament);
- instruct the committee he appointed to write new electoral laws to make them equitable ones; and
- reinstate the Constitutional Court so that there is

some minimal guarantee of rule-of-law procedures in the electoral process.

Even if Yeltsin exhibits such political decorum, not a trait for which he has been known, what will he do if local legislatures and other regional authorities, which overwhelmingly opposed his September overthrow of the constitutional order, refuse to conduct new elections or comply with any of his decrees on their territories? It is a scenario for nuclear-laden Russia's further disintegration and a civil war. The larger corps of military officers—those not drawn into the Moscow shootout—are already deeply divided politically. Local commanders, many of them full of loathing for the president and the entire four-year democratization experiment, may not remain so passive.

Indeed, now that Yeltsin has made the army and other security forces the arbiter of Russia's political fate, how will he diminish their role to what it must be in any democratic system? Or, to take a special U.S. interest, will he reduce their already large role in Russian foreign policy?

Why, then, was it necessary to put Russia's fledgling democracy at such great risk? According to Yeltsin, the Parliament, full of reactionary Communists and fascist-like nationalists, has been the "hard-line" obstacle to all market and democratic reforms and thus the cause of Russia's deepening crisis since the Soviet breakup in 1991. The charge is ritualistically echoed in the American press, much of which repeatedly confuses this Russian Parliament with its 1989 Soviet counterpart, and almost none of which bothers to study it carefully. Furthermore, even if the Parliament was as bad as Yeltsin claimed, were his actions really better than simply waiting for its term to end by law in 1995?

There is very little to admire in the legislature's leadership, composition, or recent behavior, but its real history and membership are much more complex. It is the same Parliament, chosen in a generally acclaimed free election in 1990, that defied Gorbachev and the Soviet Communist Party by making Yeltsin its first chairman. It is also the Parliament that adopted a constitutional amendment enabling Yeltsin to become Russia's popularly elected president in June 1991, gave him sanctuary in its White House during the failed August 1991 coup, ratified his abolition of the Soviet Union in December of that year, and empowered him, for twelve months, to reform the economy by decree.

For reasons that remain less than fully clear, and against the advice of Russia's leading pro-market economists, Yeltsin opted for the policies known as "shock therapy." By late 1992, these policies had impoverished the majority of Russian families, generated a Klondike "capitalist" profiteering in state goods and natural resources—"corruptalism," as many Russians call it. They also shattered any popular consensus about the nation's post-Communist future and thus eroded Yeltsin's support in the Parliament and political class generally.

As the social pain grew, extremists on both sides of an already raucous political spectrum became more zealous, undercutting centrists and inflaming legislative and executive branch leaders alike with contempt for any compromises. One of Russia's eternal political questions—"What is to be done?"—gave way to another: "Who is to blame?" These deep-rooted realities, not the Parliament or Soviet-era constitution, underlie the country's crisis, and they will be reflected in any new, freely elected legislature.

But Yeltsin will have much to answer for in a court of history. As Russia's first popularly chosen president, his highest duty was to exemplify and nurture democratic practices, not just rhetoric, in a nation where support for them remains thin and where ancient demons of despotism still stalk the land. It was his special responsibility to lead a nation of citizens already tormented and torn by profound shocks—the loss of their country in 1991 and of their life savings and living standards in 1992—toward social consensus and political compromise, not more pain and confrontation that only exacerbate Russia's towering economic problems and arouse its anti-liberal, anti-Western, anti-Semitic specters.

Yeltsin's apologists insist that he always sought compromise with the Parliament, but consider the highly typical one he proposed this past summer. Rejecting the Parliament's draft for a new separation-of-powers constitution, he demanded one whose legislature would either rubber-stamp the president's laws or be subject to dissolution, and which abolished the office of vice president. Even his own handpicked "constitutional assembly" rejected it. In reality, well before provoking this latest and most dangerous polarization throughout the country, Yeltsin had reverted to Russia's old tsarist and Communist tradition of a "strong-hand" leader who exercises the "people's will" against malevolent dissenting ideas, institutions, and rivals.

Striking down Parliament was squarely in that leadership-cult tradition, which has also played a very large role in Yeltsin's electoral successes and on which he is still counting heavily. Six Russian or Soviet legislatures now have been disbanded in this century—four since 1917 in the name of a higher democracy. But only Yeltsin has set one ablaze, generating a television image and cry that will be long remembered: *Parliament is burning!*

The twofold lesson is unmistakable and ought to be especially pondered by all those members of the U.S. Congress now wildly applauding Yeltsin's actions: No authentic democracy is possible anywhere, least of all in Russia, without a truly independent and fully sanctioned parliament or congress, no matter how disagreeable or unpopular it may become. And once abolished, such parliaments do not reappear easily and quickly in Russia.

Yeltsin's Russian and American apologists will argue that none of these historical lessons matter. Let them explain, then, just a few of the many recent developments that collide with their spins and history writing. The coup makers who plotted against Presidents Gorbachev and Yeltsin in August 1991 dared not order their tanks to fire on the Russian Parliament. Yeltsin did so. The two men who stood defiantly alongside Yeltsin against the 1991 putsch, Rutskoi and Khasbulatov, now sit in the infamous political prison Lefortovo, threatened with capital charges, while all the 1991 putschists remain untried and at liberty. And among the deputies who refused to leave the Parliament building on October 4 was thirty-three-year-old Oleg Rumyantsev, whose heroic efforts to write a truly democratic constitution for

Russia—his draft was rejected by Yeltsin—led the *Washington Post* in 1990 to call him "the James Madison of Russia" and the U.S. National Endowment for Democracy to award his committee a grant and honor him as a featured speaker at its 1991 biannual conference.

As for the Clinton administration, it has lent America's name to a strong-arm coup, encouraged the dissolution of a legislature that was supposed to ratify desperately needed nuclear disarmament treaties, further inflamed the growing backlash against our intrusive role in Russia's internal affairs, and contemptuously dismissed several parties and leaders with whom one day we, or our children, will have to deal. The administration replies that it was surprised by Yeltsin's decision to shut down Parliament and had to support him then and now as the best or only pro-democracy hope.

If Clinton and his advisers were really surprised, which Russia have they been observing since March 20, when with unflagging U.S. support Yeltsin first tried to abolish the Parliament? Well before he struck again on September 21, there was plenty of plain evidence that he intended to do so.

Moreover, if the administration is right that Yeltsin is the only Russian leader fit to support or even properly acknowledge, on whom or what will it base U.S. policy if this sixty-two-year-old man in dubious health suddenly leaves the scene? Above all, if the Clinton administration really believes that Yeltsin's methods are the "best hope for democracy in Russia," it is saying, in effect, there is no hope. That prophecy is false, but it is quickly becoming a self-fulfilling one.

[*Washington Post*, October 10, 1993]

POSTSCRIPT

After the destruction of the Parliament, then known as the Supreme Soviet, Yeltsin reneged on a promise he had made during the conflict to hold an early presidential election in the summer of 1994. (The election took place instead in 1996, as originally scheduled.) But elections for a new Parliament, now called the Duma, and a referendum on Yeltsin's proposed constitution were held in December 1993.

The constitution, which greatly empowered the presidency at the expense of other branches of government, particularly the Duma, was officially adopted, but the results of the referendum were almost certainly falsified. (The more than 50 percent of eligible voters required for ratification probably did not actually participate.)[10] In 2000, it nonetheless remained Russia's constitution, and Vladimir Putin inherited the super-presidency created for Yeltsin.

To the shock of the Kremlin and its Western supporters, opposition parties overwhelmingly defeated pro-Yeltsin ones in the December 1993 parliamentary elections. Two months later, the new Duma voted an amnesty that freed Rutskoi and Khasbulatov from prison. In 1996, Rutskoi was elected governor of Kursk province and moved toward Yeltsin politically. In 2000, he supported Putin. Khasbulatov, an academic economist, returned to that profession, while aspiring to a political role in his war-torn native Chechnya. Later in 2000, he offered himself as an alternative pro-Moscow leader of Chechnya, and there were some indications that Putin considered the possibility.

The full consequences of the bloody events in the center of Moscow on October 3–4, 1993, the first such violence there since 1917, will occupy historians for years to come. A strong case can be made that freeing himself from any effective parliamentary restraints led Yeltsin to more unwise and fateful decisions, including a privatization program that resulted in oligarchical ownership and asset looting, the first Chechen war, in 1994–96, and thus the second one, in 1999–2000. Other historians will continue to argue that Yeltsin's actions against the Parliament saved post-Communist Russia from a "Red-Brown" takeover.

Meanwhile, Russians themselves do not even agree on the number of casualties. The Yeltsin government reported that about 150 people were killed and 800 to 1,000 wounded. Advocates of the destroyed Parliament insist there were many more victims. Anti-Yeltsin forces continue to glorify the memory of the "martyred Parliament and its defenders" and included its destruction in the unsuccessful 1999 impeachment charges against the president. A personal friend retains a more ironic perspective. She has kept her "worthless" privatization voucher issued in 1992 because it was printed with an illustration of the soon-to-be-assaulted Parliament building.

Along with the Western democracies, particularly the United States, most self-professed Russian democrats supported Yeltsin's use of force against the Parliament, but some soon decided that it had been "a terrible mistake."[11] No such public reconsideration has taken place in the United States.

At the time, Russian democrats who sided with the Parliament often declared, "We will not forget and we will not forgive what the West did during these terrible days." A new U.S. policy that included a bit of even tacit regret would probably bring forgiveness. In June 2000, in Moscow for a summit meeting with President Putin, President Clinton addressed a successor Russian Parliament, but without mentioning the events of 1993. The Duma gave his speech a cool reception and many deputies did not attend the session, apparently in protest.

A change in the official American position on what happened in October 1993 seems unlikely for at least two reasons. A new U.S. administration would in effect have to repudiate the Clinton administration, which pointedly gave Yeltsin "full support" and congratulated him after he used tanks against the Parliament. Second, influential American newspapers continue to characterize that Parliament misleadingly as an "openly seditious Russian legislature" that undertook a "Communist revolt" or "mutiny against the Kremlin," and Yeltsin's decision to use tanks against it as "easily defended."

Many Russians, on the other hand, will long remember that less than three weeks after the first such assault on a European parliament since the German Reichstag fire in 1933, President Clinton's   secretary of state arrived in Moscow to praise Yeltsin's Russia as a country "being reborn as a democracy."[12]

America's Failed Crusade (February 1994)

The worst and most predictable U.S. foreign policy failure of the late twentieth century has been unfolding in post-Communist Russia ever since the Soviet breakup in 1991. All the desirable outcomes in a country that remains so essential to American security—democracy, a prospering economy, a political establishment friendly to the West, major reductions and safeguarding of nuclear missiles and other weapons of mass destruction—have been undermined by the U.S. government's own policy.

American politicians and pundits are belatedly awakening to that failure, but not to its full magnitude or the real reason behind it. Pointing a "Who lost Russia?" finger at one another, zealous promoters of a profoundly unwise policy, initiated by the Bush administration in 1992 and greatly expanded by the Clinton team since 1993, insist that this policy failed because the West did not give sufficient or timely financial aid to Russian reformers. Their self-serving excuses ignore the lessons that must urgently be learned if the American debacle in Russia is not to become a full-scale disaster.

At fault, as I have argued repeatedly, is the basic premise that has guided American policy since 1991: that the United States can and should intervene deeply in Russia's internal affairs to transform that nation into an American-style system at home and a compliant junior partner abroad. That preposterously missionary idea is in almost total conflict with Russia's historical traditions, present-day realities, and actual possibilities, and thus is dangerously counterproductive.

Essentially, the United States said to the post-Communist Russian leadership of Boris Yeltsin: If you follow our "free market" prescriptions for economic reform—a leap-to-capitalism "shock therapy"—and our lead on international issues, we will give you ample financial aid, on-site adviser-therapists, and a place by our side (or in our shadow) in world affairs. For his own complex reasons, President Yeltsin accepted or pretended to accept the offer, which both sides immediately anointed as a "strategic partnership and friendship." And on that romantic assumption, the Clinton administration, with more ideological gusto and less restraint than its predecessor, has stuck to Yeltsin like Krazy Glue.

Consider how badly this missionary American policy has already failed:

- Prospects for peaceful development toward stable markets and democracy in Russia are worse today than they were two years ago, and much worse than they were when President Clinton took office only a year ago. The Russian economy is in free fall, ravaged by an extraordinary multiple collapse of production, capital investment, consumption, legal transaction, and the ruble. Moreover, since Yeltsin destroyed the constitutional order by force last fall, Russia has had no real political system at all, only his current efforts to create a personal regime of power. As a result, antidemocratic, military, and other security forces now play a much larger role in domestic and foreign politics than they did a year ago.
- Nor has Russia's foreign policy conformed to U.S. prescriptions. Its opposition to the proposed expansion of NATO eastward and to Western action against Serbia is just the latest evidence that Russian policies can be made and sustained only in Moscow, not in Washington. Meanwhile, almost nothing concrete has been

done to reduce the various nuclear threats on former Soviet territory, which are greater today than they were under the Soviet regime. Not all of the much bally-hooed weapons-reduction treaties, for example, have yet been fully ratified.

- As for the U.S. wager on Yeltsin as the popular instrument of the American crusade, 85 percent of Russian participants in the December 1993 elections for the new Duma voted against his policies and party, even though Yeltsin wrote the rules, controlled television, and lavished money on his supporters. Still worse, a significant part of that anti-Yeltsin vote was a backlash against America's intrusive role there, which included various gestures by President Clinton on behalf of "my friend Boris."

- More recently, the administration's apparent remoteness from Russian realities allowed President Clinton to be embarrassed by a Potemkin-village summit meeting with Yeltsin in Moscow. Promises made by Yeltsin about the composition and direction of his government were immediately violated. The "breakthrough" on persuading Ukraine to give up its nuclear weapons looks even more dubious as Ukrainian-Russian relations worsen in the aftermath of the election of a Crimean president who campaigned for returning the combustible Black Sea region to Russia. And in Belarus, where Clinton visited after Moscow, the pro-Western president was removed just after his departure.

- Finally, here in the United States, the Clinton administration has created so many illusions and false expectations that current developments are generat-

ing an anti-Russian backlash in our own country—
certainly against more aid for reform. Inveterate Cold
Warriors are already rebuilding their barricades.
"We gave bear stroking a try," Charles Krauthammer
declares in *Time*. "It did not work." A new U.S.-Russ-
ian Cold War may not yet be on the horizon, but a
chilly or cold peace is now more likely than the
vaunted "era of partnership and friendship." (And
imagine the U.S. reaction if some new Russia-cen-
tered union emerges with one or more former Soviet republics, as is also likely.)

But there is worse news. Not even those of us who
warned about the dangers inherent in U.S. policy foresaw how deeply the Clinton administration would intervene in the cauldron of Russian politics. It is said that
the United States must support Yeltsin because he is
Russia's elected president. But Clinton and his top aides
have gone far beyond that norm of international relations, becoming his cheerleader, accomplice, and spin
doctor, and thus implicating America in some of his
most ill-advised and even wicked deeds.

To understand that complicity, we must see Yeltsin's
leadership through the eyes of a great many Russian
citizens. For them, he has been an extremist leader
imposing from above—an old Russian tradition—
exceedingly radical policies for which they never voted.
Yeltsin's most extreme measures have come as three
traumatic shocks to society. In 1991, he suddenly abolished the Soviet Union, the only country most Russians
had ever known. (American opinion of that state isn't
relevant to a serious analysis of the consequences.) In

1992, his economic "shock therapy" took away the life savings and living standards of most Russian families. And in 1993, his tanks overthrew the elected Parliament and constitutional system previously presented to citizens as the legitimate post-Communist order.

Not surprisingly, Yeltsin's shock leadership has produced not the much-heralded "Russian transition" but a polarized society, devastating all varieties of moderation and centrism in political life. Extremism always begets extremism. Yeltsin's policies led, for example, to the victory of the extreme nationalist Vladimir Zhirinovsky in the December 1993 elections.

Recall now the American role in those events, even leaving aside any covert involvement. The U.S. government wildly applauded Yeltsin's precipitate abolition of the Soviet Union without real concern for its psychological, economic, or bloody impact on ordinary citizens, including its potential for unleashing several civil wars in a land full of nuclear stockpiles and reactors. When his shock therapy then impoverished tens of millions of Russians (including prospective middle-class investors in economic privatization), our government urged him to do more of the same, scorning other pro-market but anti-Yeltsin economists for not being "real" reformers. When parliamentary opposition to Yeltsin grew in 1992 and 1993, the U.S. administration echoed his charge that it was a "citadel of Red-Brown reaction," thus helping to undermine what Russian democratization needs most— an established Parliament and accepted opposition. The Clinton administration then supported Yeltsin's first attempt to shut down the elected Parliament in March 1993, shunned Russian moderates who tried to prevent a more fateful confrontation, and cheered even more loudly when Yeltsin finally resorted to a tank-backed coup, thereby endorsing Russia's long antidemocratic tradition of unfettered executive power. And now that Yeltsin has contrived a new "constitution" without an authentic separation of powers, the administration heralds it as a "democratic breakthrough."

Given this dismal record, can there be any doubt that the intrusively missionary U.S. policy—supported no less enthusiastically by Congress, the media, and many academic specialists—has both undermined our purposes in Russia and compromised our best values? The crusade to macromanage Russia's present and future (along with new suggestions by the administration that it might try the same folly in Ukraine) must end, but what kind of policy should be adopted? The answer must be found this time in Russia, not in Washington, international banks, or American universities.

Deeply wounded, polarized, and angry, Russia desperately needs moderate, consensual, gradual reforms. Any more shocks may send some rough beast slouching toward the Kremlin. A broad coalition of Russian moderates—"centrists" who see themselves trapped between Yeltsin, extreme nationalists, and hard-line Communists—is struggling to emerge as a political force capable of reshaping the reform process, with or without Yeltsin. To do so, its leaders will have to overcome their own past conflicts and future ambitions. Though Prime Minister Viktor Chernomyrdin's recent pledge to blend market economics with "the special characteristics of our state, people, and Russian traditions" embraces their philosophy, for example, other important moderates, notably Valery Zorkin, the ousted chief justice of the Constitutional Court, have not forgiven his crucial supporting role in Yeltsin's assault on the Parliament in October 1993.

Nonetheless, some such moderate bloc is Russia's best hope for democratic and market reform, even if it does not conform to U.S. dogmas about what that must mean. If so, it is also America's best hope for a Russia engaged in progressive change at home rather than a pursuit of lost power abroad.

But how will the Clinton administration, which despite its devotion to centrism at home has been an opponent of moderation in Russian politics, react to any centrist opposition to Yeltsin's policies? If the administration heeds the lessons of its missionary failures in Russia, it will adopt the new and moderate principle that I have urged many times: The United States lacks the wisdom, right, or power to intervene in Russia's internal affairs; all attempts to do so will backfire perilously. On that principle, the United States would withdraw its excessive presence in Russia, cease its dogmatic sermons and dollar-laden ultimatums, and encourage Russia to find its destiny, as it must, within its own circumstances and possibilities.

And when—or for pessimists, if—Russia finds its own way toward political and economic reform, even if it is not ours, the United States will be able to give generous financial assistance, as it must, that is both productive and honorable. Otherwise, America may find itself with few friends, partners, or democrats in post-Yeltsin Russia.

[*The Nation*, February 28, 1994]

POSTSCRIPT

As I noted earlier, Ukraine eventually transferred its nuclear weapons to Russia, but relations between these largest former Soviet republics remain unsettled and most of the other problems discussed here have only grown worse.

Vladimir Zhirinovsky's peculiar role in Russian politics is another example of misleading American media coverage. After his incongruously named Liberal Democratic Party won more votes than any other in the December 1993 parliamentary elections, nearly 23 percent, this ostentatiously ultranationalist, even quasi-fascist, figure was regularly cited by the Kremlin, the Clinton administration, and the U.S. press as an example of what awaited Russia, and the world, if Yeltsin lost power. Even after Zhirinovsky's party lost almost half its voters in the December 1995 elections, he remained a stock bogeyman in U.S. media coverage, along with the Communists, who became the largest party in the Duma.

In reality, Zhirinovsky and his party voted in Yeltsin's favor on almost every crucial occasion during the rest of the 1990s, just as he has since supported President Putin. In turn, Yeltsin's Kremlin helped maintain Zhirinovsky as an electoral factor by giving him financial assistance and exposure on television networks it controlled. By comparison, the Communist Party's voting record in the Duma was much closer to that of Grigory Yavlinsky's pro-democracy Yabloko Party. Here too Russia's complex realities did not fit American simplistic stereotypes.

"Who Is to Blame?" (December 1995)

An explosive issue in Russian politics today has gone largely unreported in the American media. It is the demonic question that has arisen since the nineteenth century whenever Russia has plunged into epic misfortune: *Kto vinovat?*—"Who is to blame?" The wrathful passions it has generated have repeatedly polarized political life, engulfed the country in frenzied searches for "enemies of the people," and helped perpetuate dictatorships inveighing against new enemies at home and abroad.

It could happen again. Many members of Russia's political class and intelligentsia as well as a growing number of ordinary citizens now view what President Boris Yeltsin and his Western supporters have called "radical reform" since 1991 as a "criminal revolution" whose perpetrators should be removed from power and punished.

Nor is this call for a reckoning merely a remnant of a historical tradition. It is a widespread response to specific contemporary policies and their consequences. They include Yeltsin's sudden and surreptitious abolition of the Soviet Union in 1991; the economic "shock therapy" measures he has enacted since 1992 that have plunged at least half the country into poverty or to the brink of it while unleashing a bacchanalia of official corruption and enriching perhaps 5 to 8 percent of "New Russians"; his tank-backed destruction of a popularly elected Parliament and indeed the entire first post-Communist constitutional order in 1993; and the war he launched against the separatist republic of Chechnya in 1994, which has killed tens of thousands of civilians (many of them elderly ethnic Russians unable to flee the bombing) and left its capital city of Grozny, once a thriving metropolis of some 400,000 people, in ruins.

Most Western commentators evidently believe that all of those deeds were virtuous or necessary, as the Clinton administration has often argued, and that only Russian extremists think otherwise. It is true that an "irreconcilable opposition"—as ultranationalists and Communist fundamentalists are called—has always considered Yeltsin an agent of Western powers who plotted the breakup of the Soviet Union and now are exploiting Russia's economy by turning it into a deindustrialized exporter of natural resources and dumping ground for excess goods. For such extreme oppositionists, Russia under Yeltsin has been "murdered, plundered, raped, spat upon, humiliated."

But it is also true that significant charges in that indictment are now regularly echoed in Russia's political mainstream. Influential anti-Communist and pro-democracy newspapers, once Yeltsin's enthusiastic supporters, have called his economic policies a "crime against the country's national security" and the resulting decline in the nation's health an "unfolding catastrophe . . . as in wartime," denounced the "thorough corruption of the executive branch," characterized Prime Minister Viktor Chernomyrdin as the "chief mafioso," and condemned the Chechen campaign as a "criminal war."

Earlier this year, for example, *Obshchaya Gazeta,*

whose editor was formerly Yeltsin's close ally, ran a two-page headline: "Boris Yeltsin Is Guilty—Before the Law, Before the People, Before History." More recently, it reported a mainstream insider as saying of the Yeltsin government, "No one will escape the people's retribution. All plunderers of Russia await their own Nuremberg trial."

Not surprisingly, as I have emphasized for more than a year, the Yeltsin regime has begun to fear its own people and dread the day it might lose power. No Russian or Soviet leader has ever left office voluntarily; Yeltsin, given the traumas he has inflicted on the country, may not chose to be the first, at least without guarantees of a safe retirement. Having ruled mostly by decree (issuing as many as 2,300 in a single year), often in open defiance of Parliament and the constitution, and having used tanks to arrest his own former allies in 1993, a powerless Yeltsin would risk becoming the target of any politics of retribution that ensued. Nor would he be alone. Similarly endangered are many of his high-level appointees and other servitors along with a number of "oligarchs" and other "New Russians" who have profited so grandly from his largesse with state property and exclusive licenses.

That is why Yeltsin's representatives have for more than a year considered ways to cancel elections, particularly the presidential contest scheduled for June 1996, or to install a successor tied to the regime "by blood and property." (Many Russian analysts think that the Chechen war may be such a pretext.) With Yeltsin in poor health and his approval ratings in single digits, much may now depend on leaders of the opposition parties. Several declared presidential candidates whom I recently interviewed, ranging from liberal democratic to Communist and nationalist, warned against repeating Russia's history of savage retribution, but none of them ruled out some kind of "legal" accounting for what has happened since 1991. And all of them worried that the Kremlin nay not permit a presidential election to take place next year, at least not a fair one.

The Yeltsin regime's best hope for a safe exit from power, with or without elections, may actually be the pervasive corruption it has engendered. Various forms of corruption have enmeshed so many politicians and bureaucrats, pro-government and oppositionist, that few can want any precedents set for punishing abuses of power. The current Parliament, or Duma, for example, has adamantly refused even to diminish the deputies' full immunity from prosecution, and many parliamentary candidates seem to run only to obtain that protection.

The billions of dollars of state property that Yeltsin's Kremlin has handed over to a small segment of the former Soviet ruling class and others could also play a perverse role. Elites excluded from that fabulous "plunder" have generally backed various anti-Yeltsin oppositions but may settle for a second redistribution benefiting themselves. Unless the economic condition of millions of families improves significantly, however, such an intramural deal is likely only to make the question of "who is to blame" even more clamorous.

How the question is eventually answered will be fateful for Russia and the world. The Clinton administration may be tempted to do all it can to help Yeltsin, its greatly valued "partner," or his associates remain in power. Many Russian politicians and commentators are convinced that the United States will close its eyes to any pro-Yeltsin irregularities in the presidential election, as occurred in the national voting in December 1993, and even to its cancellation.

To do so would be a great mistake. With virtually the entire Russian political spectrum already offended by the U.S. plan to expand NATO eastward and the impending Western military presence in the Balkans, even tacit American support for any attempt by the Yeltsin regime to evade democratic judgment could only further poison our relations.

The Clinton administration has endorsed almost everything Yeltsin has done on the grounds that he represents reform and stability in a Russia still laden with nuclear devices. But what kind of stability actually exists if those changes have awakened a historical demon and caused so many citizens to see them as criminal? The only hope is that this time Russia will decide who is to be blamed in a democratic way.

[Full text of an abridged version in
New York Times, December 11, 1995]

POSTSCRIPT

After a protracted struggle inside Yeltsin's entourage over whether or not to cancel the 1996 presidential election, it took place as required by the constitution.[13] In the first round, Yeltsin and the Communist Party candidate Gennady Zyuganov finished far ahead of the other contenders with 35.3 percent and 32 percent of the vote respectively; Yeltsin then won the runoff 53.8 percent to 40.3 percent.

Considering the president's use of his almost tsar-like powers of incumbency, from financial expenditures far exceeding the legal limit and control of national television to appointment of electoral officials, the election could not be called "fair," but it was incomparably better than a canceled election. No serious observers doubted that Yeltsin had actually won, but many were convinced that the margin of his final victory had been padded.

More important as an indicator of political culture at the time, many Russians, perhaps most of them, did not believe that Yeltsin would leave office voluntarily if defeated. Yeltsin fed the suspicion himself by telling a group of Western well-wishers, "I may not win the election, but I certainly will not lose." When I put the question directly to a Kremlin insider just before the runoff, he answered unambiguously, "Better resistance and even a civil war than Communists back in power."[14]

The Clinton administration went out of its way, certainly well beyond propriety, to help Yeltsin win. It arranged a booster-summit meeting in Moscow and a $10 billion IMF loan shortly before the election, justified the ongoing Chechen war by comparing it to the American Civil War and Yeltsin to Lincoln, and sent U.S. campaign experts to serve as his advisers. The American ambassador in Moscow, Thomas Pickering, even tried to pressure Grigory Yavlinsky to withdraw from the first round in favor of Yeltsin.[15]

But as readers already understand, Yeltsin's reelection in 1996 did not vanquish the wrathful question "Who is to blame?" The Duma's attempt to impeach him failed, but Western news reports that Kremlin officials, possibly including Yeltsin and his relatives, had secret bank accounts abroad further inflamed the issue. Of those Russians surveyed in late 1999, 90 percent did not trust Yeltsin and 53 percent wanted him put on trial. Harking back to the Stalin era, street protesters carried banners charging, "Yeltsin is an enemy of the people."[16]

High-level fear of retribution continued to grow and played an even larger role in the politics of 1999–2000. (More and more highly placed candidates for the Duma in December 1999 sought a seat for its immunity from criminal prosecution than had been the case in the 1993 or 1995 elections.) Yeltsin's Kremlin believed it had finally found in Vladimir Putin, head of the former KGB, and in his conduct of a renewed Chechen war, the successor tied to it "by blood and property" it had sought since 1995. Putin's first act upon becoming acting president was to issue a decree stating that Yeltsin "may not be prosecuted on criminal charges" or even asked to give evidence about any crimes.[17]

In early 2000, the Communist Party failed to persuade the Duma to nullify the decree. But in light of what happened in the 1990s, it is unlikely that Yeltsin's immunity will go unchallenged in the years ahead. As for the Clinton administration, as we saw before, it hurriedly endorsed Putin and the Kremlin's "democratic transfer of power."

Transition or Tragedy? (December 1996)

A terrible national tragedy has been unfolding in Russia in the 1990s, but we will hear little if anything about it in American commentary on this fifth anniversary of the end of the Soviet Union. Instead, we will be told that Russia's "transition to a free-market economy and democracy" has progressed remarkably, despite some "bumps in the road." Evidence alleged to support that view will include massive privatization, emerging financial markets, low inflation, "stabilization," an impending economic "takeoff," this year's completed presidential election, a sitting Parliament, and a "free press."

Few if any commentators will explain that Russia's new private sector is dominated by former but still intact Soviet monopolies seized by ex-Communist officials who have become the core of a semi-criminalized business class; that inflation is being held down by holding back salaries owed to tens of millions of needy workers and other employees; that a boom has been promised for years while the economy continues to plunge into a depression greater than America's in the 1930s; that President Yeltsin's reelection campaign was one of the most corrupt in recent European history; that the Parliament has no real powers and the appellate court little independence from the presidency; and that neither Russia's market nor its national television is truly competitive or free but is substantially controlled by the same financial oligarchy whose representatives now sit in the Kremlin as chieftains of the Yeltsin regime.

In human terms, however, that is not the worst of it. For the great majority of families, Russia has not been in "transition" but in an endless collapse of everything essential to a decent existence—from real wages, welfare provisions, and health care to birthrates and life expectancy; from industrial and agricultural production to higher education, science, and traditional culture; from safety in the streets to prosecution of organized crime and thieving bureaucrats; from the still enormous military forces to the safeguarding of nuclear devices and materials. These are the realities underlying the "reforms" that most U.S. commentators still extol and seem to think are the only desirable kind.

Fragments of Russia's unprecedented, cruel, and perilous collapse are reported in the U.S. mainstream media, but not the full dimensions of insider privatization, impoverishment, disintegration of the middle classes, corrosive consequences of the 1994–96 Chechen war, or official corruption and mendacity. Why not? Why don't American commentators lament the plight of the Russian people as they did so persistently when they were the Soviet people? The United States has thousands of professed specialists on Russia. Why have so few tried to tell the full story of post-Soviet Russia? Indeed, why, despite incomparably greater access to information, do most reporters, pundits, and scholars tell us less that is really essential about Russia today than they did when it was part of the Soviet Union?

There are, it seems, several reasons, all of them related to the American condition rather than to Russia's. As during the Cold War, most U.S. media and academic commentators think (or speak) within the parameters of

Washington's policies toward Russia. Since 1991, Russia's purportedly successful "transition" and the U.S. "strategic" role in it have been the basic premises of White House and congressional policy.

American business people, big foundations, and academics involved with Russia also have their own stake in the "transition." For the business community, it is the prospect of profits; for foundations, another frontier of endowed social engineering; for academia, a new paradigm ("transitionology") for securing funds, jobs, and tenure. Confronted with the fact that the results of Russia's "transition" continue to worsen and not improve, most of its U.S. promoters still blame the "legacy of Communism" rather than their own prescriptions, or insist that robber baron capitalism will surely reform itself there as it did here, even though the circumstances are fundamentally different.

More generally, Americans once again see in Russia, for ideological and psychological reasons, primarily what they seek there. This time it is a happy outcome of the end of Soviet Communism and of our "great victory" in the Cold War. How many of us who doubt that outcome, who think the world may be less safe because of what has happened in the former Soviet Union since 1991, who believe that ordinary Russians (even those denigrated "elderly" Communist voters) have been made to suffer unduly and unjustly, who understand that there were less costly and more humane ways to reform Russia than Yeltsin's U.S.-sponsored "shock" measures—how many of us wish to say such things publicly, knowing we will be accused of nostalgia for the Soviet Union or even of pro-Communism? Crude

McCarthyism has passed, but not the maligning of anyone who challenges mainstream orthodoxies about Soviet or post-Soviet Russia. And the presumed "transition to a free-market economy and democracy" is today's orthodoxy.

But does it even matter what Americans say about Russia today? Those of us who oppose the Clinton administration's missionary complicity in the "transition," and its insistence that Russia "stay the course," may wish the United States would say and intervene less. In one respect, however, U.S. commentary matters greatly. Eventually, today's Russian children will ask what America felt and said during these tragic times for their parents and grandparents, and they will shape their relations with our own children and grandchildren accordingly.

[*The Nation*, December 30, 1996]

POSTSCRIPT

The above article, an earlier statement of an argument developed more fully in the first section of this book, was probably the most widely reprinted of my writings of the 1990s—and the most controversial. Certainly, it aroused the broadest and most heated reaction in the form of letters sent to *The Nation* and to me personally, messages to an e-mail list devoted to Russian affairs, and articles commenting on what I had written.

Many of the responses were favorable and can be summarized in two words that appeared in several letters—"Amen!" and "Bravo!"—but many were not. Not surprisingly, some of the negative responses relied heavily on the hoary insinuation that anyone so critical of U.S. policy, Yeltsin's leadership, or Russia's "transition" must regret the end of the Soviet Union and favor today's Communist Party,[18] or fail to understand, as two letter writers explained, "one cannot make an omelette without breaking a few eggs."

The most interesting objections, however, were from professionals who were participating in the "transition" and sincerely believed in it, as was clear from their substantive and civil replies. An English-language newspaper published in Moscow by pro-Yeltsin expatriates, for example, ran not one but two editorial rejoinders to my article in the same issue.[19] I interpreted it as a tribute but also a sign that the editors already sensed the impending collapse of their cause, even though Yeltsin had recently been reelected and Russia's financial meltdown was still more than a year and a half away.

But I was moved and troubled most by a late-night international phone call I received in Moscow, just after the article's publication. The caller, a European mid-level official at the IMF, wanted to speak in confidence. He had gone to the trouble of tracking me down, he explained, to express gratitude that "you wrote what urgently needed to be said but which I and my colleagues cannot say." He was, he added, circulating copies of my article at the IMF and the World Bank.

I was pleased by his assurance that I and others highly critical of U.S. policy toward Russia had sympathizers in official circles, but I remain troubled that they did not themselves speak out, at least not until much later, and even then only a very few of them. Their

silence reminds me too much of the many decent people I knew in the old Soviet party-state bureaucracies
who kept their dissident views private, but who at least
had compelling reasons for doing so.

The Other Russia (August 1997)

Anyone who thinks that Soviet-style propaganda, with
its determined disregard for Russian realities, is a thing
of the past should visit Moscow this summer of 1997.
In July, the large part of the "free press" controlled by
the Kremlin and its oligarchical supporters seized upon
the first anniversary of President Yeltsin's reelection to
celebrate the government's alleged successes, particularly those since he returned to office from bypass surgery
several months ago.

Among the loudly touted official claims of a general
"stabilization" were that Yeltsin had regained his
"youthful vigor" in politics and Russia its "great-power
standing" in the West, as illustrated by "normalized
relations with NATO" and Yeltsin's participation in the
May G-7 (now nominally G-8) summit in Denver. But
the most startling assertion was that the Russian economy, after six years of shrinkage and near collapse, is
at the beginning of a major recovery. As Yeltsin put it
in his anniversary radio address to the nation, "the tide
has turned and the slump has been stopped."

During a three-week stay in Moscow, we found little
evidence to support any of these claims, several of
which are being echoed by the Clinton administration

and in the U.S. press. Every political figure we met—liberal, Communist, and nationalist, as they are somewhat misleadingly typecast in the Western media—agreed that the country's fragile political stability rests largely upon Yeltsin's tenure in office, but no one knew the real state of his health. Few believed the official reports and many thought his bout of "fatigue" in Denver was actually a sign of his newly deteriorating condition. Certainly his current long vacation away from Moscow, given his previous absences from office, seems more restorative than recreational, tales of his epic fishing achievements notwithstanding. And the flagrantly nepotistic (even by Russian standards) appointment of his thirty-seven-year-old daughter, Tatyana Dyachenko, as a Kremlin adviser only strengthened the widespread perception that Yeltsin is almost totally dependent on a small group of personal appointees currently led by First Deputy Prime Minister Anatoly Chubais.

As for the country's relations with the West, most Russian foreign policy specialists speak of a looming crisis, not normalization. They point, above all, to the symbolism of the Russian president's absence from the July NATO summit in Madrid, where President Leonid Kuchma of Ukraine, the second most populous and strategically important former Soviet republic, signed a highly publicized agreement with the Western alliance. Nor did they minimize statements by U.S. officials that NATO's expansion eastward has only begun and that its doors are open to three other former Soviet republics—Lithuania, Estonia, and Latvia—a move adamantly opposed by Moscow. Even Yeltsin's Russian supporters believe that the real threshold of conflict with NATO, and thus the United States, lies ahead.

For the great majority of Russians, however, the government's least credible boast is that the country is on the verge of an economic boom. Western visitors to Moscow who repeat the assertion seem to be misled by the capital's special status. Moscow may have more Mercedes cars per capita than any other city in the world and is in the noisy throes of a peculiar kind of gentrification. Along with glittery new buildings, pre-revolutionary mansions are being transformed into opulent banks, lavish offices for multinational corporations, and high-security housing for the newly and fabulously rich. Western-style stores and cafés are full of these "New Russians" wantonly spending several times a typical citizen's monthly salary on a single purchase. And Moscow's small and economically unrepresentative stock market, fueled by foreign investors looking for bargains, has recently soared. Meanwhile, in another tenacious Soviet tradition, the city is getting an expensive facelift in connection with its upcoming 850th anniversary, which has less to do with municipal services—even here they are crumbling for most citizens—than with the national political ambitions of Mayor Yuri Luzhkov, sometimes dubbed "the Moscow Mussolini."

But apart from the relatively small number of native beneficiaries and Western boosters, few Russians think Moscow's economy rests on anything more substantial than massive high-level corruption. Protected by an intensely unpopular system of oligarchical politics and finance, the takeovers, mergers, and confiscation of former Soviet state assets churn on in the guise of "free-market privatization." (In a July article about a merger that would create Russia's largest investment bank, the *New York Times* neglected to mention that one of the financiers behind the deal, a former Yeltsin deputy minister, is being investigated for the embezzlement of $500 million in state funds.) Suffice it to say that annual capital flight, estimated even by the Russian government that abets it to be $2 billion a month, continues to exceed all foreign investment, aid, credits, and loans, including those from the IMF and the World Bank.

Whatever the full explanation, Moscow is an island of relative prosperity—a "fiefdom of thieves," as it has been called—in a decaying country. Most of the privatized wealth accumulated since the 1991 breakup of the Soviet Union has been concentrated in the capital through a semi-criminal and oligarchical banking system, along with nearly 80 percent of all the country's new investment. The rest of Russia remains in the throes of the twentieth century's greatest depression—even according to the government's own statistics. The fall in production, down nearly 50 percent since 1991, continues, and unemployment is expected to exceed at least 10 percent by next year. Capital investment dropped another 18 percent last year and 8 percent in the first quarter of this year.

In conversations with Russians from the provinces, we found none who could report any signs of improvement. On the contrary, several spoke despairingly of a "dying nation"—idle factories, decaying farms, polluted rivers, malnourished children, and collapsing professions, education, and health care. According to official statistics, at least 25 to 30 percent of Russians now live in actual poverty, but even those astonishing figures give little indication that a large twentieth-century middle class is being transformed into nineteenth-century subsistence farmers, who must grow on tiny garden plots what they need to survive but can no longer afford to buy.

By all accounts, there is no stability in these provincial wastelands. Tens of millions of citizens, among them workers, teachers, doctors, and soldiers, still have not received months of salaries. In some of the most stricken areas, there is a growing pattern of direct citizen action and violent protest so dramatic (though still episodic) as to remind observers of the recent uprising in Albania. In the Kuzbass region, miners protesting unpaid wages threatened to take up arms. In the Far East, workers and pensioners blocked railway lines and bridges while wives of unpaid officers closed a military airbase by lying down on runways. Workers at a nuclear submarine facility sealed off the yard and took the managing director hostage until wages were flown in from Moscow. Teachers and doctors in the city of Kimry occupied the city hall, blockading administrators inside until adequate supplies and back salaries were promised.

It was in this context that the specter of a military "mutiny" suddenly and unexpectedly emerged inside the Yeltsin camp itself. All but unreported in the U.S. press, the Rokhlin affair, as it became known, shook Moscow in June and July. In a seven-page open letter to the "Commander in Chief," which he sent to garrisons across the country and then published in opposition newspapers, General Lev Rokhlin accused Yeltsin of surrounding himself with brazenly corrupt advisers, willfully destroying the army and the defense industries, betraying Russian national interests, and acceding to NATO expansion and thus to America's "diktat over Europe's political and military order."

Such charges have long been leveled by Communists and radical nationalists, but Rokhlin is neither. Previously a top army commander under Yeltsin and now chairman of Parliament's Armed Forces Committee, he was elected to the Duma as a member of the main progovernment party. Two points in his open letter were therefore a bombshell. Yeltsin, he wrote, was purposely impoverishing the army in favor of Interior Ministry troops, which are to be used as a praetorian guard in the event of popular unrest. "Russia is being turned into a police state," he insisted. And he called upon the military to "close ranks" and defend itself against the Yeltsin government.

The Kremlin's reaction bordered on panic. Yeltsin's men likened Rokhlin's letter to "mutinous" Communist agitation in the army in revolutionary 1917, and the president immediately appeared on television to promise payment of all military back salaries by September. (The government did manage to pay back pensions in early July, but officials admit to having no idea how the nearly bankrupt state will be able to pay all the months of civilian back wages, much less future salaries and pensions.) For all its talk about stability, the Kremlin's alarm is understandable. In a recent survey, 60 percent of Russian experts on military affairs responded that a coup, mutiny, or complete disintegration of the army is likely within eighteen months. Indeed, several ranking political figures remarked privately that by comparative political science criteria, the Russian military should have taken power two or three years ago.

In light of all this, can Yeltsin's reconstituted "young reformer" government, headed by Chubais and Boris Nemtsov, really be serious about imposing a new round of economic "shock therapy," this one by abolishing long-standing state subsidies for housing and utilities? "Another dose of this so-called therapy," warned former Soviet President Mikhail Gorbachev during a conversation with us at his foundation, "is likely to generate a social explosion. People don't receive their wages, and now the government is going to raise their rents! What is it thinking?"

Various explanations are circulating in Moscow. One is that the "young wolves" currently in power really believe that their radical monetarism will "shock" the economy into growth, or that they must comply with the IMF's austerity guidelines in order to continue to receive loans needed to keep it afloat. Another widespread view, fueled by Yeltsin's threat to remove Lenin's body from the Red Square Mausoleum along with more than two hundred Soviet-era urns from the Kremlin walls, is that he wants to provoke a showdown with the Communist-dominated Parliament in the fall, its dissolution followed perhaps by the imposition of a praetorian regime, as Rokhlin warned. There is even a belief, which points to the aggressive new round of "privatization," that all talk of "more reform" is really camouflage for a final looting of state assets before the oligarchy flees to its Western villas and bank accounts.

(According to Moscow newspapers, many government officials and other influentials already have their children safely ensconced in foreign schools.)

Yeltsin's Western supporters may find this latter charge outrageous, but their hero and de facto head of the Russian government, Chubais, is already endangered by documented charges that he has done some considerable looting of his own. (Virtually no one in Moscow, not even pro-Yeltsin journalists, takes seriously the Kremlin's recent "anti-corruption" campaign, promoted by the recently arrived thirty-seven-year-old Nemtsov.) On July 1, *Izvestia,* Moscow's most authoritative and generally pro-Kremlin newspaper, reported that Chubais had received a $3 million interest-free loan from a leading bank, which he then helped to win control of a large oil company. And suspicions that Chubais may have personally pocketed U.S. Agency for International Development funds channeled through Harvard University's Institute for International Development to a network of quasi-private centers he and his cronies created are being investigated in Washington and Moscow. If Chubais, the architect of privatization since 1992 and patron saint of Russia's ruling political-financial oligarchy, is not safe, can any Yeltsin regime insiders really feel secure?

If they do, it is largely because Russia lacks an effective opposition. Under strong pressure from more radical activists, the leadership of the Communist Party, which remains by far the largest and best organized in the country, has called for a nationwide "political strike" in the fall, but many observers doubt its resolve. Since losing the presidential election to Yeltsin in 1996,

its leader, Gennady Zyuganov, has repeatedly prevented a parliamentary vote of no confidence in the government, despite the efforts of two otherwise dissimilar
young leaders of smaller opposition parties in the
Duma—the liberal democrat Grigory Yavlinsky and the
nationalist Sergei Baburin. Nor have any effective opposition leaders emerged outside the Moscow political
establishment. A television blackout has largely muffled
the angry roar of General Aleksandr Lebed, and trade
union officials seem unwilling to mobilize their membership fully.

In stricken nations, new leaders often appear only
when desperate circumstances finally beckon them.
Russia's future leaders may already be emerging in the
remote provinces—in local unions, political movements,
even army garrisons—but are still not visible to the
nation or to us. It may also be, however, that today's
opposition, like the Kremlin, fears the people, who by
all accounts and nearly every criterion now live worse
than before 1991. Widespread analogies with 1917 and
Albania may be for political effect, but there is a pal-
pable anxiety across the political spectrum that the
fabled patience of the Russian people has limits, and
when they are reached the result could be beyond anyone's control. Indeed, it is surely indicative that while
all the Moscow-based leaders and parties are already
preparing for the next parliamentary and presidential
elections, scheduled respectively for 1999 and 2000,
once again no one is certain when or even whether they
will actually take place.

[Co-authored with Katrina vanden Heuvel,
The Nation, August 11–18, 1997]

POSTSCRIPT

In July 1998, General Rokhlin, whose political popularity had continued to spread, was shot to death in circumstances that remain mysterious. Authorities charged his wife with the murder—she initially gave a confession but quickly withdrew it—and imprisoned her. As required by Russian law, she was released in January 2000, still proclaiming her innocence and pending a trial that was then postponed. Many Russians continue to believe she was framed and that Rokhlin's death was a political assassination. For their part, the authorities, first under Yeltsin and then under Putin, showed little interest in the case.

The army did not "mutiny," but some Russian political analysts thought generals might do so if the Kremlin tried to deprive them of a complete military victory in the new Chechen war that began in 1999. It is also worth noting that the seven national oversight districts created by Putin in May 2000 to monitor the heads of Russia's eighty-nine administrative-territorial units correspond exactly to the location of the country's regional military garrisons. The Movement in Support of the Army, which Rokhlin founded, moved closer to the Communist Party after his death and failed in the December 1999 election to receive enough votes to make it into the new Duma.

Financial scandals implicating Chubais and his personal team finally led to his fall from high office,[20] but Yeltsin put him in charge of the state's powerful (and wealthy) electricity monopoly and he remained an influential Kremlin insider. Predictably, in 1999, Chubais and other "liberal" reformers became strong supporters of the new prime minister, former KGB chief and soon-to-be president Putin. Despite everything, many U.S. officials, journalists, and scholars still regard Chubais as Russia's exemplary "reformer" and hope for his return to power. The electoral coalition he formed with other "young reformers," Union of Right-Wing Forces, which Putin endorsed along with the larger pro-Kremlin alliance called Unity, got 8.5 percent of the vote in the December 1999 election, enough to enter the new Duma.

The retired but still youthful General Lebed, who had finished third in the 1996 presidential race and endorsed Yeltsin in the runoff in return for being made his national security chief, negotiated an end of the first Chechen war. Manifestly ambitious, Lebed soon broke with the Kremlin, or the Kremlin with him, and in 1998 was elected governor of the vast Krasnoyarsk province. Though still denied regular access to state television, and despite having fallen in popularity polls, Lebed remains a formidable political figure.

After 1997, two new national leaders emerged in response to circumstances, Primakov and Putin, but both were created by Yeltsin and neither came from the provinces. Provincial governors played a large role in national politics, but primarily in blocs backing various Moscow politicians such as Zyuganov, Primakov, Putin, and the city's mayor, Luzhkov. In 1999 and 2000, most of them quickly fell in line behind Putin.

The pseudo-economic "stabilization" we reported in this August 1997 article was, of course, confirmed by

Russia's financial collapse a year later, when the number of people living in poverty again greatly increased, bringing the total in the Potemkin village of Moscow to 50 percent. As for the "final looting of state assets" anticipated in 1997, many Russian politicians and commentators charged that it got under way in earnest in 1999—either as an amassing of funds for the March 2000 presidential campaign or as a last pillaging in case Yeltsin and his entourage lost the Kremlin, or both.

Meanwhile, Yeltsin has left the Kremlin, but Lenin's body remains in its Red Square mausoleum. Having embraced a number of Soviet-era symbols and made an alliance with the Communists in the Duma, Putin has given no indication of acting on Yeltsin's repeated threat to remove the body.

Why Call It Reform? (September 1998)

As Russia's economic collapse spirals out of control, rarely if ever has American discourse about that country been so uncaringly and dangerously in conflict with reality. With its endless ideological mantra of a purported "transition from Communism to free-market capitalism," almost all U.S. government, media, and academic commentary on Russia's current troubles is premised on two profoundly wrong assumptions: that the problem is essentially a "financial crisis" and that the remedy is faster and more resolute application of the "reform" policies pursued by President Yeltsin since 1992.

Treating Russia's agony as a case of the "Asian flu"—

as merely a matter of bolstering a faltering stock market, banking system, and currency with more budgetary austerity and tax collection, ruble devaluation, and Western financial bailouts—is like rearranging deck chairs on the *Titanic.* Russia's underlying problem is an unprecedented, all-encompassing economic catastrophe—a peacetime economy that has been in a process of relentless destruction for nearly seven years. GDP has fallen by at least 50 percent and according to one report by as much as 83 percent, capital investment by 80 percent, and, equally telling, meat and dairy livestock herds by 75 percent. Except for energy, the country now produces very little; most consumer goods, especially in large cities, are imported.

So great is Russia's economic and thus social catastrophe that we must now speak of another unprecedented development: the literal demodernization of a twentieth-century country. When the infrastructures of production, technology, science, transportation, heating, and sewage disposal disintegrate; when tens of millions of people do not receive earned salaries, some 75 percent of society lives below or barely above the subsistence level, and millions of them are actually starving; when male life expectancy has plunged as low as fifty-eight years, malnutrition has become the norm among schoolchildren, once-eradicated diseases are again becoming epidemics, and basic welfare provisions are disappearing; when even highly educated professionals must grow their own food in order to survive and well over half the nation's economic transactions are barter— all this, and more, is indisputable evidence of a tragic "transition" backward to a premodern era.

Even if economic growth were miraculously to resume

tomorrow, Russia would need decades to regain what it has lost in the nineties, and nothing can retrieve the millions of lives already cut short by the "transition." Indeed, as a careful statistical study by Professor Stephen Shenfield of Brown University shows, an even greater and possibly inescapable economic and social disaster may be approaching.

Why call this "reform," as does virtually every U.S. commentator? Certainly, very few Russians any longer do, except to curse Yeltsin and his policies, especially those long and zealously promoted by the Clinton administration. Russian economists and politicians across the spectrum are now desperately trying to formulate alternative economic policies that might save their nation— ones more akin to Franklin Roosevelt's New Deal than to the neoliberal monetarist orthodoxies of the State and Treasury departments, the IMF, World Bank, and legions of Western advisers, which have done so much to abet Russia's calamity.

But when President Clinton goes to Moscow in September 1998, he will no doubt tell Yeltsin publicly, as he often has done in the past and Vice President Gore did when he visited in July, "Stay the course!" For most Russians, it will mean that America welcomes what has happened to their country and does not care about their ruined lives.

[*The Nation*, September 7–14, 1998]

POSTSCRIPT

In 2000, as we saw in the first section of this book, most American officials, journalists, investors, and scholars

still considered Yeltsin's U.S.-sponsored economic policies of the 1990s to be the only authentic program of
reform for post-Communist Russia. Hence their lament
that Russia did not fully "stay the course" and their
hope that it will do so under Putin. Inside Russia, on
the other hand, very few people believe in those policies any longer. Meanwhile, the demodernization of the
country, the loss of much it had achieved in the twentieth century, continues, along with the tragic human
consequences of "reform."

"Who Lost Russia?" (1998–2000)

Ever since the U.S. government launched its crusade to
transform post-Communist Russia into a fascimile of
the American system, it was only a matter of time
before that missionary arrogance led to disaster and
clamorous shouts of "Who lost Russia?" The unfolding
disaster has been evident from the very beginning,
especially its impact on the Russian people, but the
American finger-pointing began in earnest only with
Moscow's financial meltdown in August and September
1998.

Moreover, the question arose not as an effort to
understand why things have gone so wrong in U.S. policy and post-Communist Russia but out of self-serving
and potentially dangerous motives. Fifty years ago,
American politicians and media demanded to know
"Who lost China?," with malignant consequences that
seem to have been forgotten. The result then was viru-

lent McCarthyism and a political "mainstream" as narrow and barren as a dry creek.

The question about Russia must therefore be answered wisely before it too becomes politically cancerous. The collapse of Yeltsinism—particularly those U.S.-backed shock-therapy, monetarist policies that helped bring about the worst economic and social devastation ever suffered by a modern country in peacetime—was also the final collapse of the Clinton administration's Russia policy, though the administration stubbornly refused to acknowledge it.

But this does not mean that the administration or the United States lost Russia. If by that is meant squandering prospects for Russian democracy, prosperity, and social well-being, it was President Yeltsin and his "radical reformers" who lost Russia. Nothing and no one forced them to impose the U.S. government's wrongheaded, dogmatic prescriptions on their nation, especially in the face of warnings by many of their best pro-reform economists. No wonder most Russians looked angrily to Yeltsin's Kremlin as their own "accursed" question—"Who is to blame?"—resounded ever more insistently across that tormented land.

But America is in grave danger of losing something equally important in Russia—its moral reputation. For nearly a decade, in the name of a sectarian economic dogma and Yeltsin's purported "reforms," the U.S. government has closed its eyes and heart to the suffering of the great majority of the Russian people, whose quality and even duration of life have fallen almost yearly. Yeltsin may have lost Russia, but we are losing our soul there.

For "realists" indifferent to moral considerations in foreign affairs, there is something else. Clinton's Russia policy and Yeltsin's leadership put international and American security in great potential jeopardy. For the first time in history, a country laden with nuclear weapons, reactors, materials, and other deadly devices is collapsing, its economic, social, administrative, and political institutions in various stages of disintegration. If the process continues, and with it inescapably Russia's nuclear safeguards, we will increasingly be faced with an unprecedented peril. In fact, the dangers emanating from Russia today already exceed those of the relatively stable and predictable Cold War era, though this too the Clinton administration refused to acknowledge.

Indeed, the administration turned its back on a major opportunity to change course in 1998 and 1999. The near total collapse of Russia's financial system in the summer of 1998 compelled Yeltsin to dismiss the last of his ballyhooed cabinets of "young radical reformers"—this one headed by the unqualified and inept thirty-seven-year-old Prime Minister Sergei Kirienko. (Some U.S. officials and commentators had called it the "best Russian government ever," probably because their favorite "young reformers," Yegor Gaidar and Anatoly Chubais, though discredited and despised in Russia, exercised considerable influence behind the scenes.)

Yeltsin first tried to reappoint former Prime Minister Viktor Chernomyrdin, another widely discredited loyalist whom the Clinton administration had once favored and still hoped might eventually be Russia's next president, but he was blocked by broad opposition in the Duma. Sensing that his own position was now threatened by the economic crisis and lacking credible alternatives, Yeltsin turned to sixty-eight-year-old Evgeny Primakov, who had played no role in the Kremlin's failed economic policies or its nourishing of powerful financial oligarchs. A top official in Gorbachev's Soviet reform government, Primakov had served as Yeltsin's head of foreign intelligence and most recently as foreign minister.

Primakov inherited a country in the throes of an economic disaster. Even before the financial meltdown, seven years of depression had halved GDP, badly eroded essential infrastructures of everyday life, and left the state bankrupt and saddled with $168 billion of foreign debt. By now, some 75 percent of Russians, perhaps more, lived below or barely above the poverty line, their wages unpaid, bank savings frozen, money in hand greatly devalued, and Soviet-era welfare provisions all but evaporated. The nation was awash in corruption, crime, disease, alcohol abuse, and premature deaths.

Understandably, Primakov's priorities upon becoming prime minister in September 1998 were helping his stricken people, stopping some $24 billion in capital flight a year, reviving domestic production, and stabilizing the country—not the monetarist shibboleths of "radical reform." A centrist by nature, he formed a coalition cabinet that included two nominal Communists as well as a member of the anti-Communist, liberal Yabloko Party. After years of imposed measures and bitter conflict, Primakov sought consensual ways to overcome the nation's crisis.

Primakov's government was the first under Yeltsin

since early 1992 to have majority support in the Parliament. Relying on that support, Primakov proposed, in addition to his economic initiatives, to curb high-level corruption by opening investigations of several financial oligarchs with close ties to the Kremlin, create a broad centrist alliance against growing extremism on both sides of the spectrum, and guarantee the holding of scheduled elections and immunity from prosecution for the beleaguered, unpopular Yeltsin when his legal term of office ended in mid-2000. As a result, by early 1999, Primakov had become the country's most popular political figure.

The Clinton administration should have eagerly embraced Primakov's government as an opportunity for a fresh start in U.S.-Russian relations. It was a chance to help stabilize that nuclear country, rehabilitate America's reputation there, and cultivate new partners for the post-Yeltsin era. The administration refused to do so, even beginning the NATO bombing of Serbia, Russia's fellow Slav nation, just as the new prime minister was in flight to Washington for his first visit since taking office, compelling him to turn back.

The history of the Clinton administration's relations with Primakov's government is not fully clear, but the new Russian prime minister seems to have had almost as many enemies in Washington (and in the American press) as he had in Moscow. Some U.S. officials distrusted him because of his personal relationship with Saddam Hussein going back to Primakov's early years as an Arabist and Soviet correspondent in the Middle East, said to have been a KGB position, or because he had remained loyal to Gorbachev throughout the last Soviet leader's time of office.[21]

Above all, however, the "long-despised" Primakov (as an American insider labeled him) seems to have been feared in Washington on grounds that he headed or fronted a "Communist government"—a false characterization but one assiduously promoted by ousted "radical reformers" in Moscow and a number of influential U.S. officials and journalists. If true, the advent of such a Russian government, said to be the Clinton administration's "worst foreign policy nightmare," would have dramatized the failure of the White House's policy and, amid the clamor over "Who lost Russia?," gravely endangered Vice President Gore's chances for the presidency in 2000.[22]

Whatever the full explanation, the administration was at best cold to Primakov and probably actively encouraged Yeltsin's growing inclination to remove him, as he did in May 1999, after only eight months. In particular, the Clinton administration, despite having enthusiastically bankrolled every previous government appointed by Yeltsin, including the one that waged the first murderous war in Chechnya, from 1994 to 1996, refused Primakov's pleas for financial help. The main reason given, and routinely echoed in U.S. editorials, was that his team had "abandoned reform."

Primakov's cabinet did move away from the purportedly free-market, rigidly monetarist policies that Washington had made a condition of aid for nearly six years—not because it was antireform or antimarket but because those measures had contributed greatly to Russia's economic collapse. Desperately seeking ways to save its people, Primakov's government proposed to move instead toward forms of state regulation and deficit spending akin to Franklin Roosevelt's anti-Depression reforms of the 1930s.

But not even this explicit appeal to America's own experience softened the Clinton administration's hard-line stance, giving the impression that Washington preferred Russia's ever-growing human suffering to two Communists in its government. No less incongruous, the administration maintained that any new financial aid would be lost to corruption, even though many of its Russian protégés previously in power, the "radical reformers," had been both inept and corrupt. In contrast, Primakov's team had not created Russia's meltdown or stolen anything. (Not surprisingly, after Primakov's ouster, the IMF resumed its loans to the Kremlin.)

The circumstances of Primakov's removal, which occurred during the U.S.-led NATO bombing of Serbia, did more damage to America's reputation in Russia. With most citizens and virtually the entire political class outraged by the air war against a small fraternal nation in Russia's backyard, Primakov's personal popularity and broad international experience would seem to have made him the ideal head of government in the worst confrontation with the West since the end of the Cold War.

Suddenly, however, Yeltsin named the U.S. favorite Chernomyrdin as his personal envoy to the warring parties and a month later replaced Primakov as prime minister with Sergei Stepashin. Stepashin's apparent credentials were having served Yeltsin faithfully through a series of policy calamities, including the disastrous Chechen war in 1994–96, and having made his career in the Ministry of Internal Affairs, where he held the rank of general. On the eve of an attempt by Parliament to impeach him, which only barely failed, Yeltsin clearly felt the need for an avowed praetorian minister, not a popular one with extensive political and diplomatic experience as well as majority support in the Duma.[23]

As for Chernomyrdin, his astonishing role in helping the U.S. alliance achieve all of its war aims without any casualties or significant concessions—the capitulation of Yugoslav President Slobodan Milosevic and NATO occupation of Kosovo—shocked many Russians. Dubbed the "Balkan Munich,"[24] it became yet another source of widespread suspicions about sinister American influence in Yeltsin's Kremlin and the country's misfortunes.

As events unfolded from May 1999 through the spring of 2000, the Clinton administration nonetheless clearly believed that its anti-Primakov policy had paid off. But have the consequences actually been in the interest of Russian reform or the United States? Primakov had represented hopes for civil peace, social justice, and stability in Russia. What followed was civil war, oligarchical intrigue, and a politics based on public fears.

Behind Primakov's downfall were powerful Russian forces that wanted a special kind of prime minister and successor to Yeltsin—one who would protect them and their interests, a Kremlin praetorian or a Pinochet, as was being said in Moscow.[25] Yeltsin, for whatever reason, did not trust Primakov's promise of immunity guaranteed by Parliament. Russia's financial oligarchs, who in light of recent money-laundering scandals could no longer count on a safe haven in the West, feared Primakov's investigation of their privatization deals and wealth. The "young radical reformers" hated and feared his denunciation of the shock therapy they had imposed on the country. These were, in effect, the Clinton administration's allies in 1999 and 2000.

Increasingly fearful, Yeltsin and his Kremlin entourage of relatives, personal servitors, and financial tycoons, known in derisive Mafia-like terms as "the Family," soon concluded that even General Stepashin, a politically conflicted man, lacked "sufficient resolve" for their needs. In August 1999, less than three months after his confirmation, they replaced him as prime minister and heir apparent with the unconflicted but nearly unknown head of the KGB successor agency, Vladimir Putin.

A career KGB officer, the forty-seven-year-old Putin had "retired" in 1991, working for two prominent political figures (themselves later investigated for corruption) before being appointed by Yeltsin to head the agency in July 1998. In contrast to the U.S. treatment of Primakov, President Clinton welcomed Putin as prime minister, as he had Stepashin, creating the impression that Washington also preferred a Russian Pinochet to a Roosevelt.

Something worse than Pinochet's bloodletting in Chile was being prepared in Moscow, actions that would soon make Primakov seem "pro-democratic" by comparison. As early as March 1999, contrary to later official claims that it only responded to provocations in August and September, the Kremlin had begun secretly planning a new military campaign in breakaway

Chechnya.[26] (NATO's ongoing war against Yugoslavia, Moscow professed to believe, legitimized its own plan.) What ensued, as Russians who had seen the popular movie said, was a "wag-the-dog war" contrived to put Yeltsin's chosen successor in power: "It is not a war for the Caucasus, but for the Kremlin. The victory to be gained is getting the Kremlin candidate [Putin] elected president and maintaining the ruling clan of kleptocrats in power."[27]

The original plan was to occupy only the northern half of Chechnya bordering Russia. But still mysterious events in August and September—an uncharacteristic Chechen guerrilla raid on neighboring Russian Dagestan and, most important, unprecedented nighttime bombings in residential buildings in Moscow and other cities killing almost three hundred people—charged the atmosphere more than enough for an all-out war to occupy the whole of Chechnya and reimpose a pro-Moscow regime.

Waging merciless war against Chechen "terrorists and bandits"—"We'll waste them even in their outhouses"—was the centerpiece of Putin's electoral campaign in the parliamentary voting in December 1999 and then the presidential election in March 2000. (He flatly refused to divulge any economic program.) Skillfully playing on public fears in the wake of the bombings and popular yearnings for "order" in the aftermath of Yeltsin's policies, Putin's handlers quickly turned him into the country's most popular politician, displacing the aging Primakov. Considering their control of national television, it was not difficult.

The blood-tinged strategy succeeded well enough in

December to set the full scenario in motion. A pro-Putin "party" conjured up on the eve of the parliamentary elections received 23 percent of the vote, almost as much as the previously dominant Communist Party. Assured by the result that his handpicked successor would win a presidential election, Yeltsin (voluntarily or under pressure) suddenly resigned.

His resignation, in accord with the constitution, made Prime Minister Putin acting president with all the tsar-like powers of Kremlin incumbency and automatically moved the presidential election forward from June 2000 to March, when the war was likely to still have popular support. On the same day, Putin issued a decree giving Yeltsin full immunity from any kind of prosecution. Three months later, a man virtually unknown until recently was elected to the super-presidency of Russia that had been created in 1993 for Yeltsin, defeating his Communist rival, Gennady Zyuganov, according to official returns, with nearly 53 percent of the vote to 29 percent. (Zyuganov claimed that he actually received just over 38 percent and Putin about 43.5 percent. If so, a runoff would have been required.)

It was that carefully contrived chain of events which the Clinton administration and too many American journalists and academics hailed as Russia's "first ever democratic transition of power." Echoing the administration's claim that its crusade and Russia's "transition" were still on course because Putin was a "leading reformer," a senior historian assured *Wall Street Journal* readers that Yeltsin had triumphantly found a "like-minded successor" and brought his own era to "this promising finale."[28]

The story began to fall apart almost immediately. U.S. Russia-watchers had cheered the success of Putin's "party" in the December 1999 parliamentary elections as the long-awaited anti-Communist breakthrough that would finally lead to more "radical reform." In January 2000, when Putin struck a deal in the new Duma with the Communist Party, at the expense of U.S.-favored "liberals," even usually recalcitrant American newspapers had to offer some rare if oblique self-criticism: "The unexpected deal . . . suggested that, rather than a centrist parliament, which many had predicted after the December elections, the Communists might again be able to dominate the chamber in alliance with the pro-Putin party."[29]

It was far from the worst American misrepresentation of Yeltsin's "promising finale." Putin's electoral ascent was, of course, neither "democratic" nor a "transfer of power." As a number of observant Russian and U.S. observers understood, it included elements of a "coup d'etat" and Soviet-style "de facto uncontested elections" carefully organized to retain power in the hands of Yeltsin's Kremlin entourage—that is, to prevent its being transferred to outsiders. To say the least, the process was "neither free nor fair."[30]

Indeed, most aspects of Putin's rise were further setbacks for Russian democratization. A pro-democracy Russian scholar pointed out that Yeltsin's ability to appoint his own successor was more "absolute" than that of any Soviet leader. The Kremlin's gross misuse of the national media, several monitors reported, further undermined the idea and practice of a "free press." A Russian constitutional lawyer and journalist were especially alarmed by how reflexively Putin's appointment as heir-designate had elicited from ordinary citizens and elites alike a "submissive acceptance" and pre-Gorbachev Soviet-like "'Yes' in unison."[31]

Still worse, the Kremlin's new Chechen war in 1999 and 2000 was the essential factor in Putin's rise to power. Politics explains the Clinton administration's decision to excuse or minimize Moscow's atrocities in the tiny Caucasus province, but some American journalists and scholars also did so. A *New York Times* correspondent characterized it as "Russia's first real democratic war," and according to an eminent Berkeley historian its "basic cause was that Russians wanted a strong reform government." As for the Kremlin commander, Putin, another Western journalist had the "reassuring impression that, in him, Russia has found a humane version of Peter the Great."[32]

Some Russian democrats had a different impression, among them Andrei Sakharov's widow, Elena Bonner. For her, the Kremlin's indiscriminate use of missiles, bombs, and heavy artillery against Chechen towns and villages, leading to thousands of deaths, the complete destruction of the capital Grozny, and some 300,000 refugees, constituted "methods of genocide" and "crimes against humanity." International human rights organizations also concluded that the Kremlin was guilty of "war crimes."[33]

Such atrocities cannot be minimized by Moscow's legal sovereignty over Chechnya, its right to fight terrorists, or the war's popularity among Russian voters. They were no better than Yugoslav President Milosevic's actions in Kosovo, to make the pertinent comparison, and arguably much worse. Still less can they be called "reform."

Nor did the consequences of the Kremlin's Chechen campaign end with Putin's election. Despite the destruction wrought by Moscow and its repeated claims of victory, the war goes on, now in circumstances favoring Chechen guerrilla fighters, and with it the growing role of military and other security forces in Russian political life. Putin's politically opportune but historically unusual alliance with army generals eager to avenge their humiliating 1996 defeat in Chechnya—the KGB and military had never been natural allies—may not be short-lived.

Furthermore, as it becomes clear that the war cannot be won on Moscow's terms, public support will fade and Russia will be left with still more "accursed questions." Who, it will be asked, sent thousands of young, ill-trained soldiers, for the second time in five years, to die or be maimed in Chechnya, and why? Who was responsible for the killing of so many elderly ethnic Russians in Grozny? And even, as is already being asked, who really placed the bombs in Moscow that detonated the carnage in Chechnya?[34] Russian history is full of such questions about high-level criminality, for which there is rarely any political statute of limitations, only endlessly bitter division.

All of these developments are inextricably linked to Putin's "democratic transition" to power and its actual meaning. We need not accept overwrought charges in Moscow and elsewhere that with him the KGB returned to power and Russia is again becoming a police state to understand that his occupancy of the

Kremlin has special historical and political significance.[35]

For the first time in Russia's centuries-long history of repressive police culture, a career secret policeman has become the nation's supreme leader. Indeed, in the aftermath of Stalin's twenty-year police terror, the Soviet elite resolved that no professional KGB officer should ever rise to supreme power, and none did. (Yuri Andropov, the Soviet leader briefly from 1982 to 1984, had previously headed the KGB, but it was not his original or primary profession and he had to leave the agency in advance in order to become Brezhnev's successor.)[36]

Why did the post-Communist "democratic" elite break with this tsarist and Soviet tradition? As a Moscow insider told readers, Putin's "accidental ascent wasn't accidental." Behind it lay the two defining economic and social realities of the 1990s—the plundering of the country's richest assets by a tiny group of Kremlin-backed insiders and, at the same time, the impoverishment or near impoverishment of most of their fellow citizens. Two other Russian traditions thus came to the fore in acute and unprecedented ways: the question "Who is to blame?" and the Moscow elite's fear of the *narod* (the people). Hence the need for a praetorian president willing to use "totalitarian force," as one oligarch demanded, if necessary to protect his creators.[37]

It does not mean that "Putinism" must inevitably be the "highest and final stage of robber capitalism in Russia."[38] A relatively young man, Putin may well turn out to be something different from what he was created to be. History is full of political leaders who rose on behalf of their nations above their former selves. But upon his formal inauguration as president on May 7, 2000, having given Yeltsin immunity and terminated most investigations of the Kremlin-backed oligarchs, he ruled Russia as their protector, or at least those he favored, although the arrangement soon proved to be unstable and temporary.

Finally, there was the Clinton administration's claim, also echoed by some journalists and scholars, that Putin's election was a victory for American goals and U.S.-Russian relations. If so, it was a bizarre revision of those goals and relations.

In 1999 and 2000, it was widely understood in Moscow that "Putin's anti-Western insinuations" were a popular and crucial factor in his rise to power.[59] And in fact, little if anything now remains of the American-Russian "strategic partnership and friendship" so often proclaimed in the 1990s. Putin did quickly schedule summit meetings with Western leaders, including one held with President Clinton in Moscow in June 2000, and had the Duma finally ratify START II, but such steps were normal features of the Cold War as well.

More fundamentally, Putin's ascent exposed a false premise of U.S. policy. The Russian "liberal" values and politicians the administration supported throughout the 1990s turned out to be something different. Believing they had realized "their dream of a Russian Pinochet," the "young radical reformers"—Anatoly Chubais, Boris Nemtsov, Sergei Kirienko—rallied eagerly behind Putin and his Chechen war.[40] Even longtime supporters now had to admit that their heroes had entered "into an unnatural embrace of military nationalism . . . strengthening the political influence of army and intelligence officials."[41]

Meanwhile, the Clinton administration continued to risk losing if not America's soul in Russia, certainly its reputation. By embracing Putin so eagerly and uncritically, the U.S. government raised a new question among Russia's opposition democrats: "Why have American leaders fallen in love with Putin?" As the administration's enthusiasm for the post-Yeltsin "democratic transition" grew more persistent, so did the answer: "The West is seduced by the prospect of a Russian Pinochet ensuring Western investors' rights in Russia."[42]

All these factors behind the Putin phenomenon, from plunder and poverty to war, yearnings for a strong-arm ruler, and anti-Americanism, were the logical, not "unnatural," consequences of the "great transition." Thus did America's crusade to remake another civilization end in disaster in post-Communist Russia and in cold peace, or worse, in its relations with that nuclear-laden, crisis-ridden country.

[Expanded and updated version of two articles in *The Nation*, October 12, 1998, and January 11–18, 1999]

PART III

TOWARD A NEW
RUSSIA POLICY

The experience of the 1990s demonstratively shows that a truly successful revival of our Motherland without excessive costs cannot be achieved by simply transferring abstract models and schemes taken from foreign textbooks to Russian soil . . . Russia will not soon become, if it ever becomes, a second edition of, let's say, the United States or England.
Russian President Vladimir Putin[1]

The Owl of Minerva spreads its wings only with the falling of dusk.
Hegel

The United States desperately needs a new and fundamentally different policy toward post-Communist Russia. Having failed to achieve any of its main objectives, the missionary crusade of the 1990s was not only the worst American foreign policy disaster since Vietnam; its consequences have contributed to new and unprecedented dangers. At the start of the twenty-first century, Russia, U.S.-Russian relations, and international nuclear security all are in much worse condition than they were a decade earlier.

Enacting a new policy will not be easy. It requires a reformation of American thinking about post-Communist Russia and a president willing to provide the necessary leadership, beginning with truth telling about what has really happened in that country and in U.S.-Russian relations. Opportunities already lost make essential U.S. goals considerably more difficult to achieve than they were in the early 1990s. Still more, the legions of proponents of the failed American crusade—in government, academia, and the media—will continue to resist any fundamental changes. Before turning to the nature of a new Russia policy, we must therefore review the perilous damage done by the old one, especially during the years of the Clinton administration.

U.S. Policy on the Wrong Side of History

Given the abrupt breakup of the vast Soviet state in December 1991, the overriding American goal had to be a Russia stable enough to control and maintain its enormous Cold War array of nuclear weapons and other instruments of mass destruction. Anything less would be, as it remains, the gravest imaginable threat to everything else. "If Russia destabilizes," a leading Clinton official once reminded us, "the costs to the United States are going to be vastly greater than anything we can possibly think of."[2]

When the Clinton administration took office in January 1993, it inherited historic opportunities to avert that danger in post-Communist Russia. The best way was, of course, by giving generous U.S. support for an expansion and consolidation of the democratization and economic market reforms begun by the last Soviet leader, Mikhail Gorbachev, and professed by the new Russian president, Boris Yeltsin. The White House also inherited a chance to develop the uniquely cooperative Russian-American relationship initiated by Gorbachev along with Presidents Reagan and Bush into, as the administration repeatedly promised, a lasting "strategic partnership and friendship" that would radically reduce, perhaps even eliminate, most nuclear dangers.

Instead, by the missionary and counterproductive ways the Clinton administration chose to pursue those historic opportunities, it squandered them. Still laden with every device of mass destruction, Russia has entered the twenty-first century, as readers know, in a state of profound instability—political, economic, social, military, even territorial—and in an increasingly hostile relationship with the United States.

The essential requirement for any nation's stability is a fair degree of general economic and social well-being. In 2000, despite the trumpeted but probably temporary modest growth of industrial output as a result of high world prices for the country's oil and a devalued ruble favoring domestic goods, Russia remained in the grip of the worst economic depression of its kind in history and continuing human immiseration. Infrastructures and other essentials needed for a minimally decent life were still disintegrating. Nearly twice as many Russians were dying, most of them prematurely, than were being born. The country, according to medical authorities, was "on the verge of a population catastrophe."

The reason, of course, is that in 2000 most Russians are impoverished. According to official statistics, about

40 percent of the people live in poverty, but the actual figure is at least 50 percent, and several usually reliable Moscow newspapers report that it could be 85 to 90 percent. Considering the conflicting figures, it seems reasonable to assume that some 75 to 80 percent of Russians now live below or barely above the minimum subsistence level. In a national survey, only 14 percent, for example, said they could afford necessary medical treatment. Whatever the exact number, a newspaper reported the essential reality: "The people are growing poorer before our eyes."[3]

At first glance, Russia's post-Communist democratization may seem to be in better health than its economy and people, even consolidated. Numerous proponents of this superficial view point out that another parliamentary election was held in December 1999 and a presidential one in March 2000, as called for by the constitution. The media, they add, are full of conflicting opinions; candidates compete for votes at the national, regional, and local levels; and citizens are allowed to assemble, organize, and travel abroad.

But it is very far from the full story. Russia today has elements of democracy, but it does not have a democratic system. Among the essentials missing are a constitution providing for a meaningful separation and balance of powers; real national political parties other than the Communists; reliable rule of constitutional, civil, or criminal law; any serious effort by ruling elites to curb systematic high-level corruption and other abuses of office, much less prosecute them; and guarantees of elementary human rights, which are being violated on a massive scale everywhere from the streets of

Moscow and Russia's prisons to Chechnya. (Russian human rights activists, their leader reports, now "are considered the country's primary internal enemies.")[4]

Moreover, as we have seen, the elements of democracy that do exist, most of them products of the Gorbachev, not Yeltsin, years, are being steadily diminished. Nationwide television and newspapers, almost entirely controlled by the Kremlin and a few self-interested financial oligarchs, are less free and objective than they were a few years ago, and both central and provincial authorities are redoubling efforts to repress independent journalism. Security and military forces are playing a larger political role than at any time since 1991, while the power of local bosses over their citizens is growing. Working-class people are being systematically deprived of elementary rights. The Russian Parliament is less autonomous than it was before and still lives in the shadow of executive decrees. And the national elections of 1999 and 2000 were less fair than preceding ones and their results perhaps even more falsifed.[5]

Again, these regressive authoritarian developments do not mean that post-Communist Russia has become a police state or is inevitably headed toward a Weimar-like descent into a new totalitarianism, as is feared by some in Moscow. But they do explain why many pro-democracy Russians—real ones, not those designated by the U.S. government—now speak of a "manipulative democracy," in which "democratic institutions exist but produce only results ordered by the state," a "democracy without alternatives," and "pseudo-democracy."[6]

The most important instance of manipulating the

political system to exclude real alternatives was, of course, the "Putin phenomenon"—the Yeltsin regime's successful scheme to deliver the nation's presidency to its handpicked, previously obscure successor in order to retain power and avoid the risk of criminal prosecution. Even if the regime did not actually stage the 1999 bombings and other events that led to the new Kremlin war in Chechnya, its cynical use of a nearly genocidal military campaign as an electoral strategy is not an indicator of democracy or stability.

Nor was Putin's prior political biography or the steps he took following his inauguration in May 2000. Two were especially ominous. On May 11, "tax police" wearing ski masks and carrying assault weapons raided the financial offices of the country's only semi-independent national television network, whose owner was then briefly arrested a month later. The raid sent a chill through the diminished independent press and led one editor to remark, "The face of Russia at the beginning of the twenty-first century is a black mask."

A few days later, Putin announced far-reaching measures to rein in the heads of the country's eighty-nine administrative territories. Some assertion of federal authority across Russia was needed, but Putin's plan seemed exceedingly regressive. By proposing to create seven overriding administrative districts headed by his personal and fully empowered appointees, five of those viceroys announced being army or security police generals, and depriving governors of their ex officio seats in the Parliament's upper chamber and perhaps their electoral autonomy, Putin threatened to restore the tsarist and Soviet tradition of ruling Russia's vast

provinces directly from the Kremlin, perhaps even relying heavily on the military to do so.

Behind Putin's rise to power were not only pro-
Kremlin oligarchs and security forces that had been
assiduously "patriotizing" their historical reputation
since 1991, and may be disposed to "using totalitarian
force,"[7] but ominous changes in Russian political attitudes. For several years, as we saw earlier, the country's
U.S.-backed "liberals" had been "yearning for . . . an
energetic Pinochet" to impose and defend what they
call economic reform. Intensifying their search in the
twilight of Yeltsin's presidency, they believed they had
found him in Putin.

In response to the imposed traumas of the 1990s,
mass attitudes have also shifted in favor of a "strong-
hand" ruler—though in this popular "yearning," one
who would restore both order and "fairness" in the
country.[8] Even a leading U.S. architect of the crusade
finally admitted that its impact has "given a bad name
to democracy, reform, the free market, even liberty
itself" in post-Communist Russia.[9]

Popular antidemocratic sentiments should not be
exaggerated, but the trend is unmistakable. By 2000,
sizable majorities of Russians surveyed favored "order"
over democratic practices and trusted the military and
political police more than they did elected institutions.
Earlier, nearly half thought that if Stalin was a candidate, he would win the upcoming presidential election.
Not surprisingly, in May 2000, the Putin regime also
seized the occasion of the fifty-fifth anniversary of the
Soviet victory in World War II to promote Generalissi-
mo Stalin's official reputation for the first time since

the pre-Gorbachev years. (At about the same time, Putin and other leaders meeting in the Kremlin drank a toast to the murderous despot on what happened to be his 120th birthday, perhaps in tribute to Stalin's ruthless 1944 mass deportation of the Chechen people.)[10]

Such yearnings reflect what Russians have traditionally, and fearfully, called a *Smuta,* and which has occurred more than once in their history. Although the term is blandly translated as a "Time of Troubles," its actual historical meaning is the collapse of central state authority followed by chaos, violence, and widespread human misery, as during the Russian Revolution and civil war of 1917–21. Many Russians believe that the post-Communist "transition" has plunged their country into a new *Smuta,* which is the very opposite of political, economic, and social stability.[11] If so, it is the first *Smuta* in a nuclearized Russia.

Defenders of U.S. support for Yeltsin's "reforms" in the 1990s still insist that these dismal outcomes are only a "rocky" patch in the transition and that America has been "on the right side of history" in post-Communist Russia.[12] It is not the opinion of most Russians. When Yeltsin resigned in December 1999, only 10 to 15 percent of those asked said there had been any positive aspects of his rule, and that figure was inflated from his usual single-digit favorable rating by the sentimentality of his New Year's farewell address. Almost half thought his leadership had been fully "catastrophic."[13]

Nor are historians likely to judge Yeltsin's leadership and thus U.S. policy favorably. If journalism is a first rough draft of history, consider the editorial opinion of a Western-owned, pro-capitalist newspaper in Moscow:

"Everyone talks about the Yeltsin years as the reform years. But the fact is, there is not a single major reform that was not begun by Gorbachev and at least slightly tarnished or rolled back under Yeltsin." For this and other reasons, the editors think Russia deserves "an American apology."[14]

A number of widely respected scholars—all of them anti-Communist, lest readers wonder—have reached similar conclusions. A senior Anglo-American political scientist characterizes the Yeltsin years not as an era of reform but of "counter-reform" and "missed opportunities." His opinion is shared by many Russian scholars, among them the country's own preeminent political scientist and the foremost dissident historian in Soviet times. Equally telling, the head of Russian studies at a Washington foundation that had been enthusiastically pro-Yeltsin during most of the 1990s now concludes that his leadership was a "monumental failure."[15]

It is not even certain that any of the achievements boasted by Yeltsin's American promoters were authentic or will endure. Another Russian scholar thinks that because of political developments in 1999 and 2000, "a lot of so-called democratic achievements will be lost."[16] Some pro-democracy Russians believe, as we just saw, that they have already been lost.

As for the post-Communist "economic transition," much of it was Potemkin-village reforms all but swept away by the financial collapse in August–September 1998. Others, such as the privatization of major industries, will almost certainly be revised to some degree because they were unfairly enacted by decree and because, as happened with the legacy of every departed Russian leader in the twentieth century, some kind of de-Yeltsinization is already unfolding.[17] More generally, Yeltsin's economic system is unlikely to endure because it has been so cruelly unfair and unproductive that almost no Russians value it, except its oligarchs and their retainers. Most see it as a kleptocracy or, as a retired American CIA specialist terms it, "phony, crony capitalism."[18]

When all else has failed, the bottom-line claim made for Yeltsin's leadership and U.S. policy in Russia is that they kept the Communists from regaining power and, by implication, the Soviet Union from reemerging. It too is a bogus "achievement."[19] After 1991, the Communist Party had no chance of returning to the Kremlin, certainly not by force.

In fact, it was Yeltsin's U.S.-sponsored economic policies that made the Communist Party more important today than it would otherwise be. Largely as a result of those cruel measures, Communists received more votes in every successive parliamentary election, from 12.4 percent in 1993 to nearly 25 percent in 1999, showing signs that its appeal was broadening beyond its "elderly" electorate and might not soon "die off." And it was Putin, whose ascension was the direct outgrowth of Yeltsinism, who made a parliamentary alliance with the Communist Party in January 2000, giving it more potential influence over Kremlin policy-making than at any time since Gorbachev dismantled its dictatorship in 1989 and 1990. To this indictment may be added, as readers will recall, the suggestion by a once pro-Yeltsin Western journalist that he turned out to be "worse than the Communists we helped him overcome."[20] (Will this also be said one day even more of Putin?)

To conclude this grim inventory of the failed crusade, not a single large American objective in U.S.-Russian relations themselves has been realized since 1993, only the opposite. There is no strategic "partnership"—the Kremlin struck the word from its revised national security doctrine in 2000[21]—but instead the worst relationship since the Cold War ended in the late 1980s. There is no Russian integration into the West, but instead, as viewed by many in Moscow, a new kind of iron curtain being imposed by NATO; an encroaching military, diplomatic, and economic encirclement led by the United States; and real allies to be sought in the East.

Still worse, there is less international security and much more nuclear danger, as we will see further on. U.S. policies and Russia's economic collapse have provoked Moscow into relying more than ever before on its nuclear stockpiles, whose safeguards are less reliable than ever before, for its national defense. In 2000, the Putin government even broadened the stated circumstances in which it would resort to nuclear weapons.[22]

Meanwhile, Washington has less real influence and thus genuine cooperation in Moscow on crucial security issues than it had during some détente chapters of the Cold War. (For that matter, in June 1999, at the Pristina airport in Kosovo, Russian and NATO soldiers came closer to actually shooting at each other—"World War III," said a British commander—than they had in Cold War times.)[23] Any expanded agreements to reduce nuclear and other weapons of mass destruction are now hostage to Moscow's assumption that Washington will eventually unilaterally abrogate the 1972 Anti-Ballistic Missile Treaty by deploying forbidden missile defense systems.

Predictions of a new Cold War on both sides may be wrong, but an increasingly cold peace has descended on America's relations with post-Communist Russia. It is codified in Moscow's new national security and military doctrines adopted in 2000, which for the first time in years again view the West as a threat and the United States as a potential enemy. Underlying the cold peace on the Russian side is the unprecedented anti-Americanism among elites and ordinary citizens alike that I noted earlier.[24]

Widespread anti-Americanism in post-Communist Russia is not a legacy of the Cold War—despite ritualistic Soviet propaganda, it did not really exist in those years—but a direct reaction to U.S. policies since the early 1990s.[25] It began with Washington's intrusive role in the Kremlin's economic policy-making, which caused so much "shock therapy" pain. It deepened as U.S. promises of large foreign investment failed to materialize and instead Moscow's foreign debt grew so burdensome that the state stopped paying pensions and wages in order to comply with Western budgetary conditions. It grew broader and angrier with NATO expansion in 1998, which was rightly seen as violating previous American promises, and virtually universal and furious with the U.S.-led NATO bombing of Yugoslavia in 1999.

By then, anti-Americanism was so popular, the "spread of anti-Western sentiments so universal," that almost every Russian political party incorporated it to some degree in its electoral strategy, even the "liberals" so favored by the Clinton administration. Frightened and marginalized by the surge of this kind of nationalism, Chubais and the other "young radical reformers" clung not only to Putin's brutal war in Chechnya but to the "same anti-Western, anti-American card" that helped his rise to power.[26] The United States still has crucial national security interests in Russia, but no longer any real friends of political consequence. The cool formality with which Putin greeted Clinton at their June 2000 summit meeting, compared to the American president's reception at events with Yeltsin, illustrated the change.

In short, the Clinton administration put America on the wrong side of history in post-Communist Russia. For this, most historians will judge it very harshly, as some of us already do. The indictment will include not merely missed opportunities but politically reckless and even immoral policy conduct that helped create a "Frankenstein's monster" system in Russia today[27]—a "transition" of the 1990s that has already reawakened the nation's historical demons and will be yet another "accursed question" tormenting its political life, and thus endangering all of us, for decades to come.

The indictment will charge that the U.S. government, enthusiastically supported by many American journalists and scholars, actively encouraged a Yeltsin regime that enabled a small clique of predatory insiders to plunder Russia's most valuable twentieth-century assets, a process that continued during the early months of Putin's rule, while most of its people were being impoverished and millions of them dying prematurely for lack of elementary resources. It will find that the White House, in the name of American interests and values, urged on and applauded Kremlin "reformers" whose "disgusting ethics" showed "the same neglect and contempt for 'the masses' as their Communist predecessors." By 2000, a group of former Soviet dissidents including Andrei Sakharov's widow had already reached its verdict, charging that Washington supported Yeltsin "despite the anti-democratic and criminal actions of his administration. . . . Now the same policy is beginning with regard to Putin."[28]

History will also record that the president of the United States in effect twice endorsed or forgave Kremlin war crimes against its own citizens in Chechnya by equating them with Lincoln's war against secession and slavery and then using the word *liberate* to characterize the destruction of Grozny.[29] And it will conclude that all these decisions and acts, by contributing to the destabilization of a nuclear country, left the United States itself, in the words of the Clinton administration's own CIA director, "at greater risk than it [has] ever been."[30]

A charge of criminal misconduct may also have to be added to the indictment: Hundreds of billions of ill-gained dollars flowing from Russia to the West since 1992, owing significantly to U.S.-designed policies adopted in Moscow, may have corrupted American institutions themselves well beyond the few cases of bank malfeasance already known. That possibility has been raised by a number of commentators, but none so expansively and authoritatively as by a recently retired top CIA specialist on Russia, who may know more than he is permitted to tell us.[31]

Pointing out that such sums of money could buy influence over "the content of our policy toward Russia," he asks, "What did Washington know and think when this plundering was going on? For the U.S., the saga . . . was either one of the most expensive blunders in recent memory or something more complicit. . . . It is hard to escape the suspicion that the mammoth stake of American investment houses played a role in U.S. government and IMF behavior." At issue, he concludes, may be "a pattern of business and government misbehavior." If so—the question cries out for a full investigation at the highest level[32]—it means that the Clinton administration squandered not only prospects for democracy, prosperity, strategic partnership, and nuclear stability in Russia but also America's reputation and integrity.

And yet, as we saw in the first part of this book, almost none of the people who influence and make U.S. policy blame the ill-conceived crusade itself for any of these calamitous outcomes. Even harsh critics of the Clinton administration explicitly or implicitly share its missionary premise that there is no "constructive" alternative to a policy that seeks to remake Russia according to American precepts, only "disengagement" and Cold War.[33] For virtually all opinion shapers and policymakers, as a ranking U.S. senator declared, this "debate now is over," even though, as we also saw earlier, the most fundamental questions have yet to be debated.[34]

In reality, the United States has misengaged post-Communist Russia from the beginning, and there have always been alternative ways to engage it that are both necessary and possible. On the eve of becoming Russia's president, Putin announced that his nation was entering the new millennium with feelings of profound "alarm and hope."[35] There is a kind of U.S. policy, which can and must engage that hope, but there is also a growing number of influential Americans who astonishingly see no reason at all for alarm.

Does Russia Still Matter?

In public as in private life, failure ought to be followed by a rethinking of what led to it. That has not been the case with U.S. failures in post-Communist Russia. Instead, it is increasingly argued in policy circles that those failures do not really matter, because Russia, pitiably weak at home and abroad, no longer really matters. A former U.S. intelligence chief and specialist on the region tells us, to take an influential example, that Russia is "virtually irrelevant" and "ain't worth worrying about."[36]

In this view, the product of misconceived Cold War triumphalism and frustrated expectations rather than rational thought, our onetime superpower adversary now requires no special priority in American foreign policy. The United States can operate for the most part in "a world without Russia." It can adopt "a minimalist policy," even "do little more than watch . . . from the sidelines."[37]

There could hardly be a worse misperception, larger analytical mistake, or graver political folly. Russia not only still matters; it matters even more than it did as Soviet Russia during the Cold War in at least three crucial respects.

Above all, the greatest potential threat to American and international security, in the most essential sense of physical safety, is located inside post-Communist Russia. Ever since the early 1990s, the Clinton administration, as well as many academics and journalists who should know better, has alleged that the United States and the world are much safer from nuclear and other lethal disasters than they were when the Soviet Union existed.

Architects of the administration's missionary crusade boast that "the American people are safer as a result of our policy"—indeed, "immeasurably more secure." According to a prominent journalist and Russia expert, we can now worry "considerably" less about "being vaporized into radioactive mist" or, as another puts it, about "a nuclear holocaust." A leading policy intellectual tells us that "American security is vastly improved," and an academic specialist that as a result of post-Communist reform, we have been "liberated from thinking about worst-case scenarios."[38]

These assurances are manifestly untrue and, coming from U.S. officials, editorialists, and scholars, inexplicably myopic and irresponsible. Even leaving aside post-Soviet Russia's enormous stockpiles of chemical and biological weapons, "all of the major fault lines of nuclear danger are growing," as we learn from a number of largely unheeded experts, and U.S. policy "simply has not kept up with the expansion of nuclear dangers inside Russia."[39] The truth may not be politically correct or palatable, but the breakup of the Soviet state and Russia's "transition" have made us immeasurably less safe than we have ever been.

To understand how unsafe, we must explore more fully a generalization made earlier in this book: What does it mean for our security when a nuclear-laden nation state is, depending on how we choose to characterize Russia's condition today, disintegrating, collapsing, or merely "highly unstable"?[40] The short answer is, no one fully knows, because it has never happened before, which itself means that compared with the relative predictability of the Soviet system and the Cold War, we now live in an era of acute nuclear uncertainty. The longer answer is that any significant degree of disintegration, instability, or civil warfare, all of which exist in Russia today, creates not one but several unprecedented nuclear dangers.

The most widely acknowledged, almost to the point of obscuring the others, is proliferation—the danger that some of Russia's vast accumulation of nuclear weapons, components, or knowledge might be acquired by non-nuclear states or terrorist groups through theft and black-market transactions, scientific brain drain, or a decision by a money-starved Moscow regime to sell them. The threat derives primarily from Russia's decade-long economic collapse. The government has lacked sufficient funds to safeguard storehouses of nuclear materials properly or to pay maintenance personnel and scientists adequately, even regularly. (Nuclear workers actually went out on strike over unpaid wages several times in the 1990s and again in 2000, even though it is against Russian law.)

Almost all of the existing U.S. programs to reduce nuclear threats inside Russia focus on proliferation. But even here, according to their official sponsors and other experts, the programs are "woefully inadequate" if we are "to prevent a catastrophe." By the end of 2000, for example, barely one-sixth of Russia's weapons-usable materials will be considered secure, and the "risks of 'loose nukes' are larger today" than they were when the programs began. Moreover, Moscow seems to have no full inventory of such materials or perhaps even of its thousands of tactical nuclear weapons, and thus no sure way of knowing whether or not something is missing.[41]

Proliferation is the pinup of Russia's nuclear dangers, the subject of Western novels and movies, but it may not be the most serious. If a nuclear explosion is waiting to happen, it is probably somewhere among Russia's scores of Soviet-era reactors at electrical power stations and on decommissioned submarines. Reactors, we are told, can be "no less dangerous than nuclear weapons." And as the Senate's leading expert informed his colleagues in 1999, Russia's "reactors suffer from deficiences in design, operator training, and safety procedures." Indeed, according to a Russian specialist, "none of our nuclear stations can be considered safe."[42]

The bell began tolling loudly on reactor catastrophes with the explosion at Chernobyl in 1986, the worst nuclear accident in history. Releasing more than a hundred times the radiation of the two atomic bombs dropped on Japan in 1945, its lethal consequences are still unfolding fourteen years later. Since the early 1990s, many reports, including one by the Russian government itself in February 2000, have warned of the possibility of another "Chernobyl-type disaster" or, more exactly, of several accident-prone Russian power stations, even faulty research reactors.[43] (The world's most dangerous nuclear plants are said to be located in post-Communist Russia and other former Soviet republics.)[44]

Scores of decommissioned but still not denuclearized Soviet-built submarines decaying in the far north greatly worsen the odds in this new kind of Russian roulette. Here too firsthand reports of "a nuclear accident waiting to happen" are increasingly ominous. Ill-maintained floating reactors are highly vulnerable, and many submarines are already leaking or dumping radioactive materials into the seas "like little Chernobyls in slow motion."[45] Active-duty Russian nuclear ships also pose a serious threat, their aging missiles susceptible to explosions, one likely to detonate others. If that happens, a Russian expert warns, "We can end up with hundreds of Chernobyls."[46]

Why, then, all the U.S. official and unofficial assurances that we are "immeasurably more secure" and can stop worrying about "worst-case scenarios"? They clearly derived from the single, entirely ideological assumption that because the Soviet Union no longer exists, the threat of a Russian nuclear attack on the United States no longer exists and we need now worry only about "rogue states." In truth, the possibility of such a Russian attack grew throughout the 1990s and is still growing.

Leave aside the warning that "a Russian version of Milosevic . . . armed with thousands of nuclear warheads" might come to power[47] and consider the progressive disintegration of the country's nuclear-defense infrastructure. Russia still has some six thousand warheads on hair-trigger alert. They are to be launched or not launched depending on information about activity at U.S. missile sites provided by an early-warning network of radars, satellites, and computers that now functions only partially and erratically. Russia's command-and-control personnel, who are hardly immune to the social hardships and pathologies sweeping the nation, have barely a few minutes to evaluate any threatening information, which has already been false on occasion. (In 1995, a Norwegian weather rocket was briefly mistaken by Russian authorities for an incoming enemy missile.)

These new post-Soviet technological and human circumstances of the nuclear age are, as American scientists have warned repeatedly, "increasing the danger of an accidental or unauthorized attack on the United States" from Russian territory. It is "arguably already the greatest threat to U.S. national survival." Assurances to the contrary, scientists emphasize, are "a gross misrepresentation of reality."[48]

Readers may choose to believe that intentional nuclear war nonetheless remains unthinkable. In post-Soviet Russia, however, it has become not only increasingly thinkable but speakable. The Kremlin's new security doctrine expanding conditions in which it would use such weapons may be merely semantic and nothing really new. But Russia's ferocious civil war in Chechnya, which did not end with the destruction of Grozny in 2000, is, as I have pointed out before, the first ever in a nuclear country.

It has not yet included nuclear warfare, but both sides have crossed a rhetorical Rubicon. Since 1999, several Russian deputies and governors, and even a leading "liberal" newspaper, have proposed using nuclear, chemical, or biological weapons against Chechnya. Said one, "I think nuclear weapons should stop being virtual." Russian military spokesmen, we are told, "do not exclude that a nuclear attack could be carried out against the bases of international terrorists in Chechnya."[49] And with that tiny republic in mind, the military has officially adopted a new concept of "limited" nuclear warfare in a single region, a threat against the Chechen resistance still being discussed in May 2000.[50]

From the other side, there were persistent reports that terrorists serving the Chechen "holy war" might blow up Russian nuclear power plants or weapons sites. The reports were serious enough to cause Moscow to redouble security at its nuclear facilities and 90 percent of Russians surveyed to say they fear the possibility.[51] Such threats on both sides may also be merely rhetorical, but it is an exceedingly dangerous rhetoric never before heard. If nothing else, there has been more loose talk in Russia since 1999 about using nuclear weapons than measures to prevent loose nukes. And it will likely increase if the Chechens expand their new guerrilla tactics farther into Russia itself, as they have promised to do.

And so, post-Soviet Russia still matters to America in the most fateful of ways. The Clinton administration has worsened the dangers incalculably by taking step after step that pushes a Russia coming apart at the nuclear seams to rely more and more on its nuclear stockpiles and infrastructures—by making financial aid conditional on economic "reforms" that impoverished and destabilized the state; by expanding NATO's military might virtually to Russia's borders; by provocatively demonstrating during the bombing of Yugoslavia the overwhelming superiority of U.S. conventional weapons; and more recently by threatening to withdraw from the Anti-Ballistic Missile Treaty in order to build a missile defense system.

Rarely, if ever, has there been such a reckless official disregard for U.S. national security or leadership failure to tell the American people about growing threats to their well-being. The Clinton administration and its many supporters in the media, think tanks, and academia never seem to connect the dots between their missionary zeal in Russia and the grave dangers being compounded there. In early 2000, one of the crusade's leading policymakers suddenly told us, after seven years of "happy talk," that "disasters are inescapable in the short run." He neglected to say that the disaster is unfolding in a country laden with twentieth-century devices of mass destruction and regressing toward the nineteenth century.[52]

Russia's potential for lethal catastrophes is the most important but not the only reason it still matters. Even in crises and weakness, Russia remains a great power because of its sheer size, which stretches across eleven time zones from Finland and Poland (if we consider Belarus) to China and nearby Alaska; its large portions of the world's energy and mineral reserves; its long history of world-class achievements and power; its highly educated present-day citizens; and, of course, its arsenals. All this makes Russia inherently not only a major power but a semi-global one. A "world without Russia" would therefore be globalization, to take the concept du jour, without a large part of the globe.

Nor can many large international problems and conflicts be resolved without Russia, especially in a
"post–Cold War order" that has at least as much international anarchy as order. From the Balkans and the
Caspian to China and Iraq, from nuclear proliferation to
conventional-arms transfers, from the environment and
terrorism to drug trafficking and money laundering,
Russia retains a capacity to affect world affairs for better or worse. On the one hand, it was Moscow's diplomatic intervention in Yugoslavia in 1999 that enabled
a desperate Clinton administration to avoid sending
American ground troops to Kosovo. On the other, the
1990s also brought the passage of narcotics westward
across Russian territory, a flood of illegal Russian
money into U.S. banks, and growing markets for
Moscow's weapons and nuclear capabilities among states
that already worry Washington.[53]

And then there are the vast geopolitical ramifications
of developments in what is still the world's largest territorial country. Nearly a fourth of planet Earth's population lives on the borders of the Russian Federation,
including most of its major religions and many of its
ethnic identities. Many, if not all, of these nations and
peoples are likely to be directly or indirectly affected by
what happens in post-Communist Russia, again for better or worse—first and foremost the "near abroad," as
Moscow calls the other fourteen former Soviet republics,
but not them alone.

Finally, there is a crucial futuristic reason why U.S.
policy toward Russia must be given the highest priority and changed fundamentally. Contrary to those Americans who have "rushed to relegate Russia to the

archives," believing it will always be enfeebled and may even break into more pieces, that longtime super-power will eventually recover from its present time of troubles, as it did after the revolution and civil war of 1917–21, indeed as it always has.[54]

But what kind of political state will rise from its knees? One that is democratic or despotic? One open to the West and eager to play a cooperative role in world affairs—or one bent on revising an international order shaped during its weakness and at its expense? One safeguarding and reducing its nuclear stockpiles or one multiplying and proliferating them among states that want them?

The outcome will depend very significantly on how Russia is treated during its present-day agony, particu-larly by the United States. Whether it is treated wisely and compassionately or is bullied and humiliated, as a growing number of Russians believe they have been since the early 1990s. The next American president may make that decision, but our children and grandchildren will reap the benefits or pay the price.

Toward a New Russia Policy: Priorities and Premises

Transforming U.S. policy toward Russia is exceedingly difficult, pessimists might say politically impossible, and only the American president can do it. The transforma-tion has to begin with presidential truth telling about the failures and consequences of the old policy. Official myths and "happy stories" lead, as they already have, to "warped" media, diplomatic, and even intelligence reporting, disillusion with post-Soviet possibilities, a revival of elite and popular Cold War attitudes, and the obscuring of grave dangers to U.S. national security.[55]

Exposing the official fictions of the 1990s therefore has to be the president's first step. Foremost among them are that post-Communist Russia has been in a benevolent "transition"; that the immiseration of a nation may be called reform, progress, or an American interest; that Russia's problems are due solely to its Soviet past, present-day Communists, Parliament, elderly voters, lack of resolve, or Yeltsin's shortcomings—not to any wrongheaded policy-making in Washington; that Moscow politics is a Manichaean choice between reformers and antireformers, democrats and "Red-Brown" nationalists; and that only programs made in the U.S.A. can reform Russia.

The president's second step must be to establish clear and constant foreign policy priorities. When it came to Russia, the Clinton administration had none at all. If it had really sought stability, it would not have insisted on "shock" economic experiments. If it had wanted Moscow to ratify the START II Treaty quickly in order to speed the reduction of nuclear weapons, it would not have shunned and denigrated the Parliament that had to approve it. If it had hoped to bring Russia into the West, it would not have erected barriers by expanding NATO. If it had wanted Moscow to settle conflicts without using force, it would not have bombed Yugoslavia, which encouraged the Kremlin to do the same to Chechnya—or earlier, and also to no good effect, Iraq, Sudan, and Afghanistan.[56] And if it had wanted Russia to rely less rather than more on its crumbling nuclear infrastructures, it would have done none of those things.

Indeed, the Clinton administration's Russia policy was either devious or dysfunctionally schizophrenic. In its profusive talk of friendship and shared values, it was the most pro-Kremlin administration since the U.S.-Soviet alliance during World War II. In the actual steps it took against and in defiance of Moscow, it was the most anti-Russian U.S. administration in modern history.[57]

The overriding goal of U.S. foreign policy today has to be, as I trust readers will agree, the stabilization of Russia and its many devices of mass destruction. Disasters once unthinkable now are fully possible in that crisis-ridden land, from nuclear explosions and launches to a larger civil war in the heart of the country (as almost happened in October 1993) and widespread social unrest in regions dotted with nuclear facilities. (In light of the many direct-action protests over unpaid wages and even against "privatization" since the mid-1990s, especially in the destitute provinces, tales of the Russian people's passivity are considerably exaggerated.)

The only way the United States can promote permanent stability in Russia is to help Moscow bring about its economic and human recovery. Doing so, however, requires not only new economic approaches but political rehabilitation of the idea of U.S.-Russian cooperation, which has been badly degraded and discredited. Almost from the beginning, despite boundless talk of partnership, the Clinton administration never really cooperated with the Kremlin but, while going through pseudo-diplomatic rituals, compelled it to bow to U.S. decisions and conditions. On the Russian side, the result has been growing resentment, humiliation, and distrust of American proposals, from arms control to financial agreements. Having created these attitudes in Moscow, it is for Washington to find ways to dispel them.

But a new kind of Russian leadership is also needed—one devoted to economic recovery and its citizens' well-being instead of "grab-it-ization" of the nation's riches, one that will declare, as Franklin Roosevelt so famously did, "The hopes of the Republic cannot forever tolerate either undeserved poverty or self-serving wealth." American pundits and politicians who now suddenly maintain that Russia is incapable of producing such leaders have, as a would-be Russian president pointed out, gone from one false perception to another: "All Western papers were writing that all the Russian people were undertaking reforms. Now they are writing, with the same enthusiasm, that all Russian people stole that money. It wasn't the truth then and it isn't the truth now."[58]

The current American view is historically uninformed and even a kind of ethnic slur. In the twentieth century, Russian governments had to rebuild the economy more than once—recovery from the devastation of World War II remains a prideful memory—and social justice is among the oldest and most enduring Russian popular beliefs. The need for "decent and responsible people" in power is a constant subject of elite discourse in Moscow, and in my own personal observations, such potential leaders are present across the mainstream political spectrum. For many Russians, the possibility of an honorable leadership was exemplified by then Prime Minister Primakov's effort in 1998–99, aborted by Yeltsin, to crack down on plundering oligarchs and develop the "real economy."[59]

Less certain is whether Russia's economic recovery is still possible in at least minimally democratic conditions. Russians themselves sometimes frame the question, as we have seen, as a choice between their version of Pinochet and FDR, or alternatively de Gaulle. Although seriously endangered by the events of the 1990s, democratization is not yet a lost cause. Thus Putin's oligarchical backers want a praetorian Pinochet to protect them and their wealth, but millions of other Russians hope he will turn out to be their Roosevelt or de Gaulle.[60]

In that connection, two circumstances are clear. As was true during the Cold War, hard-line and intrusive U.S. policies toward Russia abet the political fortunes of Moscow's own hard-liners, who are inveterate opponents of democratization and a pro-Western orientation in general. The growing revival of this unholy axis between American and Russian cold warriors in the 1990s is yet another unintended but dangerous legacy of the Clinton administration that must be overcome.[61]

We may still hope that the other circumstance is only hypothetical. If democracy turns out to be the inescapable price of nuclear stability in Russia, the United States will have to accept the new regime, assuming it is not itself a destabilizing extreme form of authoritarianism and while hoping it will be short-lived. American missionaries whose policy contributed greatly to this tragic possibility continue to insist that "democracy in Russia is a precondition for cooperation."[62] But without cooperation, some kind of nuclear catastrophe is increasingly likely, and the fallout will not discriminate between democrats and despots or leave behind soil in which any kind of democracy can grow.

Several factors will determine whether or not post-Communist Russia confronts the world with such a dire choice, but one of the most important is whether or not the United States adopts a wiser policy toward that fateful country. Lack of wisdom usually derives from false assumptions. In this case, it has been four false premises that informed the failed crusade of the 1990s and now must be discarded.

One is the ideological presumption that a truly reformed Russia could have no large national interests different from American ones. In reality, any Russian government, because of the nation's geography and history, will have its own special interests in, to take obvious examples, the Balkans, the Baltics, Ukraine, Central Asia, the Caucasus, and China. Apart from ideology, there is no reason why such legitimate interests should be construed as threats or litmus tests in U.S.-Russian relations. As in relations with other major powers, reconciling them with American interests is supposed to be the purpose of diplomacy.

For much the same reason, it is time for U.S. policymakers, journalists, and academics to stop equating "real" Russian reformers only with ones who "do favors for the United States" and thus are regarded as "an enormous asset for the U.S."[63] Any Russian leaders so perceived at home will never be secure, only distrusted, as Yeltsin and his reformers soon came to be. A leadership able to stabilize Russia has to find support in its own country, not the United States, and its policies have to be made in Moscow, not Washington.

In that respect, the Yeltsin leadership's extraordinary dependency on the West, particularly the United States—psychological, political, and financial—was an aberration in Russian history. No such supplicant or compliant Kremlin leadership is likely to appear again. Subsequent ones, as was clear as soon as Putin took over from Yeltsin, will be considerably more nationalistic, at least to the extent of giving proud and loud priority to Russia's interests at home and abroad, as do most governments everywhere regardless of ideology. This too should be seen not as a threat but as an opportunity for a new beginning in U.S. relations with post-Communist Russia.

The second false assumption has been that the "free market" or "neoliberal" economic reforms demanded by the United States throughout the 1990s would have broad popular backing, find a post-Yeltsin generation of political leaders, and thus form Russia's future. In fact, as was pointed out earlier, those characteristic American ideas (though not practices) never had mass support in Russia and now, after all the pain inflicted in their name, have even less. In almost every survey of public opinion done since the late 1980s, most Russians have wanted political and economic liberties, but also many of the cradle-to-grave benefits provided by the latter-day Soviet system, which responded to older native values as well.[64]

It does not mean, contrary to U.S. declarations about

"no third way," that Russia's only alternative is a return to the Communist past. The dismantling of Soviet Communism was begun by Gorbachev more than a decade ago. The product of historical circumstances, it cannot be restored. Nor do many Russians want to do so, not even most Communists. From left to right, no significant political movement any longer believes, for example, in a state-monopoly, command economy. All of them, including today's Communist Party, understand that in order to prosper Russia needs some kind of market economy and large private sector.[65]

A debate over what kind of "mixed" economic system should emerge from the traditional and the necessary has long been under way in Russia, and with special intensity since Yeltsin's U.S.-sponsored policies collapsed beyond dispute in 1998. It will broaden and deepen with the unfolding process of de-Yeltsinization. The decision is Russia's to make, not the West's. And unless the outcome has a Russian face, it too will be unstable.

The third false premise informing the American crusade is exceedingly dangerous. It assumes that because post-Communist Russia is bankrupt and weak, it has no choice except to adapt to U.S. wishes at home and abroad. Barely more than a cultural conceit, it insists that apart from the West, Russia "hardly has anywhere else to go."[66] This assumption is especially myopic. Russia has options, and the one gathering support in the political class today is profoundly alarming.

Reacting to a decade of Western security policies and financial conditions, proponents of this alternative would turn Russia away from the West—back toward the nation's older Eastern traditions and a strategic alliance with the world's largest non-NATO countries, China and India. It is a "nightmare scenario," as some Western specialists understand: "Then you basically have the world's heartland—2 billion people in China and India—allied with a formidable technological power in Russia. That would be a disaster for the United States."[67]

For Eurasian Russia, it would not be a giant step. After all, as Putin once told an audience of supporters, "You and I live in the East, not the West."[68] Since becoming president, Putin has indicated a preference for a revised Western orientation focused on Europe rather than the United States, but the Eastern alternative—turning an "Asiatic mug" to the West[69]—is already being tried out. Against a backdrop of growing bilateral diplomatic, economic, and intelligence ties, Russia has developed a near-monopoly on the Chinese and Indian arms markets and is selling them increasingly sophisticated weapons, which already account for about 60 percent of all its arms sales. In February 2000, to take an example that bears directly on U.S. commitments, Moscow supplied Beijing with the first of perhaps four guided-missile destroyers that will be a new factor in the conflict over Taiwan.[70]

Advocates of this alternative to Yeltsin's failed pro-West policy of the 1990s argue that it serves another essential purpose. By making Russia the arsenal of non-Western states—not only China and India but Iran, Libya, North Korea, Serbia, possibly Iraq, and others—its military-industrial complex, including science and technology, will become the engine of the nation's economic recovery. (Though still far behind those of the United States, Moscow's arms sales grew from $2.5 billion in 1998 to more than $4 billion in 2000 and are projected to reach $5 billion by 2003, which does not include roughly $1 billion for each nuclear reactor it constructs abroad.)

The result would not resemble the economic "reform" envisaged by Washington, but military-industrial priorities drove Russia's recovery after World War II, and their present-day proponents maintain that they can and should do so again. The domestic and international implications of this strategic option hardly need to be emphasized, only that it is a direct response to the Clinton administration's Russia policy and that its political appeal is growing.

Finally, there is the largest U.S. fallacy of all—the assumption that America has the right, wisdom, or power to remake an enormous country whose history predates its own by many centuries. It produced the tutelage approach that led the Clinton administration to intrude so deeply and unwisely into the internal affairs of post-Communist Russia—into its most basic domestic policy-making, choice of ministers, budgetary priorities, "civil society," even parliamentary and presidential elections. If common sense is not enough, the 1990s left behind abundant evidence that such a crusade is inherently doomed from the outset and dangerously counterproductive in the end. Without an entirely different approach, the unprecedented perils created during that decade will only grow worse.

The proper and necessary approach was adumbrated fifty years ago by George F. Kennan, the esteemed

American diplomat and historian of Russia. In 1951, anticipating the eventual waning of Soviet Communist rule, he warned,

> Let us not hover nervously over the people who come after, applying litmus paper daily to their political complexions to find out whether they answer to our concept of "democratic." Give them time; let them be Russians; let them work out their internal problems in their own manner. . . . The ways by which peoples advance toward dignity and enlightenment in government are things that constitute the deepest and most intimate processes of national life. There is nothing less understandable to foreigners, nothing in which foreign interference can do less good.[71]

Had Kennan's advice been heeded in the early 1990s, Russia and U.S.-Russian relations would certainly be in much better condition than they are today. But even if they were not, America would be less complicit.

It may not be too late. Adapting Kennan's approach today would mean, among other changes, letting Russians themselves, instead of the U.S. Treasury or State Departments, decide what constitutes reform in their country and how to achieve economic recovery. It would mean letting Russian voters choose their Parliament and president without U.S. public or secret involvement. It would be to understand that the stabilization of nuclear Russia, and still more democratization, can come only from the "deepest and most intimate processes" of Russian life, not America's.

That understanding would withdraw most of the official U.S. missionaries still encamped in Russia. Along with high-living private "advisers" funded by the U.S. government, they have done more harm than good. If nothing else, their activities are a constant source of the anti-American backlash. If there are exceptions, there is a simple rule of thumb: Americans should do nothing in Russia that we would object to a foreign state doing in our own country. If any U.S. advice is really needed, e-mail is less intrusive and cheaper. (What private foundations and universities do, however unwise, is their business, but Washington sets the example.)

And because "words are also deeds," as Russians say, Kennan's approach would change the verbal atmospherics of U.S. policy. It would end the incessant public judgments passed on Russia's internal affairs by the American president, vice president, and their appointees, as occurred throughout the 1990s, and yet again by President Clinton in June 2000, even while they were guests in Moscow. It would mean that the U.S. government, from the White House to its Moscow embassy, would no longer play the role of sponsor, cheerleader, or agitprop department for any faction or ism in Russian politics. It would mean, in a word, the end of the American crusade.

Reengaging Russia

Sentiment and ideology aside, the United States has only one truly vital interest in Russia today—the reduction and eventual elimination of the nuclear and possibly other lethal perils growing there. No major progress is possible in that direction without reengaging the

Russian government in genuinely cooperative rather than missionary ways.

Unreconstructed American crusaders will no doubt protest. In reaction to the failure of their excessively pro-Kremlin stance of the 1990s, they have decided that their only mistake was not having "allied directly with the Russian people." They now propose to remake post-Communist Russia from below—to "assist Russian society, not the Russian state," or what they yearningly call "civil society."[72]

The idea may be "warm and fuzzy,"[73] but it is also inappropriate and reckless. It perpetuates the intrusive arrogance that Russians cannot be democratic or entrepreneurial without American guidance. Moreover, "civil society," as I noted before, can be made to mean almost anything. According to Putin, the Kremlin's brutal war against civilians in Chechnya was launched "to restore civil society."[74] And if the term really means grassroots organizations operating apart from the state, as its Western proponents say, the Communist Party is its largest embodiment in Russia today.

In practice, a "civil society" policy is usually an excuse to give U.S. funds and political support exclusively to "our guys"—to Russian individuals, media, parties, and other groups that profess pro-American ideas. Doing so in defiance of the Russian government will only arouse even more suspicion of U.S. motives and target recipients of American largesse for abuse, especially by local authorities. In any event, "civil society" cannot take the steps urgently needed to stabilize Russia's economy and nuclear-related facilities.[75] Only the state and its Moscow leadership can do that.

Economic and nuclear stability being no less in Russia's interest, Putin or any rational Kremlin leader is certain to welcome new, non-missionary proposals to achieve them. To be effective, an American president does not need a best friend or protégé in the Kremlin, as the Clinton administration evidently believed was necessary, only a leader committed to those essential purposes. (The administration therefore again needlessly put America on the wrong side of history by rushing to endorse Putin for the Russian presidency even before the March 2000 election and while he was escalating atrocities in Chechnya.)[76]

Nor can the U.S. government, including Congress, conduct a virtual boycott of the Russian Parliament, as it did in the 1990s. Whatever the term *civil society* may mean, popularly elected assemblies, no matter their political complexion, to borrow Kennan's phrase, are its product and reflection—and, of course, the only institution absolutely essential for representative democracy.[77] Without the participation of Parliament, or the Duma, programs designed to stabilize Russia and cope with its nuclear threats will not themselves be stable.

Reengaging Russia has to begin with its half-dead economy. It is both the primary source of the country's perilous instability and the focus of the failed but unrelenting American crusade. For the sake of stabilization and real cooperation, a fundamentally different U.S. approach is needed. It even requires a new vocabulary. The word *reform*, now thoroughly discredited in Russia and having no meaningful relation to realities, should be replaced by *recovery* and *development*.[78]

The new approach will mean abandoning American

dogmas about Russia's "transition." Instead of dictating Moscow's economic policies as a condition for financial assistance, the most intrusive form of tutelage, Washington should invite the Russian government to propose its own programs for economic recovery. If the proposals seem plausible to a range of U.S. and European economists rather than to the sectarians who have controlled policy—eminent American economists have already urged a different approach for Russia[79]—the U.S. president, as the self-professed world leader, would lead an international campaign to raise funds for them.

This non-missionary initiative, the centerpiece of a new U.S. policy, has several important virtues. Politically, it would show the post-Yeltsin Russian leadership that the post-Clinton American leadership has renounced tutelage for real cooperation, and not only in the economy. The mutual interest on which it is based and the collaboration it involves would extend to Russia's nuclear dangers and international affairs as well.

The new approach would also ground U.S. policy in Russian realities instead of fictions. Few if any Russian politicians or economists any longer believe in the neoliberal, monetarist measures dictated by the IMF since the early 1990s, though some still pretend to do so. For the most part, the IMF's main conditions—minimizing the state's role in favor of purported free-market forces, maximizing privatization at any cost, putting government budgetary austerity, tight money, and other anti-inflation indicators above investment, production, employment, and welfare—are now broadly rejected as unworkable, destructive, and even having (perhaps intentionally) cost Russia its economic sovereignty.[80]

Sooner or later, Moscow will no longer "stay the course," whether Washington approves or not. Its new course, to have any chance of stabilizing the economy, will have to be designed at home. Russia has scores of professional pro-market economists who, unlike most Western missionaries, know the country and its possibilities but were shunned in the 1990s. If their programs cause hardship or fail, at least America will no longer be complicit.

In that important respect, a non-missionary, or non-dogmatic, approach would be in the spirit of the finest moment of American international assistance—the Marshall Plan for the recovery and development of Western European nations devastated by World War II. The plan was generously funded by the United States, but it was drafted, at the invitation of the U.S. government, by the recipient states themselves.[81] Based on this fundamentally different approach (and on different economic principles), it worked, unlike U.S. prescriptions in post-Communist Russia.

If solicited, Russia's economic proposals would also echo America's historical experience. As the "Washington Consensus" has failed, a Moscow consensus—sometimes hopefully called "Putin's Third Way" and "Russia's Truth"—has been developing across much of the political spectrum. In opposition to the IMF's Hoover-like policies, which predictably plunged Russia into an even greater economic depression, the emerging consensus recalls the New Deal's Keynesian measures to extricate America from its own economic crisis of the 1930s. Hence the growing references to Franklin Roosevelt, beginning with the Primakov cabinet and continuing under Putin.[82]

Jettisoning IMF axioms of spontaneous prosperity through painful deprivation, a new Moscow economic policy would be an avowedly "anti-catastrophe course."[85] It would strive, in the language of the American 1930s, to put factories, farms, and people back to work by adopting once-standard methods of overcoming economic depressions—reviving production by direct investment in industrial and agricultural enterprises and by putting money in the hands of would-be consumers to create domestic demand for those products. The private sector would be preserved and even encouraged to grow, as required in a "mixed" economy, but the nationalized sector would be revitalized and the state brought back to guide economic recovery and development.[84]

To guardians of the U.S.-IMF dogmas of the 1990s, requisite measures adopted by the Russian state would be heresy, even though once they were orthodox Western practices. They would include, to one degree or another, deficit spending for investment, unpaid wages and pensions, and other government arrears, as well as restored subsidies for defense industries, education, science, and welfare; tariffs on imported goods to protect domestic enterprises; tightened controls to stop bank malpractices and capital flight; regulation of some prices; and possibly selected renationalization of privatized enterprises, particularly ones producing oil, gas, timber, strategic metals, precious stones, and vodka.

For its own sake, the United States must do everything possible to help finance any such unprecedented and fateful attempt to restabilize a nuclear country, if it is undertaken by Moscow. The only condition should

be that the Kremlin refrain from any more destabilizing actions of its own, such as its Chechen war of
1999–2000, which, in addition to the financial cost,
was so extreme militarily and immoral that it provoked reckless nuclear threats on both sides. In such
an event, Moscow should receive no Western funds
except ones earmarked for nuclear safety. In the
absence of such events, the West must provide however much is needed.

Many influential Americans will strongly oppose new
financial aid to the Russian government. Some actually
argue that "it is in our interest that their economy *not*
recover," even though this Cold War relic myopically
puts U.S. and international security in grave jeopardy.[85]
Others say that any new funds will also be stolen, even
though Washington's own IMF measures fostered the
Klondike plundering and official Ponzi schemes, and its
own protégés and oligarchical creatures did much of the
looting. New funds, or at least most of them, can be
safeguarded by different policies and cautionary lessons
learned from the 1990s.

Above all, opponents of more financial aid still insist
there is no alternative to the IMF economic policies of
the 1990s and therefore the new approach taking shape
in Moscow cannot work. But the U.S.-sponsored program having manifestly failed, why should not one akin
to the American New Deal of the 1930s now be tried
in Moscow? Nuclear Russia cannot risk any more
"shock" measures or disintegration of its twentieth-century infrastructure, which is all the modernity it has,
into "rubble." No other alternative has been put forth.
And the one being proposed, by ending years of official

indifference in Moscow (and Washington) to the "miserable fate" of the poverty-stricken Russian people, will at least have popular support. (Putin, for example, has repeatedly emphasized the terrible dimensions of poverty.)[86]

How much money would Russia need to revive and stabilize an economy that remains half or less the size it was in the early 1990s? Estimates vary, depending on calculations of technology and other infrastructure already lost during a full decade virtually without investment, in many cases even in bare maintenance. We may take as a rough approximation the estimate of a Russian economist admired for his moderation and good sense who puts the figure at $500 billion over a ten-year period.[87]

Is $500 billion a year a small or large sum? Compared with the roughly $65 billion the West lent or gave post-Communist Russia from 1992 to 1999, it may seem a lot. But compared with the trillions of dollars the United States spent building nuclear and other weapons during the Cold War, to the projected $836 billion to $1.9 trillion U.S. budget surplus during the same ten years, and to the essential national security it would buy, it is very little.

Nor would the United States have to provide most of this annual cost of Russia's economic recovery. The wealthy nations of Western Europe, Scandinavia, and Japan are more directly endangered by Russian instability, particularly by Chernobyl-like nuclear disasters. Given U.S. leadership, they may be expected to pay their fair share. More significantly, Moscow proponents of an indigenous economy policy, wary of falling deeper into foreign debt and doubting the prospect of meaningful foreign investment in the near future, are now determined to find most of the necessary funds at home.

Relying on the power and reach of a resurgent state, they propose to recapture huge foreign-currency earnings of Russia's oil, gas, timber, and other natural-resources monopolies from self-aggrandizing oligarchs and corrupt directors; regain traditionally large profits from domestic vodka sales; snare at least part of the $18 billion to $24 billion fleeing abroad each year; reform commercial banks in order to entice billions of dollars in private savings from under mattresses into the economy; and make inflation benefit the government budget, which is less than 5 percent what it was a decade ago, instead of speculative banks and foreign portfolios.[88]

How much money the Russian government could actually mobilize at home would depend on political factors as well. One is its willingness—it still has sufficient power, contrary to widespread perceptions—to crack down on the financial oligarchy and high-level official corruption that cannibalized the nation under Yeltsin. Closely related is the question of renationalizing lucrative enterprises that were wrongfully privatized or plundered, which the state would either manage itself or resell for their actual value. (In the early and mid-1990s, former Soviet state assets worth some $200 billion were handed over to insiders for only $7 billion.)[89]

Considering Russia's abundant wealth and what Putin calls the nation's statist "genetic code," a determined Kremlin leadership probably could mobilize internally a substantial part of the estimated funds needed for economic recovery, but not all of them.[90] If stabilization of the world's largest nuclear country really is our highest priority, the West has to encourage rather than obstruct any such effort by Moscow and take steps to assure that it receives funds it cannot muster on its own. If there is leadership, there are ways to do so, from making outright financial grants or long-term, interest-free loans to providing relief from crushing debt.

The United States, as the presumed leader of the international campaign, could take a first step of considerable economic and political importance. It could immediately give the Russian government enough money, probably less than $1 billion, to pay all the back pensions and wages it still owes to the people, which includes doctors, teachers, strategic-weapons officers, and nuclear maintenance workers. Even better would be an additional sum enabling the Kremlin to raise the many pensions and salaries that are below the subsistence level of about $30 to $35 a month.[91]

By underwriting such an act of financial restitution and social justice—instead of "free market" policy, let us call it fair-market economics—the U.S. government would achieve three purposes truly worthy of "the only superpower." It would prevent or reduce inflationary consequences of printing the necessary rubles, which the Russian government will eventually have to do anyway. It would put money in the hands of those consumers who most desperately need it. And it would go a long way toward rehabilitating America's reputation in post-Communist Russia.

Helping the country's impoverished masses is necessary not only because so many Russians blame the United States but because their "miserable fate" is a major source of instability. Washington should organize, for example, international pharmaceutical relief—food assistance is less needed and hinders the recovery of Russia's badly depressed farm sector—for the most afflicted of the 86 percent of Russians who cannot afford medicine they need. And considering the large number of unemployed people, low wages, and devalued ruble, a modest-size Western grant would enable Moscow to initiate a New Deal–like program putting people back to work rebuilding the nation's crumbling infrastructures, another source of instability.

Other stricken segments of society also need help. The Soviet and post-Soviet middle classes, which have to be the mainstay of the stable democracy the West professes to want in Russia, have been decimated by U.S.-sponsored economic measures. Meanwhile, Western programs to provide start-up capital for small private firms and mortgages for aspiring homeowners remain on the drawing board or underfunded.[92] It is time to implement them seriously but in nonintrusive ways—in rubles (not dollars) and through select Russian banks (not Western offices) able to introduce these commercial practices in a country that generally lacks them.

Further steps can be taken to narrow the gap between the West's financial resources and professed political goals. By paying off the $7 billion former Soviet republics owe Russia, mostly for energy, the United States and its allies would at once bolster the fragile independence of those new states and put more funds for economic recovery in Moscow's hands. Similarly, if the West wants a negotiated stable peace in Chechnya, it should offer in return to help finance the rebuilding of that shattered territory.[93]

Such initiatives would help put Russia on the road to economic recovery, but they would not be enough for the long journey. Many more billions of dollars will be needed. Even without appropriating new funds, the West can enable Russia to obtain those larger sums by giving Moscow substantial relief from its crushing foreign debt and by helping it retrieve some of the billions of dollars that have fled to Western havens since the early 1990s.

Moscow's foreign debt of perhaps $168 billion—eight times its annual budget and requiring payments in future years of some $15 billion to $16 billion a year—makes economic recovery virtually impossible.[94] No matter how much money the government manages to mobilize at home, it will have to choose between paying the West and investing in its own economy and people. Restructuring deals only perpetuate Moscow's debt bondage. Eventually it will compel the Kremlin to make a more profound choice—between perpetual economic decline and defaulting on its debt, in effect Russia's self-banishment from the West.

The only solution is to forgive a large part of Russia's foreign debt and defer payment on the remainder. In addition to a broad-based international campaign to abolish the debt of all poor countries, there is a relevant precedent. The West canceled half of post-Communist Poland's prior debt; nearly two-thirds of what post-Communist Russia owes is Soviet-era obligations. Moreover, about $25 billion of its post-Communist debt, owed to the IMF and World Bank, was undertaken at U.S. urging and granted to Yeltsin for essentially political, not economic, reasons. Above all, however, there is the security imperative: unless the West frees Russia from this crushing burden, that vast nuclear country will grow increasingly unstable and resentful.

No less important is "following every lead to help Russia recover funds spirited out by corrupt officials and Western co-conspirators," as a *New York Times* columnist has urged.[95] Most estimates of capital flight from Russia since 1992 range from $150 billion to $350 billion. Even the lesser figure nearly equals Moscow's entire foreign debt and far exceeds all past, present, and imaginable foreign investment in Russia, which was barely $2 billion in 1999.

The United States, whose policies and financial institutions have abetted the theft, has an obligation to lead a Western effort to repatriate as much of this enormous sum as possible. (The excuse for doing nothing, which insists the funds will return automatically when Russia has a stable investment environment, minimizes the criminality involved and has the cart before the horse.) Here too there are precedents. Mexico and other states have asked foreign governments to confiscate illicit capital flight, and in 1998 the U.S. FBI assisted Moscow in locating stolen gems and gold coins.[96]

Every $1 billion the United States helps Russia bring home for economic recovery is a direct investment in American and international nuclear security. The imperative, as a specialist emphasizes, is twofold: "Countries serving as havens for stolen money have a responsibility to the citizens of the looted state. . . . Otherwise, these billions of dollars will be endlessly plundered, and Russia's downward spiral into economic chaos will never be stopped."[97]

Even if all these new economic policies are adopted in Moscow and Washington, the United States cannot risk waiting for them to stabilize Russia. The nuclear perils already existing there—again, biological and chemical ones as well—are too grave and looming. As we have seen, a catastrophic clock is ticking in that tormented land, and no one knows what time it is—dawn, high noon, dusk, or nearly midnight.

Extraordinary American leadership is urgently needed to cope with these unprecedented nuclear dangers, which are due in significant measure to the unwise policies and negligence of the Clinton administration[98]—at least as much leadership concern as has gone into the campaign against Iraq's infinitely lesser weapons of mass destruction. Two simultaneous approaches are needed—one to reduce threats already posed by Moscow's increasingly unreliable systems of nuclear command, control, and maintenance, the other to repair those infrastructures.

When asked why there has not already been an accidental Russian nuclear strike against the United States, an expert Cassandra replied, "We've been lucky."[99] If so, there is no time to deal with this present danger through the traditional process of negotiating and ratifying treaties. (START II was stuck in the Russian Parliament for seven years, and the U.S. Senate has refused to ratify the Comprehensive Test Ban Treaty and delayed action on several START II protocols.) Instead, the American president should take a series of unilateral steps on the reasonable assumption that Moscow would reciprocate, and which would greatly diminish or even eliminate this danger.

Publicly stating his expectation that Russia will do the same, the president should begin reducing U.S. deployed nuclear warheads from the existing 7,000 not to the 3,000 to 3,500 permitted by START II as of December 2007 but to no more than 1,000, which is all Moscow probably can afford to maintain properly and considerably more than either side actually needs. He should take all deployed warheads off launch-on-warning hair-trigger alert. And he should reverse long-standing strategic doctrine by announcing that the U.S. government will never be the first to use nuclear weapons.[100]

These dramatic unilateral steps—a just-do-it approach— might offend Washington conventional wisdom, and some would require congressional approval. But by greatly relieving the stresses of lingering Cold War practices on Russia's failing early-warning system and by providing days instead of minutes to recognize false alarms, they would gain America and the world incalculable security without any cost to the U.S. ability to "deter or fight a nuclear war," as doomsday strategists like to say. (The joint Moscow center announced by Clinton and Putin in June 2000 to verify false early-warning signals at least acknowledges the growing danger of accidental missile launches, but it does not address the underlying causes and is far from an adequate safeguard.)

It follows, of course, that the United States must not

deploy a national missile defense system or otherwise abrogate the Anti-Ballistic Missile Treaty unless Russia gives its full consent. Among other counterproductive consequences, Moscow's response to this kind of unilateral act would be to rely even more heavily on its fragile nuclear stockpiles and infrastructures, indeed to build more strategic weapons in order to overwhelm any such system.[101] For the United States, the result would be a minimum of $60 billion spent on a theoretical defense against hypothetical threats from "rogue" states, coupled with an exponential growth of actual nuclear threats in Russia and possibly the undoing of three decades of arms control agreements.

The second way of coping directly with the threats requires a complete itemization of the vulnerabilities of Russia's nuclear weapons, materials, and reactors. Partial lists have been prepared by scientists and intelligence agencies of several concerned countries, including the United States, but evidently not a comprehensive inventory of all the dangers.[102] It cannot be compiled without Moscow's full cooperation. If necessary to obtain it, any foreign on-site inspections can be done by experts from non-NATO countries and under the auspices of the United Nations or another nonallied international organization.

Given an inventory of disasters waiting to happen, Western and Russian specialists would design programs to prevent them, which the United States would take the lead in funding. (The Russian ministry responsible for all this so lacks funds that it is proposing to earn money by storing nuclear waste of other countries— that is, by importing still more risks. And for the same financial reason, Putin has relaxed restrictions on the export of Russian nuclear equipment, thereby creating the possibility of more proliferation dangers.) Various projects already exist to help Russia dismantle decommissioned strategic weapons and safeguard nuclear facilities and materials, but they are woefully underfunded. New, unorthodox programs are also needed, including one to repair Russia's early-warning system, an undertaking no less in America's security interest.[103]

Without a complete inventory, no one knows how much all this would cost. Nor does it really matter. Real security, as opposed to many chimerical provisions in the nearly $300 billion U.S. defense budget, cannot cost too much. (The $10 million allocated for Russia's "civil society" media in 1999 would have been better spent paying or upgrading the salaries of nuclear maintenance workers.) But to take one important example, U.S. programs to protect and dispose of Russia's nuclear warheads and materials, budgeted at just over $1 billion for 2001, are said to need $5 billion to $8 billion over a five-year period to accomplish their mission.[104]

Again, shared with other Western countries, is this kind of expenditure large or small? Compared with the trillions of dollars spent to create these lethal dangers, or even the billions proposed for a national missile defense system, it is a small one. Or as another Cassandra warns, it is "tiny in comparison to the cost and risks of a failure to act."[105]

None of these economic and scientific measures to stabilize nuclear Russia will be effective, however, unless the United States stops pursuing other policies that convince Moscow it is being excluded, encircled, and threatened—and thus must maximize its weapons of mass destruction. Commenting on the Clinton administration, an American observer remarked, "Someone high up in Washington seems to have the task of getting up every morning and asking, 'What can we do today to make the Russians nervous?'"[106]

Fraying the strategic nerves of a government with already shaky control over its capacity to destroy America is, to be charitable, exceedingly reckless. A wiser guideline has to prevail: Every related U.S. policy abroad must be tempered by the unprecedented nuclear and other threats that exist today in post-Communist Russia. Major revisions in current American policy are therefore urgently needed.

The U.S.-led expansion of NATO eastward, which broke a Bush administration promise to the Gorbachev leadership, must stop. The inclusion of three former Soviet bloc countries in 1998—the Czech Republic, Hungary, and Poland—persuaded Moscow that Russia, post-Communist or not, was neither truly wanted nor trusted in the West. Believing that it was not only being excluded from Western security arrangements after the Cold War but again being made their primary target, the Kremlin intensified its search for strategic partners elsewhere and accelerated plans to build new nuclear weapons.

If NATO moves farther toward Russia, acting on Clinton administration statements about including the former Soviet republics of Lithuania, Latvia, Estonia, and possibly even Ukraine, it will cross a Rubicon fraught with even greater perils. If nothing else, Moscow is likely to redeploy missiles in Belarus, now in a Union with Russia, on the border of NATO Poland. The result would be a new nuclear confrontation in Europe, this time with Moscow in considerably less control of its hair-trigger weapons.

The use of NATO for offensive military purposes, a radical departure from its original defensive mission, particularly in Russia's traditional backyard, also must stop. Coming on the heels of the alliance's expansion, the U.S.-led bombing of Yugoslavia in 1999 inflicted "a deep psychological wound" on Russian political life.[107] Its consequences, all of them bad, continue to unfold.

The seventy-eight-day air war against Russia's fellow Slav nation played a major role in bringing the country's security forces back to the center of the political stage. It tipped the balance squarely in favor of the "war party" in the Kremlin debate over Chechnya. It diminished Moscow's willingness to cooperate with NATO or the United States on strategic matters. It even aroused the fear that Russia itself might be NATO's next victim—"Yugoslavia yesterday, Russia tomorrow." Unable to match the U.S. conventional air weapons it had observed over Serbia, Moscow concluded that "there remains nothing else but to rely on nuclear weaponary."[108] One immediate consequence was the new Kremlin doctrine reinstating the West as an enemy and expanding the conditions under which it would use those nuclear weapons.

Reckless U.S. behavior on the other side of Russia, in the Caspian Basin region with its large oil and gas reserves, also must end. In the 1990s, the Clinton administration began aggressively pursuing pipeline arrangements with several former Soviet republics in the Caucasus and Central Asia designed to limit or even shut off Moscow's access to those deposits. In the pursuit, there has been a growing U.S. political, financial, and even military presence in a potentially explosive region that for centuries was part of the tsarist empire and Soviet Union.

Imagine how this encroachment by faraway America is seen from Moscow. Coupled with NATO's movement toward the country's western borders, it has revived the specter of a "hostile encirclement" of Russia. Among the worst legacies of Stalinism, that fear played a lamentable Cold War and repressive role in Soviet Russian politics for four decades until Gorbachev finally exorcized it in the late 1980s. Because of U.S. policy, it has returned. Even longtime anti-Stalinists now say the despot may have been right about the "imperialist" West.

Still worse, the Clinton administration learned nothing from the infamously ill-conceived way the victorious Allies treated Germany after World War I. In effect, Washington has treated Russia similarly since the end of the Cold War, as a vanquished nation. How else to understand the administration's winner-take-all statements that the United States has "vital interests" and therefore entitlements throughout the former Soviet Union, from the Baltics and Ukraine to Central Asia and the Transcaucasus?[109]

Evidently, Russia is to be left with very little. Burdened with crushing debt and militarily excluded in the west, its energy resources challenged in the south, its former allies and republics everywhere claimed by other powers, it no longer seems to have any legitimate claims, national concerns, or zones of special interest—

not even in neighboring Slav nations, judging by U.S. protests against the new Russia-Belarus Union.

Many observers have warned that because of internal factors, post-Communist Russia may share the tragic fate of Weimar Germany. If so, they should also warn about the West's treating Russia as it did that doomed republic.[110] In today's unstable nuclear age, it would take far less than a Hitler to put the world in the gravest imaginable danger.

Nor have these unwise policies toward Russia brought any real compensatory gains. NATO expansion has not, and cannot, solve a single serious problem emanating from the former Soviet Union—not economic collapse, nuclear threats, terrorism, environmental dangers, drug and arms trafficking, international money laundering, or others. Moreover, the West could have guaranteed the security of the small inducted nations, if that really was the purpose, as it can the Baltic States, without moving its military alliance menacingly close to Russia.

The U.S.-led NATO bombing of Yugoslavia was equally unnecessary. If Russia had been given a serious mediating role before the air war was launched, there would have been other ways to restrain Milosevic. Instead, while violating international law and the United Nations Charter, and further damaging America's moral reputation, the war left Milosevic in power, much of Serbia's economy in ruins, Kosovo in destitution, the principle of resorting to force in ascendancy, and six thousand U.S. troops in a quagmire of reverse ethnic cleansing and continuing violence. Nothing has been permanently resolved, and no easy solution or escape is at hand.

As for the U.S.-backed pipeline and other anti-Russian gambits in the Caspian region, where Putin has already begun to reassert Russia's interests, they exemplify shortsighted, counterproductive American policy-making. Even if the pipeline turns out to be financially feasible—there is some doubt about this—it will be, contrary to Clinton administration boasts, a pyrrhic "foreign policy victory."[111]

Without stability in the region, American and other Western oil companies cannot operate successfully, and Russia has ways to destabilize it whenever it chooses. They range from the methods Moscow used in Chechnya to exerting its still strong influence or inciting unrest in the region's new states. Washington has alluded to U.S. military support for those regimes, mainly authoritarian kleptocracies,[112] but it cannot risk war in yet another energy zone and still less with nuclear Russia. To operate profitably in the former Soviet Union, Western oil companies will have to respect Russia's long-standing interests and cooperate with Moscow, not exclude it.

Real cooperation—a clichéd and abused word in international relations—is, of course, what has been missing in all of Washington's policies toward post-Communist Russia. Despite the Clinton administration's effusive talk about a post–Cold War era, it actually perpetuated the fundamentals of Cold War policy-making. Ideology, militarized thinking, and zero-sum assumptions were the policy hallmarks of that era. Since the early 1990s, ideology has been behind the administration's missionary crusade, militarized reasoning behind its expansion of NATO and air war against Yugoslavia (not to mention the seven other countries it bombed or otherwise attacked), and zero-sum calculations behind its escapades in the Caspian.

A new Russia policy is possible only by replacing those dangerous anachronisms with common sense, political-diplomatic thinking, and the imperative of mutual security interests—that is, authentic cooperation. Without it, nothing can be done about the perilous instability of Russia's instruments of mass destruction, or even about lesser problems. Kosovo, to take an example where Washington now has an enormous stake, will eventually require a diplomatic rather than military solution, probably political partition. It will not be achievable without Russia's full participation. And there will be other important cases, among them Iraq.

Reengaging Russia therefore means rising above the prevailing winner-take-all attitude and recognizing that even in its weakened condition, Moscow has legitimate interests, rights, and capabilities in world affairs. For the Kremlin, those entitlements are now symbolized by its seat and veto on the United Nations Security Council, the only non-nuclear parity it has left.

The Clinton administration's disregard for the United Nations in the 1990s, in favor of U.S. unilateralism and NATO, was a major element in the ways it misengaged Russia. The United States now must also reengage the United Nations and its collective approaches, and not only in order to cooperate more fully with Moscow.[113] The ominous new nuclear age created by Russia's instability threatens many nations. None of them alone, not even "the only superpower," can cope with it.

The time has come for America to restrain its super-power impulses in a larger way as well. For more than a half century, since World War II, the United States has represented, managed, and defined the West's relationship with Russia. Its proxy has long been taken for granted as normal, even natural, but in terms of geography and history, it is not. If Russia is ever to integrate with the West, it will be as a substantially European nation primarily through relations with the rest of the Continent, not America. The alternative to a new iron curtain is not Pax Americana but what Gorbachev called "our common European home."

The United States must continue to lead in safe-guarding and reducing instruments of mass destruction, but in other areas it should gradually relinquish its fifty-year role in the West's relations with Russia. Again, there will be many protests. During the Cold War, Soviet Russian overtures to Europe were denounced by U.S. policymakers and pundits as a plot to steal America's allies. That possessive anxiety no doubt played a part after the Cold War in the U.S. insistence on expanding NATO and its purposes.

There are no longer any good reasons for this habitual fretting or virtual tutelage over Europe itself. In the nineteenth and early twentieth centuries, close Russian-European relations, even royal family ties, did no special harm to faraway America, and would do none now. And if Russia is not America's to lose, neither is Europe.

In any event, the United States may have increasingly less say in this development. Since the end of the Cold War, natural affinities between Europe and Russia have been reemerging—Germany is by far Moscow's largest creditor, not America, and the European Union already accounts for about 40 percent of Russia's foreign trade—along with growing mutual resentment over what both perceive to be U.S. political and military "hegemonism."[114] Both are opposed, for instance, to Washington's plan for a missile defense system.

An exception illustrates this trend. Much more than did the U.S. government, European capitals reacted strongly against the Kremlin's brutality in Chechnya. In April 2000, the Parliamentary Assembly of the Council of Europe, which Moscow joined in 1996, even suspended Russia's voting rights. And yet, that same month Russia's new president, announcing that "we will try to integrate with Europe," made London the site of his first state visit, which the British prime minister eagerly trumpeted as a "new strategic relationship."[115] It was only the beginning of Putin's activist diplomacy toward Western Europe. Even before Clinton left Moscow after their meeting in June 2000, the Russian president had departed for Rome. Putin then made a still more important diplomatic visit to Germany.

We should see political virtue in the necessity of a historic European-Russian rapproachment. Unlike America, Europe and Russia shared the twentieth-century traumas of war on their own territory, occupation, police terror, and dictatorship. (And whereas almost no Americans have ever actually known a Communist, virtually every European has, sometimes intimately.) Kinship, understanding, and tolerance often grow out of common historical experiences. If nothing else, having suffered their own calamities, Europeans are less likely to see Russia as some kind of "calamitous nation" or perverse "enigma."

Even if it turns out that Europe cannot fully understand or integrate post-Communist Russia, it can hardly do worse than America has done since the end of the Soviet Union. After all, Europeans stopped believing in missionary crusades a long time ago.

The Owl of Minerva

We must end where this book began, with America's Russia-watchers. Do most of them now understand that they misconceived their subject for nearly a decade? In the new millennium, are U.S. policymakers, journalists, and academics finally focused on post-Communist Russian realities, particularly the dangers, instead of American fictions?

Russia's purported transition to prosperity, stability, and democracy under Yeltsin ended in an unprecedented economic depression, human catastrophe, civil war, nuclear instability, and with a career KGB officer in the Kremlin—hardly the way Russia-watchers had predicted. And yet, as we saw earlier, the outcome has not opened their eyes or changed their minds in any fundamental ways. Their standard narrative of "Russia's historic transition" remains largely the same, only somewhat revised and updated to incorporate the rise of Putin.

Indeed, Yeltsin's resignation and Putin's ascent were made an occasion, in the first months of 2000, for reaffirming the story's "standard templates." Top editors of both the *New York Times* and the *Washington Post* wrote what could be read only as apologias for the entire Yeltsin era and by implication their papers' coverage of the Russian 1990s. One of America's most eminent Russia specialists, a former ambassador to Moscow, extended those rationalizations even to Putin's savage war in Chechnya. A senior historian lent his authority to the same apologia. A leading missionary economist continued to denounce his critics for "shameless naivete or cynicism." Younger transitionologists also clung to their templates, one urging the U.S. government to acknowledge the "moral basis" of the post-Communist Kremlin's war.[116]

Nor are there any second thoughts about the American crusade, even though it is amply clear from the 1990s that, as a native observer remarked, "Russia swallows such 'missionary' efforts whole." The point of any setbacks, we are still assured, "is not that we've misengaged Russia." Thus *Business Week*'s specialist continues to applaud a Harvard shock therapist's role in privatization, "one of the most successful reforms of the Yeltsin era," though most Russians today equate it with plundering and impoverishment. And American correspondents and investors in Moscow still yearn for Kremlin appointees, now under Putin, who are impeccably "liberal"—a "market-friendly, English-speaking guy who listens a lot to financial markets."

Lest doubts arise about the American crusade, a senior political scientist warns once more against "illusions about there being some kind of 'third Russian way' " between the Soviet past and U.S. prescriptions. Indeed, a new generation of academic transitionologists appears on the scene worried, in light of IMF failures of the 1990s, "there will be no instrument left with which to guide Russia toward market reform." A billionaire American missionary is deeply disillusioned, but because the crusade did not take an even "more direct, intrusive approach." A Washington academic advises the U.S. Senate to rectify that shortcoming by funding American tutelage over Russian society itself. And a *Washington Post* editorial defiantly proclaims, "Yes, meddle in Russia's affairs."[117]

Worst of all, America's Russia-watchers are still sleepwalking through the new nuclear age, evidently unaware that lethal dangers in the country they study now exceed any in history. Testifying to a U.S. Senate committee on the situation in post-Yeltsin Russia, two leading think-tank experts do not even mention those growing threats. The head of Russian studies at a major university denounces economic proposals to stabilize the country as "neo-Sovietism." A journalist reports that NATO expansion has been a U.S. "triumph," even though it has clearly made the nuclear threats worse. A foreign affairs columnist recommends "containment vis-à-vis Russia," as though quarantine can prevent nuclear explosions and launches.[118]

Readers might say it does not matter what the "chattering class," as the English sometimes call us, thinks because it has no real power. In an important respect, they would be right. Only presidential power and leadership can enact a new Russia policy to cope with the growing dangers. Here too most of the news is bad.

The Clinton administration's reaction to Yeltsin's

ignominious departure was to reaffirm the necessity of its tutelage policy. "The very absence of clarity about Russia's future . . . in the minds of its own people and its own leaders," a top American official explained, "requires all the more clarity in U.S. policy." Having lost its designated "personification of Russian reform," the administration quickly nominated Putin for the role, angrily dismissing "psychobabble about the KGB thing."

President Clinton himself remained as missionary as ever. Visiting Moscow in June 2000, he was, as a wire service report put it, "in an instructional mode." Speaking to the Russian Parliament, he admitted that "Americans have to overcome the temptation to think we have all the answers," but, according to another report, immediately "proceeded with a catalogue of recommendations that sounded like a transplanted State of the Union address."[119]

Contrary to all appearances, the administration's crusade was said to be on track, Russia being "a work in progress" merely in need of more "reform." It meant what it had before—the U.S.-sponsored economic measures that have destabilized the world's largest nuclear country. Seeing in Putin a chance for a "second beginning" of those policies, the administration and IMF immediately tried to influence his choice of economic ministers, as they had Yeltsin's. They urged Putin, in return for loans, to appoint "genuine reformers"—the same kind who had led Russia into depression and mass poverty in the 1990s.[120] It was, again in Yogi Berra's useful malapropism, déjà vu all over again.

In democratic theory, the choosing of a new Ameri-

can president should include a discussion of failed policies. As the 2000 presidential election approached, only
an elliptical debate about Russia had taken place. Ritualistic statements about arms control aside—the Republican chairman of the Senate Foreign Relations
Committee opposed any new such agreements—neither
major candidate expressed an awareness of the full
dimensions and gravity of the nuclear threats inside
Russia, or their underlying causes, even while scientists
continued to issue urgent warnings.

The Democratic candidate, Vice President Gore,
pledged to continue NATO's eastward expansion and,
insofar as his positions were discernible, every other element of the Clinton administration's disastrous Russia
policy. The Republican candidate, Governor George W.
Bush, on the other hand, proposed a new approach to
nuclear security. He promised to explore the possibility
of unilaterally reducing deployed U.S. warheads to levels perhaps substantially below the 3,000 to 3,500 permitted by START II and taking some of the remaining
ones off high alert status, on the assumption that
Moscow would reciprocate.

Such unilateral steps, as readers know, are urgently
needed. But Bush also favored further NATO expansion
and an even more expansive missile defense system
than the limited one advocated by Gore, regardless of
Russian objections. If carried out, both proposals would
almost certainly compel Moscow, as readers also understand, to rely even more heavily on its fragile nuclear
infrastructures and to keep its missiles on hair-trigger
alert. Indeed, Bush endorsed the Republican Senate's
reckless rejection of the Comprehensive Test Ban treaty,

which had prompted delegates to a UN conference in 2000 and others to view the United States itself as "something of a nonproliferation rogue state."[121]

Above all, neither presidential candidate showed any awareness of the folly of the American crusade to reinvent Russia. As its cosponsor in the 1990s, Vice President Gore seemed eager to pursue the same intrusive policy already under way in Ukraine. Governor Bush did not object, his chief foreign policy adviser echoing the crusade's missionary premise: "The twenty-first century will be based on American principles."[122]

We are left with a woeful paradox. An unprecedented danger and a fateful failure of U.S. policy-making have brought forth little if any of the new American thinking or leadership that is needed. In this context, Hegel's bleak axiom "The Owl of Minerva spreads its wings only with the falling of dusk" seems naively optimistic. The great German philosopher believed that although we are unable to comprehend epochal events until they unfold, we do then understand them. For the first time in history, a fully nuclearized country has already been perilously destabilized, but still there is no sufficient American understanding.

Russians who once believed in a wise and compassionate America are despairing.[123] Recalling how the U.S. government pressured its collapsing Russian ally to remain in the carnage of World War I and thus on the road to catastrophe in 1917, a Moscow historian fears it is happening again:

The West is rigidly demanding that Russia march forward. This time not towards the Galician foothills of the

Carpathians but scarcely in a less dangerous direction. As in long ago 1917, the West, not wanting to open its eyes to Russia's real problems, is promising loyalty only in exchange for continuing in a direction, begun in 1992, that is objectively leading to . . . chaos.[124]

There is, however, also an optimistic historical precedent. In the mid-1980s, the world faced a lesser but grave nuclear danger. Cold War threats and military buildups had led the two superpowers to the brink of actual war. It was avoided and the Cold War ended largely because of the radical "new thinking" and leadership of Mikhail Gorbachev that emerged in the authoritarian Soviet system.[125]

Today, democratic America must provide the new thinking and leadership, but has yet to do so. Instead, the Owl of Minerva still sleeps, wings firmly tucked, while the clock of disaster inside Russia ticks toward midnight.

NOTES

<hr />

<hr />

In composite notes, sources are given in the order that they are cited in the text unless otherwise indicated. The following abbreviations are used:

JRL	*Johnson's Russia List* (e-mail)
LAT	*Los Angeles Times*
NYT	*New York Times*
NG	*Nezavisimaia Gazeta*
RFE/RL	Radio Free Europe/Radio Liberty
WSJ	*Wall Street Journal*
WP	*Washington Post*

Part I

1. Remnick, *Resurrection: The Struggle for a New Russia* (New York, 1997), p. 362; *Slavic Review,* Fall 1998, p. 625; Gore quoted by Mark Egan, Reuters dispatch, *JRL,* Oct. 8, 1999; *Charlie Rose,* PBS, Sept. 10, 1999; Voice of America, Dec. 2, 1999, *JRL,* Dec. 5, 1999; *Weekly Standard,* Jan. 17, 2000, p. 15; Michael Stone quoted in *Russian Review,* March 25, 1996, p. 39; *Voprosy ekonomiki,* no. 3, 1997, pp. 74, 76; *NG,* Sept. 22, 1999; report quoted in AP dispatch, *JRL,* July 31, 1999; *Anti-Defamation League Survey on Anti-Semitism and Societal Attitudes in Russia* (New York, 1999), p. 4; Solzhenitsyn interview, *Novaia gazeta,* May 11–14, 2000.

2. For a discussion, see Alexander Dallin in Robert O. Crummey, ed., *Reform in Russia and the U.S.S.R.* (Urbana, 1989), pp. 248–49.

3. "After the Soviet Union: Implications for U.S. Policy" (The Eighty-first American Assembly, April 23–26, 1992), p. 9; and the proposal

of Robert D. Blackwill summarized by Joseph Fitchett in *International Herald Tribune,* June 22, 1992. Similarly, see George Soros' proposal in *Open Society: Chronicle of the Soros Foundations,* April 1992, p. 5; William G. Hyland in *Foreign Affairs,* no. 1, 1992, p. 48; and *WP* editorial, Oct. 27, 1992.

4. As reported by Elaine Sciolino in *NYT,* Feb. 4, 1993. For the official, see Thomas Graham interviewed in the documentary film "Return of the Czar," PBS, May 9, 2000. Neither the officials involved nor Sciolino seemed to think it odd that such decisions, which concerned the most important political and economic issues then facing Russia, were being debated inside the U.S. government.

5. Steven Erlanger, ibid., July 28, 1993. As a critic later put it, "Metaphorically, Russia played helpless child, with the West as omnipotent adult." Lawrence R. Klein and Marshall Power, eds., *The New Russia: Transition Gone Awry* (Stanford, 2000), p. 7.

6. Quoted by Daniel Williams in *WP,* March 13, 1993. A month later, President Clinton himself was even more fulsome: "We have interests and values. They are embodied by the policies and direction of President Yeltsin." Ibid., April 5, 1993. About the same time, a chief architect of the crusade officially stated, "President Yeltsin is the personification of reform in Russia." Strobe Talbott quoted by Michael Dobbs and Paul Blustein, ibid., Sept. 12, 1999.

7. Robert E. Rubin in *NYT,* Sept. 21, 1999. Similarly, see Michel Camdessus in *Moscow News,* Dec. 15–21, 1999. For "dictating," see David E. Sanger's report on the IMF in *NYT,* Nov. 10, 1999. Even prior to the Clinton administration, American missionaries had already assigned to the IMF a primary organizational role in the crusade as the "only one in the world that has a relatively clear view of how Russia can most effectively reform its economy." Jeffrey Sachs in *New Republic,* Dec. 21, 1992, p. 23.

8. U.S. media admirers of Harvard Professor Jeffrey Sachs, who advertised himself as "an economic adviser to the Russian government" and who was especially influential in shaping American opinion on Russia, called him an "enlightened missionary" and "evangelist." See Francis X. Cline in *NYT,* Jan. 16, 1992; and Peter Passell in *NYT Magazine,* June 27, 1993, p. 60. A reviewer of Leon Aron's biography of Yeltsin characterized it as a "near-evangelistic defense." John Thornhill in *Financial Times,* Feb. 15, 2000. Similarly, see the complaint about economists "on a mission" in Joseph Stiglitz, *Whither Reform?* (Washington, D.C.: World Bank, 1999), p. 22. The "rush to

give advice," as a perceptive reporter noted sardonically, actually began considerably earlier. See James Risen in *LAT,* Sept. 5, 1991.

9. For an example of how intrusive this tutelage became, see the purloined letter written by then Deputy U.S. Treasury Secretary Lawrence H. Summers to Anatoly Chubais, then Russia's first deputy prime minister, in *NG,* Sept. 26, 1997. For other examples, see Janine R. Wedel, *Collision and Collusion* (New York, 1998).

10. Zbigniew Brzezinski in *Foreign Affairs,* Fall 1992, p. 33. I quote here from the version of the letter published in Moscow in *New Times,* no. 23, 1993, p. 26.

11. Thomas Pickering quoted in a USIA release, in *JRL,* Nov. 18, 1996; E. Wayne Merry in *WSJ,* Sept. 8, 1999; Strobe Talbott quoted by John Lloyd in *NYT Magazine,* Aug. 15, 1999, p. 64.

12. Scott Horton in *Harriman Review,* Dec. 1998, p. 30; Soros in *Open Society,* June 1992, p. 3.

13. For the businessman, see Paul Tatum, who was assassinated in Moscow two years later, quoted by AP in *NYT,* Nov. 4, 1996. Similarly, see the letter from a Russian investment adviser to *NYT* (Sept. 7, 1995) that ends, "A nation of 150 million people is on the threshold of a great burst of economic activity. Be there!" The other quoted comments are by Matthew Brzezinski in *WP,* Sept. 17, 1999.

14. "Fitch IBCA Comment," Sept. 8, 1998, March 4, 1999; Timothy L. O'Brien on Soros in *NYT,* Dec. 6, 1998; Joseph Kahn and Timothy L. O'Brien on Goldman, Sach & Co., ibid., Oct. 18, 1998; O'Brien, ibid., Sept. 5, 1999; O'Brien and Raymond Bonner, ibid., Feb. 17, 2000.

15. "A Test of the News," published as a supplement to *New Republic,* Aug. 4, 1920. The case they took was the *NYT.*

16. Jim Hoagland in *WP,* Nov. 6, 1992; Rose Brady, *Kapitalizm* (New Haven, 1999), pp. 242–43; Thomas L. Friedman in *NYT,* Oct. 24, 1999; Steven Erlanger, ibid., July 28, 1993; David Hoffman in *WP,* Sept. 19, 1999. Similarly, see *NYT* editorials of Aug. 10, 1999, and Nov. 26, 1991, on the "larger American purpose of accustoming Russia to democratic ways" and the need "to push the Russians forward."

17. Ellen Shearer and Frank Starr, "Through a Prism Darkly," *American Journalism Review,* Sept. 1996, p. 37; Anthony Olcott reviewing Rose Brady's *Kapitalizm* in *WP Book World,* June 27, 1999, p. 6. For a more general indictment of press coverage, see Matt Bivens and Jonas Bernstein, "The Russia You Never Met," *Demokratizatsiya,*

Fall 1998, pp. 613–47. For some of the best press criticism, see Mark Ames and Matt Taibbi, *The Exile* (New York, 2000), an anthology of an often scatological tabloid published biweekly in Moscow. For a few random examples of small factual errors, see Alessandra Stanley and Eric Schmitt on Otto Latsis, public opinion polls, and ruble devaluation in, respectively, *NYT,* March 21, 30, 1997, and Sept. 22, 1999; and Andrew Meier on Sergei Baburin in *Time,* July 13, 1998, p. 52. For errors of more analytical and policy consequence, see Michael Specter and Michael R. Gordon on Russian attitudes on NATO expansion in *NYT,* Feb. 24, May 2, 28, 1997; the *Newsday* editorial of Aug. 22, 1999, on Russian "faith in a free-market system"; and the very odd omission of Putin's reference to the United States in his remarks quoted by Jane Perlez in *NYT,* Jan. 17, 2000. Similarly, see below, note 92. An exasperated Russian journalist at a joint American-Russian magazine finally all but shouted, "Check your facts, for the love of God!" Masha Gessen in *JRL,* Dec. 11, 1999.

18. David Hoffman on *The NewsHour with Jim Lehrer,* PBS, July 22, 1997.

19. Leonid Krutakov interviewed by Matt Taibbi and Mark Ames in *JRL,* Oct. 23, 1999. For "giants," see Lee Hockstader in *WP,* Jan. 1, 1995. For examples of typical sources, see those cited by Steven Erlanger in *NYT,* April 9, Dec. 4, 1993; Fred Hiatt in *WP,* March 26, 1995, Dec. 10, 1996; David Hoffman, ibid., Dec. 13, 1997; and the astonishing list in John Lloyd, *Rebirth of a Nation* (London, 1998), pp. x, 451. For U.S. policymakers, a former insider tells us, the "choice was always black or white." Donald Jensen interviewed in "Return of the Czar," PBS, May 9, 2000. Favorite sources among supporters of U.S. policy, the IMF, and Yeltsin included Jeffrey Sachs, Anders Åslund, Charles Blitzer, and Michael McFaul. When not named, they were often referred to as "many analysts," "specialists," "experts," "Western diplomats," and "top advisers." Typically, a correspondent included U.S. Ambassador Thomas R. Pickering, whose misrepresentations of Russia are a matter of record, and the vice president of an investors' lobby organization among the "smartest Russia-watchers." See Fred Hiatt, *WP,* Dec. 10, 1996. On the other hand, Russia's many opposition politicians and economists were rarely quoted or interviewed, unless to be dismissed as follows: "The Communist leader, Gennadi M. Zyuganov, delivered his usual lines about the collapse of the country." (Michael Specter, who got the middle initial wrong, in *NYT,* Oct. 18, 1996.) The practice was

established early. Thus was Aleksandr Rutskoi, Yeltsin's vice president, who was moving rapidly into opposition to him, dismissed in 1993: "Mr. Rutskoi speaks only of corruption, Russia's humiliation as a 'great power' and the need to find some 'middle way' toward a gradual, somehow less painful reform." (Steven Erlanger, ibid., April 24, 1993.) The themes and subjects then being dismissed remain, of course, of crucial importance in Russia today. As this suggests, there is little evidence in the coverage that American correspondents in Moscow read the Russian press.

20. *NYT* editorial, Dec. 14, 1993. Similarly, see David Hoffman in *WP*, Oct. 1, 1995. "Extremists" sometimes took the form of "hard-liners." Early on, the *WP* decided that the Russian political spectrum was "politicians such as Yeltsin who favor an essentially Western model of development and those who would like to resurrect the authoritarian past." Michael Dobbs, ibid., Feb. 1, 1992.

21. For Yavlinsky, see Michael Specter quoting Michael McFaul approvingly in *NYT*, May 5, 1996; and similarly the *NYT* editorial on May 1, 1996, and Specter's dispatch on May 18, 1996. Yavlinsky remarked earlier that anyone who criticized Yeltsin or IMF guidelines was "already not a democrat, and you're lucky if they don't call you a Communist-Fascist." *Izvestiia*, July 12, 1995. For "clean hands," see Michael Wines on Sergei Stepashin in *NYT*, May 13, 1999. Wines's report and single partisan source are contradicted in the same issue by Celestine Bohlen and, on the op-ed page, by Amy Knight. Similarly, see Michael R. Gordon's promotion of the inexperienced and, as it turned out, inept Sergei Kirienko, ibid., April 12, 1998; and, on the general hyping of Kirienko, see Bivens and Bernstein, "The Russia You Never Met," p. 637.

The U.S. press was especially keen on the purported achievements of the "young reformers," which usually turned out to be failures or pseudo-reforms. Boris Nemtsov's governorship of Nizhni Novgorod, which was presented as a showplace of reform, is a good example. In general, affirming that Yeltsin's backers were invariably "reformers" resulted in some odd reasoning on the part of American journalists. Thus, a mayor could be "a democrat" even while being "an autocratic ruler." Another correspondent managed to include rapacious financial oligarchs: "They are reform-minded in the sense that they bankrolled Yeltsin's presidential campaign against his Communist rival . . . and they generally favor the country's rocky transition to a free-market democracy, which has made them fabulously wealthy." For another, a "reformer" could not be anyone who was "hostile to the West, opposed to free economic competition, and generally antipathetic to U.S. interests in Russia." See, respectively, Alessandra Stanley in *NYT,* June 10, 1997; David Hoffman in *WP,* Jan. 10, 1997; and Carroll Bogert in *Newsweek,* March 21, 1994, p. 51.

22. Vladimir Kvint quoted by Peter Passell, *NYT,* Jan. 24, 1993; James Ledbetter in *Village Voice,* May 28, 1996; Robert V. Daniels, *Russia's Transformation* (Lanham, Md., 1998), p. 193.

23. John Kohan in *Time,* Dec. 7, 1992; Celestine Bohlen and Thomas L. Friedman in *NYT,* April 15, 16, 1999. Similarly, see the editorial, ibid., June 6, 1999.

24. Bivens and Bernstein, "The Russia You Never Met," p. 620.

25. Michael R. Gordon and Alessandra Stanley in *NYT,* Oct. 17, 1996, Nov. 17, 1997. Similarly, see David Hoffman in *WP,* Sept. 9, 1997; Paul Quinn-Judge in *Time,* Dec. 15, 1997; Carol J. Williams in *LAT,* March 25, 1998. A *NYT* editorial on Nov. 19, 1997, finally called for Chubais's removal, but eleven days later his rehabilitation as a martyr of reform was fully under way. See Alessandra Stanley, ibid., Nov. 30, 1997. And no major U.S. newspaper protested his subsequent political comeback, which soon followed. Indeed, Chubais's reputation as "a champion of free markets" survived the twentieth century. See, e.g., Neela Banerjee, ibid., Feb. 12, 2000; and, similarly, Alessandra Stanley, ibid., Jan. 2, 2000.

26. Matt Taibbi and Mark Ames, "The *Journal*'s Russia Scandal," *The Nation,* Oct. 4, 1999, p. 20.

27. Charles Krauthammer and Jim Hoagland in *WP,* March 19, 1993. For making omelettes, see also David Remnick on *Charlie Rose,* PBS, Oct. 4, 1993; and the U.S. politician cited in *U.S. News and World Report,* Nov. 29, 1993, p. 49. For voices in unison, see, e.g., A. M. Rosenthal, the editorial, and Leslie H. Gleb in *NYT,* March 16, 22, 28, April 29, 1993; George F. Will in *WP,* March 25, 1993; and editorials in *Chicago Tribune,* May 9, 1993, and *New Republic,* April 12, 1993. After the bloody outcome, the *NYT* had no second thoughts (editorial, Dec. 6, 1993) and the *WP* began to worry (editorial, Oct. 17, 1993) only when Yeltsin shut down some newspapers as well. Nor were pro-Yeltsin journalists responding to some clamorous American opinion. In a survey, six of ten thought the United States should stay out of the struggle between Yeltsin and the Parliament. *New York Post,* March 29, 1993. For an early warning against this

view in U.S. policy and the media, see Valery Chalidze in *Newsday,* March 28, 1993.

28. See, e.g., Alessandra Stanley in *NYT*, Jan. 19, 1997; *Chicago Tribune* editorial, May 9, 1998; and Jim Hoagland in *WP*, Dec. 16, 1999. Yeltsin seriously considered using armed force against the new Parliament as well, but those plans were rarely reported in the U.S. press. See, e.g., Anatolii Kulikov's testimony in *NG*, July 23, 1999.

29. Oleg Bogomolov, *NG*, Feb. 8, 1994; and John Morrison cited in Shearer and Starr, "Through a Prism Darkly," p. 39. For an example of what they had in mind, see Steven Erlanger's upbeat report on economic prospects in Russia, especially for foreign investors, which manages to put a "salutary" spin even on pyramid schemes that had already taken the life savings of millions of Russians. See *NYT*, Aug. 5, 1994. Presumably, this is why the *NYT* could not understand the growing popularity of the Russian Communist Party. See its editorial of May 24, 1996. For exploitation, see Iraida Semenova and Aleksei Podymov in *Rossiiskaia gazeta,* Jan. 24, 2000.

30. See Steven Erlanger cited above, n. 19; for more shock therapy, *WP* editorial, March 12, 1997, and Michael R. Gordon, *NYT*, July 13, 1997; and for taxation, *ibid.,* May 28, 2000. For estimates of poverty, see below, Part III, n. 3.

31. See, e.g., Steven Erlanger, the editorials, and Richard W. Stevenson in *NYT*, Aug. 22, 1994, July 16, Sept. 25, 1995, May 24, 1996; Fred Hiatt, Margaret Shapiro, Michael Dobbs, and the editorial in *WP*, April 2, July 30, 1995, March 19, 1997; Carol J. Williams in *LAT*, Dec. 2, 1997; and Steve Liesman in *WSJ*, Jan. 28, 1998. For Gore, see above, n. 1.

32. Fred Hiatt in *WP*, July 12, 1998. For Putin, see *NG*, Dec. 30, 1999, and, similarly, *Izvestiia,* Feb. 25, 2000.

33. Carroll Bogert in *Newsweek,* May 31, 1993, p. 12. For more impatience with "doom and gloom," see Steve Liesman in *WSJ*, Sept. 26, 1996. For the provinces, see Leonid Krutakov, as cited above, n. 19.

34. Ann Hulbert in *New Republic,* Oct. 2, 1995, p. 54. For protests, see the report by Katrina vanden Heuvel in *The Nation,* Aug. 10–17, 1998, pp. 4–6; and by vanden Heuvel and me, below, pp. 147–58.

35. Fred Hiatt in *WP*, March 9, 1998; *WSJ* quoted in Bivens and Bernstein, "The Russia You Never Met," p. 631. Similarly, see Richard W. Stevenson's enthusiasm for the Russian-American investor Boris Jordan in *NYT*, Sept. 20, 1995, in light of the exposé of Jordan's activities by David Filipov and Matt Taibbi in the *Boston Globe,* Oct. 22, 1997.

36. Philip Taubman in *NYT,* June 21, 1998. In 1996, the U.S. ambassador to Moscow, and soon to be the State Department's second-ranking official, cited the same signs of progress. See Thomas R. Pickering quoted by Jonas Bernstein in *Moscow Times,* April 8, 2000. Similarly, see Steven Erlanger and Michael Specter, ibid., July 23, Oct. 12, 1995; Carol J. Williams in *LAT,* Dec. 24. 1997; the editorial credo of *Russian Review,* Jan. 29, 1996, a short-lived American-edited magazine; and David Hoffman on the lifestyle of a mayor's wife in *WP,* Sept. 16, 1999.

37. Timothy L. O'Brien quoting Nordani A. Simonia in *NYT,* Sept. 5, 1999, on, according to O'Brien, the "real dynamic that has driven events." Even Russian democrats commonly characterize the 1990s as a "great civil war over property." See Sergei Stankevich in *Novaia gazeta,* March 6, 2000; and, similarly, Vitalii Tretiakov in *NG,* Dec. 18, 1999.

38. As reported by John Donnelly in *Boston Globe,* Oct. 6, 1999. For the Parliament, see Richard Pipes in *NYT,* March 14, 1993; and Michael Scammell, ibid., Aug. 19, 1992. For two examples of poor political analysis, see Scammell's certainty that Yeltsin felt "obliged to co-exist" with his vice president and Pipes's certainty that pro-Yeltsin forces would easily win the Dec. 1993 parliamentary elections. Ibid., Aug. 19, 1992, Oct. 5, 1993. Yeltsin later arrested his vice president and lost the elections very badly.

39. E.g., Zbigniew Brzezinski and Marshall Shulman served in the Carter administration, Richard Pipes in Reagan's White House, and Ed Hewitt and Condoleezza Rice in that of George Bush.

40. For "missionaries," see Alec Nove quoted by Archie Brown in *Post-Soviet Affairs,* no. 1, 1999, p. 63; and for "apologists," Peter Reddaway in *WP,* Feb. 22, 1995. Whether dissenters were shunned or did not try hard enough to make their opinions known is another question. According to the senior economist James R. Millar, he and others who opposed shock therapy generally "failed to stand up," but when they did, "we got relegated to the 'not a real economist' category." (Private letter, Sept. 29, 1999.) Thus, journalists probably quoted Anders Åslund on the state of the Russian economy more than anyone except Jeffrey Sachs in the early 1990s. A onetime "adviser" to the Yeltsin government, Åslund was a true believer in the "reforms" as "a success story." (See below, n. 43.) So far as I know, scholars whose views were different, and their research better, were almost never cited—as, e.g., Lynn D. Nelson and Irina Y.

Kuzes, *Radical Reform in Yeltsin's Russia* (Armonk, N.Y., 1995). Typically, Åslund's book was given a favorable review in the *NYT Book Review* (July 23, 1995), and that by Nelson and Kuzes none at all. The practice of assigning reviewers with a vested interest in optimism about Russian reform under Yeltsin is widespread and ongoing. See, e.g., the review by John Chown, an adviser to the Russian government, of three books on the economy in the *Times Literary Supplement*, Jan. 28, 2000, pp. 4–5; and the reviews of Leon Aron's biography of Yeltsin cited below, Part III, n. 116.

41. John Edwin Mroz in *Foreign Affairs*, no. 1, 1993, pp. 54–55; Dimitri Simes in *WP*, Jan. 19, 1992; Nicolai N. Petro in *JRL*, Oct. 1, 1997.

42. Alexander Rahr in *RFE/RL Research Report*, Aug. 27, 1993, p. 1; Martin Malia in *NYT*, Dec. 12, 1993. Similarly, see Leon Aron, *Yeltsin* (New York, 2000), esp. pp. 688–738.

43. On Yeltsin's opponents, see S. Frederick Starr in *Baltimore Sun*, March 26, 1993; Anders Åslund in *NYT*, Dec. 7, 1992; Michael McFaul quoted by Michael Specter, ibid., May 5, 1996; and Stephen Sestanovich, ibid., Dec. 23, 1991. For versions of the "success story," see Joseph Blasi, ibid., June 30, 1994; Stephen Sestanovich, ibid., Sept. 27, 1994; Anders Åslund in *Foreign Affairs*, Sept.–Oct. 1994, pp. 58–71, and his *How Russia Became a Market Economy* (Washington, D.C., 1995): Brigitte Granville, *The Success of Russian Economic Reforms* (London, 1995); Richard Layard and John Parker, *The Coming Russian Boom* (New York, 1996); Joseph R. Blasi, Maya Kroumova, and Douglas Kruse, *Kremlin Capitalism* (Ithaca, 1997); and (on balance) Daniel Yergin and Thane Gustafson, *Russia 2010* (New York, 1993). Elements of the story also appear in Brady, *Kapitalizm*, and Thane Gustafson, *Capitalism Russian-Style* (New York, 1999). Political scientists also found reasons to be optimistic. See, e.g., Nicolai M. Petro, *The Rebirth of Russian Democracy* (Cambridge, Mass., 1995); John Löwenhardt, *The Reincarnation of Russia* (Durham, N.C., 1995); M. Steven Fish *Democracy From Scratch* (Princeton, 1995); and Marcia A. Weigle, *Russia's Liberal Project* (University Park, Pa., 2000.)

44. Åslund, *How Russia Became a Market Economy*, p. 198; Michael Mandelbaum in *WP*, March 24, 1993; Martin Malia in *New Republic*, April 19, 1993, pp. 18–20; Richard Pipes in *NYT*, March 14, 1993; Bruce A. Ackerman, ibid., March 3, 1993. Similarly, see Pipes, ibid., Oct. 5, 1993; and Malia, ibid., March 28, Dec. 12, 1993. In some later accounts, the whole episode was simply omitted. See, e.g., Michael

McFaul's preface to the memoirs of Yegor Gaidar, *Days of Defeat and Victory* (Seattle, 2000).

45. For a critical history of the field, including the totalitarianism school, see my *Rethinking the Soviet Experience: Politics and History Since 1917* (New York, 1985), chaps. 1–2. The "boo" witticism is Frederic Fleron's. See his edited volume *Communist Studies and the Social Sciences* (Chicago, 1969), p. 33, n. 82.

46. Christopher Shea, "New Faces and New Methodologies Invigorate Russian Studies," *Chronicle of Higher Education,* Feb. 20, 1998, p. A16; Thomas F. Remington, "On Teaching Post-Soviet Politics," *AAASS NewsNet,* Sept. 1998, p. 8. Similarly, see Robert C. Stuart, "Teaching Transition Economies," ibid., May 2000, pp. 15–16. Interested readers should glance at articles and book reviews in the field's main journals: *Slavic Review,* the *Russian Review, Europe-Asia Studies, Post-Soviet Affairs,* and *Problems of Post-Communism.*

47. See, e.g., Michael McFaul in *Current History,* Oct. 1994, p. 313; David Hoffman in *WP,* Sept. 19, 1999; and Thomas A. Dine in *Problems of Post-Communism,* May–June 1995, p. 27. For "rocky," see Jack F. Matlock Jr. in *NYT Book Review,* April 11, 1999, p. 11; David Hoffman in *WP,* Jan. 15, 1998; Richard W. Stevenson in *NYT,* Sept. 2, 1999; and Strobe Talbott speech, *JRL,* Oct. 2, 1999.

48. See the opinions cited and summarized in Shea, "New Faces," pp. A16–A18.

49. Ibid.

50. For the crumbling consensus, see Daniel Yergin in *WP,* Sept. 3, 1998; William Greider, ibid., Oct. 7, 1998; Richard W. Stevenson in *NYT,* Oct. 7, 1998; Roger Cohen, ibid., Nov. 14, 1998; and John Gray in *The Nation,* Oct. 19, 1998, pp.17–18.

51. See, e.g., N. Petrakov and V. Perlamutrov in *Voprosy ekonomiki,* no. 3, 1997, pp. 74–83; N. Ia. Petrakov, *Russkaia ruletka* (Moscow, 1998); L. I. Abalkin, *Vybor za Rossiei* (Moscow, 1998) and *Spasti Rossiiu* (Moscow, 1999); Sergei Glazev, *Genotsid* (Moscow, 1997); V. Kolobova, *Grigorii Iavlinskii* (Rostov, 1998); Petr Tsitkilov on Evgenii Primakov in *Svobodnaia mysl,* no. 8, 1999, pp. 6–18; and the Communist Party program in *Sovetskaia Rossiia,* June 24, 1999. See also below, Part III, n. 80.

52. Michael Mandelbaum in *WP,* April 12, 1993. More candid than others, Professor Mandelbaum is not a Russianist but writes regularly on the subject. For a journalist, see Philip Taubman in *NYT,* June 21,

1998, where we learn that the process "favors the young . . . and has little patience or compassion for those unable to adapt."

53. See, e.g., Fish, *Democracy From Scratch,* p. 234 and passim; Joan Barth Urban and Valerii D. Solovei, *Russia's Communists at the Cross-roads* (Boulder, 1997), p. 188; Gustafson, *Capitalism Russian-Style,* pp. 229–30, 234; and Taubman, cited above, n. 52.

54. The euphemism is "gradually moving off the stage." See Gustafson, *Capitalism Russian-Style,* p. 229; and similarly Strobe Talbott's 1996 speech, *JRL,* Oct. 30, 1996, where reform is tied to their "passing from the scene." In the same spirit, columnists tell us that the "demographics in Russia are on the side of reform" and that Communist Party members are "aging and dying." Thomas L. Friedman and William Safire in *NYT,* Feb. 16, Sept. 9, 1999. In the national elections of 1999 and 2000, however, the party continued to win 25 to 30 percent of the vote.

55. See the headlines in *NG,* Oct. 16 and 20, 1998; for orphans, the Agence France-Presse report in *NYT,* Nov. 19, 1998; and for livestock and imports, Petrakov, *Russkaia ruletka,* pp. 256–57, and his article in *Obshchaia gazeta,* March 2–8, 2000.

56. Garry Kasparov in *WSJ,* Oct. 16, 1998. Only a year after the crash did the *WP* seem to notice that there had been "a total divorce between the financial sector and the real economy." See David Hoffman quoting Eric Kraus in the issue of Aug. 17, 1999.

57. Mikhail Kasyanov quoted by Jonathan Fuerbringer in *NYT,* April 21, 2000. For viewing Russia's oligarchs through the American experience, see David Hoffman in *WP,* Sept. 19, 1999; and *NYT* editorial, June 16, 2000. For an exposé of the nature of Russia's "robber barons," see Mark Ames in *The Exile,* Oct. 25, 1998.

58. See, e.g., Steven Erlanger (quoted here) and Joseph Blasi in *NYT,* July 23, 1995, June 30, 1994; and the study by McKinsey & Co. reported by Jeanne Whalen in *WSJ,* Oct. 19, 1999. For productivity, see also Vladimir Tikhomirov in *Europe-Asia Studies,* March 2000, pp. 220, 224. For a case study of privatizing as asset stripping, see Matt Taibbi in *The Exile,* Oct. 16, 1999. Similarly, see Lee S. Wolosky in *Foreign Affairs,* March–April 2000, pp. 18–31. For small business, see the Itar-Tass report, *JRL,* April 23, 2000.

59. Mikhail Khodorkovsky quoted by Steve Liesman and Andrew Higgins in WSJ, Sept. 23, 1998; V. A. Lepekhin in *Obshchestvennye nauki i sovremennost,* no. 1, 1999, p. 75; Vyacheslav Nikonov quoted by Timothy L. O'Brien in *NYT,* Sept. 27, 1998; and the contingency

plans of the oligarch Vladimir Gusinsky (who was later jailed briefly in 2000) reported by Andrew Higgins in *WSJ*, Oct. 12, 1998. Similarly, see comments on Boris Berezovsky by Dikun and Kostiukov in *Obshchaia gazeta*, Dec. 30, 1999–Jan. 12, 2000. For the scholar, see Tikhomirov cited in the preceding note.

60. The analogy with serfdom was made by the Duma deputy Nikolai Gonchar, as quoted by Giulietto Chiesa in *La Stampa*, Oct. 8, 1999.

61. According to a leading minister in the government that pursued the policy, the ruble was "wildly overvalued." Boris Nemtsov in *NYT*, Oct. 27, 1998.

62. Whether or not a Western-style middle class exists in Russia today is a disputed issue, but a number of Russian analysts argue that it does not. See, e.g., Galina Sillaste in *NG*, Oct. 22, 1998; Iakov Krotov in *Obshchaia gazeta*, Sept. 17–23, 1998; and Evgenii Primakov's comments on the "legend of a middle class," *Izvestiia*, Nov. 20, 1998. For the other view, see Harley Balzer, "Russia's Middle Classes," *Post-Soviet Affairs*, April–June 1998, pp. 165–86.

63. E.g., few historians doubt that a "civil society" existed in Nazi Germany, but hardly the one professed and sought by today's transitionologists. Similarly, most of them assert that no "civil society," in the sense of social activity apart from the state, existed in Communist Russia, but this is untrue, as several pro-reform Russians have pointed out. See, e.g., Andranik Migranian, *Rossiia v poiskakh identichnosti* (Moscow, 1997), p. 189; and Larissa G. Titarenko in *Demokratizatsiya*, Summer 1999, p. 451, who also notes the "polemical" aspect of the concept. Moreover, a U.S. correspondent laments Russia's lack of a "working civil society," but excludes from the notion the country's largest electoral party, the Communist Party. (David Hoffman in *WP*, Nov. 7, 1999.) And Prime Minister Vladimir Putin says that the Kremlin's murderous war against Chechen civilians is "to restore civil society to the Chechen people." See his op-ed article in *NYT*, Nov. 14, 1999. For a critique of the concept, see David Rieff, "The False Dawn of Civil Society," *The Nation*, Feb. 22, 1999, pp. 11–16. See also below, Part III, nn. 73, 74.

64. Nikolai Petrakov in *Obshchaia gazeta*, Sept. 9–15, 1999; and Putin in *NG*, Dec. 30, 1999. For "museums," see the report by Katrina vanden Heuvel in *The Nation*, Aug. 10–17, 1998, p. 5, and confirmed by sources as diverse as Tom Bell on Magadan in *Anchorage Daily News*, April 26, 1999; and a Bloomberg dispatch on Moscow, *JRL*, Aug. 21, 1999. For an exceptional focus on poverty, see Bertram Silverman

and Murray Yanowitch, *New Rich, New Poor, New Russia,* exp. ed., (Armonk, N.Y., 2000).

65. Anatolii Kulikov interviewed in *NG,* July 23, 1999.

66. For Yeltsin and the oligarchy, see V. A. Lepekhin in *Obshchestven-nye nauki i sovremennost,* no. 1, 1999, p. 75. The degree of media freedom is a complex and debatable issue, but a leading Russian journalist thinks that because most newspapers and television networks are owned and operated for selfish purposes, the "entire media is run in the agit-prop style, Lenin-style propaganda." Leonid Krutakov interviewed by Taibbi and Ames, *The Exile, JRL,* Oct. 23, 1999. More balanced perhaps, a study found that "free press" in Russia today is actually "degrees of non-freedom," as reported by Robert Coalson in *Moscow Times,* Nov. 12, 1999. Similarly, see Matt Bivens in *Brill's Content,* July/August 2000, pp. 86–90, 124–25.

On "federalism as feudalism," see Brian Whitmore in *Transitions,* Sept. 1998, pp. 71–77. Former Prime Minister Evgeny Primakov called the formal subjects of the federal constitution "these fiefdoms." A mayor said "governors are little princes in their own fiefdoms. They don't obey anyone." And according to the president of Ingushetia, "The constitution claims there is federalism, but in practice, there is no federalism." See, respectively, Russian TV "Vesti," Sept. 29, 1998; *NYT,* Nov. 21, 1999; *East-West Institute Regional Report,* March 11, 1999; and, similarly, Konstantin Titov in *NG,* Jan. 25, 2000. For the capitulation, see the letter by three governors in *NG,* Feb. 25, 2000; and the commentaries, ibid., March 4, 2000; and in *Izvestiia,* Feb. 28, 2000.

67. For the warning, see Gordon's report, *NYT,* Oct. 8, 1998. For attitudes toward the bombing and the United States, see the ADA survey cited above, n. 1; and another reported by Reuters, *JRL,* Nov. 23, 1999; and Michael R. Gordon's report in *NYT,* March 27, 2000. For a firsthand report on student reaction to the bombing, see Karen Hewitt in *Guardian* (UK), April 24, 1999. And for the new iron curtain, see Mikhail Krugov in *Novaia gazeta,* March 27–April 2, 2000.

68. Richard E. Ericson and David Remnick, as cited above, n. 1. Similarly, see Anders Åslund in *Weekly Standard,* Dec. 29, 1997–Jan. 5, 1998, pp. 24–27.

69. Eugene Huskey in *American Political Science Review,* Dec. 1998, p. 968; Michael McFaul in *Foreign Affairs,* Jan.–Feb. 1995, p. 89; Richard Pipes in *Commentary,* March 1992, pp. 30–31; Richard E. Ericson in *Journal of Economic Perspectives,* Fall 1991, p. 26; Steven

Erlanger in *NYT,* Feb. 19, 1995. Similarly, see Martin Malia, *The Soviet Tragedy* (New York, 1994), pp. 496–98; William E. Odom in *WP,* Sept. 6, 1998; Åslund, *How Russia Became a Market Economy,* p. 52; and Mandelbaum in Michael Mandelbaum, ed., *Postcommunism* (New York, 1996), p. 11.

70. Ericson in *Journal of Economic Perspectives,* Fall 1991, p. 25; Stiglitz, *Whither Reform?,* p. 22.

71. See Murray Feshbach in *Atlantic,* Jan. 1999, pp. 26–27; and Nicholas Eberstadt in *Policy Review,* June–July 1999, pp. 3–24. Western organizations that had advised Russia to abandon its state health program for a Western insurance-based approach later had second thoughts. See Wendy Moore in *Russian Journal, JRL,* Sept. 3, 1999. For the general human consequences of the "rubble" policy, see below, nn. 96, 97.

72. Viacheslav Dashichev in *Svobodnaia mysl,* no. 7, 1999, p. 121; Grigory Yavlinsky quoted in Nelson and Kuzes, *Radical Reform in Yeltsin's Russia,* p. 21. For the purported "implosion" and "rubble," see above, n. 69.

73. The small group of specialists who see Yeltsinism as a kind of "neo-Bolshevism" are much closer to the truth. See Dmitri Glinski and Peter Reddaway in *Journal on Democracy,* April 1999, pp. 24–31; and Stiglitz, *Whither Reform?,* p. 22. It is a view widely held in Russia. See, e.g., Leonid Krutakov interviewed by Taibbi and Ames, *The Exile,* in *JRL,* Oct. 23, 1999.

74. Petrakov and Perlamutrov in *Voprosy ekonomiki,* no. 3, 1997, p. 76. For the analogies, see G. Khanin and N. Suslov in *Europe-Asia Studies,* Dec. 1999, p. 1450; Sergei Glazev, *Genocide* (Washington, D.C., 1999); and Boris Kagarlitskii in *Novaia gazeta,* Feb. 21, 2000.

75. For a comparison of the American and the Russian depressions, see James R. Millar in *Current History,* Oct. 1999, p. 323; and *Human Development Report for Central and Eastern Europe and the CIS 1999* (New York: United Nations Development Program, 1999), p. 15, from which I have taken the quoted characterization.

76. Tatyana Tolstaya in *New York Review of Books,* Nov. 19, 1998, p. 6.

77. The governor of Yakutiya quoted by Michael Wines in *NYT,* Oct. 21, 1998. For schools, see the study by Vladimir Andreev in *Russian Social Science Review,* July–Aug. 1998, p. 19; and the report by Geoffrey York in *Globe and Mail* (Canada), Nov. 24, 1998.

78. *Moscow News,* May 14–20, 1998; Boris Rasputin in *Dissent,* Winter 2000, p. 18. Similarly, see Sergei Karaganov, ibid., March 8–14, 2000.

79. For food, see Paul Goble's *RFE/RL* report, *JRL,* Feb. 2, 1999; for health, Eberstadt in *Policy Review,* June–July 1999, pp. 3–24; and for research and development, Tikhomirov in *Europe-Asia Studies,* March 2000, p. 216. For children, see below, n. 100.

80. Joseph M. Pickett in *JRL,* Jan. 27, 1999. For the "retreat," see Richard C. Paddock in *LAT,* March 13, 1999.

81. Quoted by Colin McMahon in *Chicago Tribune,* Nov. 19, 1998. For the farms, see Geoffrey York in *Globe and Mail* (Canada), Jan. 19, 2000.

82. A. V. Fadin in *Kentavr,* Jan.–Feb. 1993, pp. 92–99; similarly, see the discussion of Gorbachev's quest for a "non-catastrophic transformation" in Vadim Medvedev, *V komande Gorbacheva* (Moscow, 1994), p. 234. For the "young reformer," see Irina Khakamada quoted by Fred Weir in *Christian Science Monitor,* Sept. 9, 1999.

83. The historian Martin Malia, e.g., speaks of "Yeltsin's modernizing reform." *NYT,* March 28, 1993.

84. For a discussion of the practice, see my *Sovieticus: American Perceptions and Soviet Realities,* exp. ed. (New York, 1986).

85. For varying kinds and degrees of historical precedent, see, in addition to the study by Lippmann and Merz discussed earlier, the following studies: Phillip Knightley, *The First Casualty* (New York, 1975); James William Crowl, *Angels in Stalin's Paradise* (Lanham, Md., 1982); and S. J. Taylor, *Stalin's Apologist* (New York, 1990).

86. For Russia as a "superior laboratory," see M. Steven Fish in *Post-Soviet Affairs,* no. 3, 1998, p. 215; and for history, Jeffrey Sachs cited by William Pfaff in *International Herald Tribune,* Oct. 21, 1999.

87. See the case of Harvard University's Institute for International Development in Wedel, *Collision and Collusion,* chap. 4.

88. Steven L. Solnick quoted in Shea, "New Faces," p. A16; George Breslauer in *Demokratizatsiya,* Summer 1998, p. 597. For investors as sources, see also Lloyd, *Rebirth of a Nation,* p. 451.

89. Taibbi and Ames, "The *Journal's* Russia Scandal," p. 18.

90. For "Russia-watchers," see above, n. 19; for Sovietologists, Meg Greenfield and Ken Ringle in, respectively, *WP,* Jan. 4 and Nov. 13, 1999. Russian studies centers at some universities have actually formed partnerships with investors. See, e.g., the advertisement at the end of the *Harriman Review* (Columbia University), June 1999.

91. David Remnick in *New York Review of Books,* April 9, 1998, pp. 13–14; Michael Scammell in *NYT Book Review,* Dec. 3, 1998. Similarly, see David Hoffman on Solzhenitsyn in *WP,* Sept. 27, 1995. For

a protest against the "debunking of Solzhenitsyn [as] one of the favorite pastimes of the Western press," see *The Exile* editorial, June 18–July 1, 1998; and for an honorable exception, Celestine Bohlen in *NYT*, June 6, 1998. Offending works by the Russian writers included Sinyavsky's "Worse Than Communists," ibid., May 30, 1996, and his *The Russian Intelligentsia* (New York, 1997); and Solzhenitsyn's *Rossiia v obvale* (Moscow, 1998) and his interviews in the Russian and Western press.

92. In addition to those mentioned earlier—see above, note 17—consider the following factual errors, all of which in effect excise the Gorbachev period from the history and interpretation of Russian reform. Carroll Bogert (*Newsweek,* Oct. 19, 1992, p. 43) thinks "Gorbachev was never broadly popular in Russia"; Margaret Shapiro (*WP,* Dec. 9, 1993) thinks "Russia's first truly democratic electoral contest" took place in 1993, as apparently do two U.S. officials—Clifford Kupchan (*Harriman Review,* Winter 1999–2000, p. 46) and Under Secretary of State Thomas R. Pickering (*JRL,* April 2, 2000); and *NYT* editorials (July 4, 1996, July 19, 1999) believe that "tyranny" still prevailed in the Soviet Union in 1991 and that it was Yeltsin who "did so much to turn Russia away from cold-war nuclear arms race." Similarly, a *NYT* editorial (May 9, 2000) maintains it was Yeltsin who "set Russia on a course toward democracy and free markets," as does Michael Wines, ibid., June 5, 2000. A reading of just one well-known book, Archie Brown's *The Gorbachev Factor* (New York, 1996), one of the best on that period, would have prevented all these errors—unless, of course, they are politically inspired. Shortly before stepping down as managing director of the IMF, Michel Camdessus belatedly conceded that he might "need to learn more about Russia's history and sociology." See his June 16, 1999, speech in St. Petersburg, *JRL,* June 22, 1999.

93. Aleksandr Bovin in Stephen F. Cohen and Katrina vanden Heuvel, *Voices of Glasnost* (New York, 1989), p. 225.

94. For some recent surveys of opinion, see the Ebert Foundation's findings in *JRL,* March 27, 1999; the report by Vladimir Shlapentokh, ibid., Sept. 22, 1998; the VSTsIOM survey, ibid., Oct. 8, 1998; and the poll reported by Anna Zakatnova in *Current Digest of the Post-Soviet Press,* May 24, 2000, p. 12.

95. See the ADL survey cited above, n. 1; and the one reported by Richard Beeston in *Times* (UK), Aug. 2, 1999. For the Brezhnev years, see the pollster Iurii Levada interviewed in *NG,* May 11, 2000.

96. World Bank report cited by Robert Lyle in *RFE/RF Newsline,* April 29, 1999. For poverty in Russia, see below, Part III, n. 3. For the self-defense of these "reformers," see V. Mau in *Voprosy ekonomiki,* no. 11, 1999, pp. 4–23, and no. 12, 1999, pp. 34–47; and A. Illarionov, ibid., no. 1, 2000, pp. 4–26.

97. For reports, see the one cited in the preceding note; *Human Development Report for Central and Eastern Europe and the CIS 1999; Women in Transition* (Florence: UNICEF, 1999); and *After the Fall: The Human Impact of Ten Years of Transition* (Florence: UNICEF, 1999). How, e.g., can any Russia specialist believe that "anybody in Moscow can get . . . a plane ticket to New York or Washington" when the cost would likely exceed the average annual Russian salary? See Angela Stent quoted by Ken Ringle in *WP,* Nov. 13, 1999. Similarly, see the correspondent who reports that a mayor's wife is "typical" of a "generation that enjoys tennis and horseback riding, mobile telephones, and European vacations." David Hoffman, ibid., Sept. 16, 1999. Also indicative is the oblique mention of poverty in a correspondent's overview of Russia's "transition" and the same newspaper's editorial suggestion that as late as 1999 Russians had not yet been among "Mr. Yeltsin's victims." See, respectively, *WP,* Sept. 19 and Oct. 8, 1999. As is a reviewer's failure even to mention poverty in commenting on three books about the present-day Russian economy. See John Chown, cited above, n. 40.

98. See, e.g., what the *NYT* found "disquieting" and what, according to its correspondent, brought about a "sea change" in American views on Russia, in the editorial of Aug. 31, 1999, and Celestine Bohlen's report on Sept. 6, 1999.

99. See, e.g., Fred Hiatt in *WP,* Aug. 29, 1999.

100. For the studies, see the AP report in *NYT,* Nov. 19, 1998; the International Confederation of Trade Unions findings reported by Reuters, *JRL,* Oct. 26, 1999; and *Human Development Report for Central and Eastern Europe and the CIS 1999,* p. 6. Similarly, see *After the Fall;* and Vladimir I. Chuprov in *Sociological Research,* Jan.–Feb. 1999, pp. 56–57. For the drawings and children with defects, see Anatolii Pristavkin in *Obshchaia gazeta,* Jan. 13–19, 2000; and Harley Balzer cited in Kennan Institute for Advanced Russian Studies, "Meeting Report," no. 10, 2000. According to a widely admired Russian scholar, "The health of Russia's children has become a national tragedy." Lilia Shevtsova, *Yeltsin's Russia* (Washington, D.C., 1999), p. 207.

101. Petrakov, Perlamutrov, and Podbereskin cited above, n. 1.

102. For "coup," see Iurii Burtin in *Svobodnaia mysl,* no. 3, 2000, pp. 4–9. (William Pfaff made the same point in *International Herald Tribune,* March 25, 2000, as did William Safire in *NYT,* March 20 and June 19, 2000.) Another Russian observer called Putin's rise "a velvet coup d'etat." Grigory Lubomirov quoted by Daniel Williams in *WP,* June 4, 2000. For Soviet-style election, see Lilia Shevtsova quoted by Maura Reynolds in *LAT,* Jan. 2, 2000; and Yekaterina Grigoryeva in *Current Digest of the Post-Soviet Press,* Feb. 9, 2000. For the KGB, see Aleksandr Minkin and Oleg Kalugin cited by Ian Traynor in *Guardian* (UK), March 24, 2000; and Mikhail Krugov in *Novaia gazeta,* March 27–April 12, 2000. For U.S. statements, see, respectively, Secretary of State Albright's remarks, *JRL,* Jan. 19, 2000; President Clinton's remarks on CNN, Feb. 14, 2000; below, Part III, n. 29; and Clinton's remarks in *NYT,* March 30, 2000. In June 2000, Clinton told the Russian Parliament, which certainly knew better, that Putin had become president through "a democratic transfer of executive power." *JRL,* June 6, 2000. Similarly, see Albright quoted by Jane Perlez, ibid., Feb. 3, 2000, and by Charles A. Radin in *Boston Globe,* April 8, 2000; and National Security Adviser Sandy Berger quoted by Charles Babington and Steven Mufson in *WP,* Jan. 7, 2000.

103. Robert Kaiser as cited above, n. 1; David Hoffman in *WP,* Sept. 19, 1999; Michael Wines in *NYT,* May 8, 2000; Judith Ingram, AP dispatch, *JRL,* Jan. 4, 2000. On Russia's condition, see also Kaiser's contradictory but ultimately upbeat series of reports in *WP,* July 9, 18, 25, 1999; Richard Cohen, ibid., Sept. 14, 1999; and Eleanor Randolph in *NYT,* Sept. 19, 1999. And on hope that Putin will "finish the job," see also Rose Brady in *Business Week,* March 13, 2000, p. 14E12; and, similarly, Boris Nemtsov and Ian Bremmer in *NYT,* Jan. 25, 2000. For a critique of Anglo-American press coverage of Putin, see Matt Taibbi in *The Exile, JRL,* Feb. 4, March 2, 16, 2000.

104. For the economy, see the Reuters dispatch, *JRL,* Feb. 19, 1999; *RFE/RL Newsline,* June 22, 1999; John Thornhill's report in *Financial Times,* July 9, 1999; and Richard Beeston's in *Times* (UK), Aug. 6, 1999. Similarly, see Michael Wines in *NYT,* June 2, 2000, whose lead report of an economy "roaring back to life" is almost entirely contradicted by facts reported later in his dispatch. For the "free-market system," see *Newsday,* Aug. 22, 1999. For Chubais, see David Hoffman in *WP,* Nov. 4, March 29, 1999; above, n. 25; and for

charges against him, *Moscow Times*, Nov. 11, 16, 1999. For Putin and foreign investors, see Michael Wines in *NYT*, Feb. 20, 2000; and Maura Reynolds in *LAT*, March 24, 2000. Similarly, see David Hoffman in *WP*, March 25, 2000; and Karl Emerick Hanuska's Reuters dispatch, *JRL*, March 27, 2000. For a succinct restating of the standard narrative, see Boris Nemtsov and Ian Bremmer in *NYT*, Jan. 5, 2000.

105. Daniel Yergin and Thane Gustafson in *WP*, Aug. 2, 1998; William E. Odom, ibid., Sept. 6, 1999; Leon Aron in *Weekly Standard*, Oct. 4, 1999, pp. 24–29; Graham T. Allison in a March 29, 2000, letter to recipients of his Harvard project's publications; Martin Malia in *LAT*, Jan. 5, 2000; Anders Åslund, Voice of America, *JRL*, Jan. 4, 2000; Mark Kramer in *WP*, Jan. 2, 2000; Marshall Goldman in *Newsday*, Dec. 21, 1999. For "good news," see Malia and Åslund in *NYT*, Dec. 23, 1999, Jan. 18, 2000.

106. Barry Gewen in *NYT Book Review*, Oct. 31, 1999, p. 34; Thomas A. Friedman on the editorial pages the same day.

107. Grigory Yavlinsky quoted by Brian Whitmore in *Boston Globe*, Sept. 9, 1999.

108. See, respectively, the negative developments itemized by Representative Benjamin A. Gilman for testimony before his committee, all of them long-standing, *JRL*, Oct. 10, 1999, and House Majority Leader Richard K. Armey quoted by Steven Mufson in *WP*, Sept. 17, 1999; the Senate testimony by the former State Department official Wayne Merry, *JRL*, Sept. 24, 1999, the retired CIA official Fritz W. Ermarth in *National Interest*, Spring 1999, pp. 5–14, and the former officials interviewed in the PBS documentary film, aired May 9, 2000, *Return of the Czar;* and Jim Hoagland in *WP*, Nov. 21, 1999. (John Helmer first remarked on the "once tongue-tied Ermarth," *JRL*, Sept. 24, 1999.) For editorials, compare those before and after Aug. 1998 in *NYT, WP, WSJ, LAT, Economist,* and *Financial Times,* among many others. For bipartisan support, see then Senate Minority Leader Bob Dole's urging President Clinton to help Yeltsin against his Russian opponents, as reported by the *AP*, March 21, 1993. Later, Dole changed his mind, attacking Clinton's "Yeltsin first" policy, as reported by Elaine Sciolino in *NYT*, March 2, 1995.

109. Michael Dobbs and Paul Blustein in *WP*, Sept. 12, 1999; John Lloyd in *NYT Magazine*, Aug. 15, 1999, pp. 34–41, 52, 61, 64; Fred Hiatt in *WP*, Aug. 29, 1999; Taibbi and Ames, "The *Journal*'s Russia Scandal"; Stiglitz, *Whither Reform?* Similarly, compare Richard Cohen in

WP, Sept. 14, 1999, and Feb. 10 and May 23, 2000; and Thomas L. Friedman on Russia's necessary "model," which turns out not to be in any "textbook," in *NYT,* Oct. 24, 1999, April 18, 2000.

110. Richard E. Ericson in *Harriman Review,* Dec. 1998, pp. 3–6, and *Post-Soviet Affairs,* Jan.–March 2000, pp. 18–25; Martin Malia in *NYT,* Sept. 3, 1998; and Michael McFaul in *Current History,* Oct. 1998, pp. 307–12. Similarly, see Richard Pipes in *NYT,* Aug. 29, 1998; and Anders Åslund quoted by Michael S. Lelyveld and John Helmer in *Journal of Commerce,* Oct. 8, 1998, p. 3A. Malia soon recovered and reversed himself yet again. See above, n. 105.

111. Fareed Zakaria in *Newsweek,* Sept. 27, 1999, p. 40.

112. Representative Jim Leach quoted in a Bloomberg dispatch, *JRL,* Sept. 28, 1999; David E. Sanger's report on the IMF in *NYT,* Nov. 10, 1999.

113. John Odling-Smee in *Financial Times,* Aug. 23, 1999; Robert D. Blackwill, ed., *The Future of Transatlantic Relations* (New York: Council on Foreign Relations, 1999), p. 29; Celestine Bohlen's report in *NYT,* Aug. 10, 1999; Terrence English in *Harriman Review,* June 1999, pp. 55–56; Stanley Fischer in *JRL,* April 12, 2000. Similarly, see Ariel Cohen, "What Russia Must Do to Recover from Its Economic Crisis" (Heritage Foundation, June 18, 1999); Lawrence H. Summers in *JRL,* Aug. 14, 1999; James M. Klurfeld in *Newsday,* Sept. 9, 1999; Robert E. Rubin in *NYT,* Sept. 21, 1999; Anders Åslund in *Foreign Affairs,* Sept.–Oct. 1999, pp. 64–77; Michel Camdessus in *Moscow News,* Dec. 15–21, 1999; and below, Part III, nn. 117, 119, 120.

114. Robert Legvold quoted by Eric Schmitt in *NYT,* Sept. 26, 1999.

115. For Russians, see Thomas L. Friedman, ibid., Oct. 24, 1999; and Richard Lourie in *LAT Book Review,* March 21, 1999. Similarly, see Fritz W. Ermarth in *National Interest,* Spring 1999, p. 5; David Hoffman in *WP,* Sept. 9, 1999; Alessandra Stanley in *NYT,* Jan. 2, 2000; and Robert J. Samuelson in *WP,* April 5, 2000. A Canadian editorial writer was so carried away by anti-Russian sentiment—"Normal for Russia is filthy, corrupt, menacing, and hollow. Nothing good has ever happened there, nor will it"—he had to apologize to his readers. John Robson in *Ottawa Citizen,* Jan. 7, 19, 2000. For blaming the administration and IMF, see Jeffrey Sachs in *NYT,* Sept. 8, 1999; and George Soros in *New York Review of Books,* April 13, 2000, pp. 10–16. For Yeltsin's government, see Michel Camdessus in *WP,* Sept. 13, 1999, and in *JRL,* April 12, 2000. And for Parliament, see Rory Mac-Farquhar in *Harriman Review,* June 1999, p. 30.

116. Richard Pipes in *CDI Russia Weekly Newsletter* (e-mail), Sept. 10, 1999. Similarly, see Trudy Rubin in *Philadelphia Inquirer,* Sept. 9, 1998; Jack F. Matlock Jr. in *NYT Book Review,* April 11, 1999, p. 11; William Taubman, ibid., March 14, 1999, p. 33; Mortimer B. Zuckerman in *U.S. News and World Report,* Sept. 13, 1999, p. 68; Strobe Talbott's Senate testimony, in *JRL,* Sept. 23, 1999; Al Gore as reported by Reuters, Sept. 26, 1999; David Hoffman in *WP,* Nov. 7, 1999; Malia, *The Soviet Tragedy,* pp. 491–520 and passim.

117. Lawrence H. Summers was confirmed as U.S. treasury secretary in July 1999. For his predecessor, Robert E. Rubin, see Kathleen Day's report in *WP,* March 7, 2000. For the Harvard economist, Andrei Shleifer, see Louis Uchitelle's report in *NYT,* April 26, 1999; for the journalist, see Taibbi and Ames, "The *Journal*'s Russia Scandal." Bridgeport University gave Viktor Chernomyrdin an honorary doctorate degree and named a research institute after him. *JRL,* Sept. 29, 1999. Similarly, see the account of Chernomyrdin's U.S. visit in *NYT,* Sept. 30, 1999. For Chernomyrdin and corruption, see below, Part III, n. 32. One institution did pay a price. In January 2000, the Harvard Institute for International Development, one of the most missionary and compromised organizations, was shut down.

118. Peter Reddaway in *JRL,* Sept. 22, 1999.

119. Greenspan's speech on June 10, 1997, on the Federal Reserve's Web site; *WP* editorial, Sept. 7, 1998; Scott Blacklin quoted by Alastair MacDonald, Reuters dispatch, Sept. 7, 1998.

120. Boris Fyodorov quoted by Michael R. Gordon in *NYT,* Oct. 1, 1998. Similarly, see Fyodorov in *WP,* July 27, 1999.

121. See above, n. 118.

122. See the covers of *Newsweek,* June 17, 1996, and *NYT Magazine,* May 26, 1996; and Stephen Kotkin in *New Republic,* June 5, 2000, p. 28.

123. Senate testimony of Wayne Merry in *JRL,* Sept. 24, 1999. On the "threat," see Jane Perlez in *NYT,* Sept. 1, 1999.

124. For the groups, see Robert S. Greenberger and Andrew Higgins in *WSJ,* Aug. 27, 1998; and Janet Guttsman, Reuters dispatch, *JRL,* Dec. 1, 1998. For Putin, see Jack F. Matcock Jr. in *NYT,* March 26, 2000; and Fred Hiatt in *WP,* March 26, 2000. All along, we are told, the possibility that the Communists might win a presidential election was the Clinton administration's "worst foreign policy nightmare." Elaine Sciolino in *NYT,* March 19, 1996.

125. This passage appears in Stiglitz, *Whither Reform?,* in the version in

JRL, June 1, 1999, but is omitted from the published version (see p. 22). For journalists, see Ames and Taibbi, *The Exile,* p. 62.

126. John Lloyd, "Who Lost Russia?," *NYT Magazine,* Aug. 15, 1999, p. 52. Lloyd is an exception. The consensus view is that whatever happened in the 1990s "was the price of keeping the Communists at bay." Chrysta Freeland in *Financial Times,* May 27, 2000.

127. David Ignatius in *WP,* Oct. 3, 1999. It should be noted that Joseph Stiglitz, chief economist and vice president of the World Bank, resigned in Nov. 1999, presumably in connection with the dissenting views in his *Whither Reform?* See the reports by Richard W. Stevenson in *NYT,* Nov. 25, 1999; and by Janet Guttsman in *WP,* Nov. 25, 1999.

128. Michael Kelly in *WP,* Nov. 10, 1999.

129. Stephen S. Rosenfeld, ibid., May 21, 1999.

130. David Ignatius, ibid., Sept. 27, 1999; William Safire in *NYT,* Sept. 9, 1999.

131. Karen Dawisha quoted by D. W. Miller in *Chronicle of Higher Education,* Sept. 3, 1999, p. A24; Charles H. Fairbanks Jr. in *Journal of Democracy,* April 1999, p. 52; Yoshiko Herrera, Program on New Approaches to Russian Security (Harvard University Davis Center), Policy Memo Series, no. 85, Oct. 1999, p. 82. Another scholar thinks there may be "an emerging consensus that the original assumptions attached to 'transition' are erroneous." Glennys Young in *Slavic Review,* Summer 1999, p. 493.

132. For more on this theme, see my *Sovieticus,* pp. 35–38.

133. Vladimir Ryzhkov quoted by Celestine Bohlen in *NYT,* May 16, 1999.

Part II

1. *WP,* Nov. 8, 1998.

2. "Can America Convert Russia?" and "America's Failed Crusade" originated as congressional testimony, which served no useful purpose that I could detect. A longer version of the first article appeared as "American Policy and Russia's Future," *The Nation,* April 12, 1993, pp. 476–85.

3. "Clinton's Yeltsin, Yeltsin's Russia," *The Nation,* Oct. 10, 1994, pp. 373–76. I put the lines in "America's Failed Crusade."

4. Martin Malia in *Journal of Democracy,* April 1999, p. 41; Jeffrey Sachs in *Central European Economic Review,* reprinted in *JRL,* Oct. 27, 1999; William Pfaff in *International Herald Tribune,* Sept. 2, 1999.

Similarly, see Scott M. Blacklin in *Harriman Review,* June 1999, p. 9; and Stephen Holmes quoted by Lynnley Browning in *Boston Globe,* Oct. 10, 1999.

5. Among Russia scholars in the United States who dissented consistently throughout the 1990s (but who may nonetheless disagree with arguments made in this book) were Robert V. Daniels, Jerry Hough, Peter Reddaway, and the scholarly journalist Abraham Brumberg. For nonspecialist economists, see, e.g., Stephen S. Cohen and Andrew Schwartz in *American Prospect,* Spring 1993, pp. 99–108; David M. Kotz in *The Nation,* April 19, 1993, pp. 514–16; and the American signers of the joint statement in *NG,* July 1, 1996, five of them Nobel laureates.

6. See, e.g., Henry Kissinger in *WP,* March 23, 1993; Patrick J. Buchanan in *New York Post,* March 24, 1993; Owen Harries in *New Republic,* Oct. 10, 1994, pp. 24–31; and Rowland Evans and Robert D. Novak in *WP,* March 6, 1995. As early as 1990, former President Richard M. Nixon worried about the missionary impulse: "I'm not enthused about this idea of sending our political experts over and telling these poor people how to win an election. I think it's a little silly and even insulting." He did not, however, mind sending "economic experts." Interview in *Time,* April 2, 1990, p. 48.

7. These lines of the poet Fyodor Tyutchev, who was the subject of a master's thesis by Deputy Secretary of State Strobe Talbott, were actually quoted to a Russian audience by the secretary of state himself shortly after Yeltsin's assault on the Parliament. See below, n. 12. For the magazine, see *Economist,* Dec. 18, 1999, p. 15. For Churchill's aphorism, see Lynnley Browning in *Boston Globe,* Oct. 10, 1999; Graham T. Allison, ibid., March 27, 2000; and Martin Wolf in *Financial Times,* March 29, 2000.

8. Several of the best American correspondents of the period reworked their reporting into books. See Hedrick Smith, *The Russians* (New York, 1976); Robert G. Kaiser, *Russia* (New York, 1976); and David K. Shipler, *Russia: Broken Idols, Solemn Dreams* (New York, 1983). Smith and Shipler reported for the *NYT,* Kaiser, for the *WP.*

9. Quoted by Elaine Sciolino in *NYT,* Dec. 6, 1994. The Russian translation of my article appeared in *NG,* Nov. 12, 1992, and was frequently quoted thereafter. For the U.S. press, see, e.g., Dimitri Simes in *WP,* July 17, 1994; Thomas L. Friedman in *NYT,* April 26, 1995; and Jim Hoagland in *International Herald Tribune,* July 1–2, 1995. For an American scholar's adaptation, see Leo Cooper, *Russia and the World* (New York, 1999), pp. 3, 169, 171, and chap. 10. For the Russ-

ian press, see Aleksandr Golts in *JRL,* Oct. 22, 1999; Andrei Serov in *Izvestiia,* Jan. 27, 2000; and Aleksei Arbatov in *Komsomolskaia pravda,* Feb. 25, 2000.

10. See Valerii Vyzhutovich in *Izvestiia,* May 4, 1994; Kronid Liubarskii and Aleksandr Sobianin in *Novoe vremia,* no. 15, 1995, pp. 6–12; *East European Constitutional Review,* Spring 1994, pp. 19–20; and Shevtsova, *Yeltsin's Russia,* pp. 96–97.

11. Yuri Burtin in *Moscow News,* Sept. 20–Oct. 6, 1994.

12. Warren Christopher, speech in Moscow, Oct. 23, 1993, U.S. Department of State Dispatch, vol. 4, no. 43. For Russian democrats, see Boris Kagarlitsky in *Progressive,* Dec. 1993, pp. 27–31. For the Clinton administration in 1993, see Michael Dobbs in *WP Magazine,* June 9, 1996, p. 29; and John Lloyd in *NYT Magazine,* Aug. 15, 1999, p. 39. For the characterizations, see Bill Keller in *NYT Book Review,* March 19, 2000, p. 6; and Michael Wines and Celestine Bohlen in *NYT,* Jan. 9, 21, 2000. For a protest against this "story line," see Matt Bivens in *Moscow Times,* Jan. 20, 2000.

13. For an insider's account of the struggle, see Aleksandr Korzhakov, *Boris Eltsin: Ot rassveta do zakata* (Moscow, 1997).

14. Katrina vanden Heuvel and I reported these comments in a letter from Moscow in *The Nation,* July 18, 1996, pp. 3–5. Similarly, see Korzhakov, *Boris Eltsin,* pp. 361–86.

15. See my report with Katrina vanden Heuvel cited in the preceding note. Our source was Yavlinsky.

16. As reported by Vladimir Shlapentokh in *JRL,* Nov. 11, 1999; and *WP,* Nov. 8, 1999.

17. *Current Digest of the Post-Soviet Press,* Feb. 2, 2000, p. 6.

18. See, e.g., Evgenii Toddes, "V otvet Stivenu Koenu," *Russkaia mysl* (Paris), Jan. 30–Feb. 5, 1997.

19. *Moscow Times,* Dec. 21, 1996. I should add that the paper had reprinted my article on Dec. 17 and that its editors and editorial policy have since changed very considerably.

20. See, e.g., Aleksandr Minkin's report on Alfred Kokh in *Novaia gazeta,* Nov. 2, 1998.

21. See, e.g., Seymour M. Hersh, "Saddam's Best Friend," *New Yorker,* April 5, 1999, pp. 32, 35–41, where, among other charges and based on hearsay, Primakov is accused of being on Saddam's payroll. Hersh's unsubstantiated charges continue to circulate. See, e.g., Peter Conradi and Mark Franchetti in the *Sunday Times* (UK), May 21, 2000. Similarly, well after Primakov's ouster, the *New Yorker* char-

acterized him as "autocratic" and an "ex-spook." See David Remnick, ibid., Dec. 20, 1999, pp. 33–34. General U.S. media attitudes
toward Primakov were typified by the titles of two editorial comments, "Beware Primakov" and "Fire Primakov." See, respectively,
William Safire in *NYT,* Sept. 17, 1998; and the *WSJ* editorial of
March 12, 1999. As for official U.S. attitudes toward Primakov, an
insider remarked confidentially, "They hate him." For Primakov's
own account of his political career before becoming prime minister,
see Evgenii Primakov, *Gody v bolshoi politike* (Moscow, 1999).

22. See, e.g., Alfred Kokh quoted by Aleksandr Minkin in *Novaia gazeta,* Nov. 2, 1998; and Andrei Kozyrev in *WSJ Europe,* May 6, 1999. I
heard such assertions from Anatoly Chubais when he visited Washington and New York in 1999. See also, for U.S. journalists, Safire
and the *WSJ* editorial cited in the preceding note; for the "nightmare," Elaine Sciolino in *NYT,* May 19, 1996; and for "long-
despised," Eugene Rumer in *JRL,* Jan. 6, 2000.

23. Immediately after his appointment, Stepashin spoke as a praetorian:
"Regardless of any political situation, I shall never allow myself to leave
or betray the President." Quoted in *Moscow Times* editorial of May 20,
1999. After being fired by Yeltsin, Stepashin joined Yavlinsky's Yabloko
Party and was elected to the new Duma in Dec. 1999. In the 2000 presidential election, he deserted Yavlinsky in favor of Putin.

24. Evgenii Popov in *Sovetskaia Rossiia,* June 5, 1999; and, similarly,
Maksim Iusin in *Izvestiia,* June 4, 1999.

25. Certainly, that was Stepashin's understanding. Speaking to business
groups on a visit to the United States as prime minister, he assured
them, with no regard for possible electoral outcomes, "As a former
head of counter-intelligence for my country, I will now reveal to you
the most important secret: Communists will never again be victorious in Russia. . . . They will never return. No one will allow this to
happen." Quoted in *Sovetskaia Rossiia,* July 29, 1999. Stepashin later
felt the need to declare, "I am not Pinochet, I am Stepashin." Quoted by Dmitrii Agronovskii, ibid., Aug. 3, 1999. For the praetorian
theme, see Dmitrii Furman in *Obshchaia gazeta,* Feb. 10–16, 2000;
Pyotr Aven quoted by Ian Traylor in *Guardian* (UK), March 31,
2000; and Albats in *Novaia gazeta*, June 5, 2000.

26. Sergei Stepashin in *NG,* Jan. 14, 2000. For Primakov, see Michael
Wines in *NYT,* Jan. 20, 2000.

27. Andrei Piontkovsky in *Russian Journal, JRL,* Dec. 4, 1999. Similarly,
see Pavel Felgenhauer in *Moscow Times,* Nov. 4, 1999; Igor

Malashenko in *Newsweek International,* Dec. 20, 1999; and Sergei Kovalev in *New York Review of Books,* Feb. 10, 2000, pp. 4–8.

28. Martin Malia in *WSJ,* March 15, 2000. For the administration's statements and "democratic transition," see U.S. officials and Graham Allison cited above, Part I, nn. 102, 105. For other journalists and scholars, see ibid., nn. 103, 104; and below, Part III, n. 116.

29. David Hoffman in *WP,* Jan. 26, 2000. Similarly, see David Hoffman and Sharon LaFraniere, ibid., Jan. 19, 20, 24, 2000; and Celestine Bohlen in *NYT,* Jan. 19, 2000. Academics made the same false prediction. See, e.g., Leon Aron in *Weekly Standard,* Jan. 17, 2000, pp. 13–15; and Mark Kramer in *WP,* Jan. 2, 2000.

30. *Moscow Times* editorial, Dec. 21, 1999; and, similarly, Vyacheslav Nikonov in *JRL,* Jan. 9, 2000. For "coup" and old-style elections, see above, Part I, n. 102. This leaves aside the likelihood of electoral fraud in Dec. 1999 and March 2000. For a discussion, see Pavel Felgenhauer in *Moscow Times,* March 30, 2000; and Laura Belin in *RFE/RL Russian Election Report,* April 7, 2000. In a private conversation, the Communist presidential candidate, Gennady Zyuganov, insisted original tallies showed that he received 38.40 percent of the vote to Putin's 43.45 percent, not 29 percent to nearly 53 percent. If so, a runoff would have been required.

31. Dmitrii Furman in *Obshchaia gazeta,* Jan. 13–19, 2000. On the media, see the European Institute for the Media report, *JRL,* Dec. 22, 1999; Paul Saunders, ibid., May 2, 2000; and Robert Coalson in *Moscow Times,* March 31, 2000. On submissive reactions, see Sergei Aleksyev in *Current Digest of the Post-Soviet Press,* April 26, 2000, p. 6; Natalya Shulyakovskaya in *Moscow Times,* Jan. 18, 2000; and, similarly, Liliia Shevtsova in *Literaturnaia gazeta,* May 24, 2000.

32. Michael Wines in *NYT,* Feb. 27, 2000; Martin Malia in *WSJ,* March 15, 2000; John Lloyd in *NYT Magazine,* March 19, 2000, p. 64. Similarly, see Jack F. Matlock Jr. in *NYT,* March 26, 2000; and David Hoffman on the war as "a series of miscalculations, rather than . . . a calculated ploy" in *WP,* March 20, 2000.

33. Elena Bonner interviewed by Natalia Yefimova in *Moscow Times,* Jan. 22, 2000; Mary Robinson cited by Jamie Dettmer in *Washington Times,* Feb. 21, 2000; Peter Bouckaert in *WP,* Feb. 25, 2000; Holly Cartner quoted by Daniel Williams, ibid., March 31, 2000; Council of Europe cited by AFP in *JRL,* March 13, 2000. Similarly, see Pavel Felgenhauer in *St. Petersburg Times,* Jan. 21, 2000; and Sergei Kovalev in *New York Review of Books,* Feb. 10, 2000, pp. 4–8.

34. For suspicions about the bombs, see Will Englund in *Baltimore Sun,* Jan. 14, 2000; Maura Reynolds in *LAT,* Jan. 15, 2000; Boris Kagarlitskii in *Novaia gazeta,* Jan. 24–30, 2000; and Matt Bivens in *Brill's Content,* July/August 2000, p. 124. Questions have also been raised about who was behind the Chechen invasion of Dagestan. See ibid. and Vitalii Tretiakov in *NG,* Oct. 12, 1999.

35. For examples of these charges, see Elena Bonner quoted by AFP in *JRL,* Jan. 27, 2000; Aleksandr Minkin cited by Ian Traynor in *Guardian* (UK), March 24, 2000; Mikhail Krugov in *Novaia gazeta,* March 27–April 2, 2000; and the document reported by Michael Wines in *NYT,* May 5, 2000.

36. Equally to the point, Andropov, a longtime party politician, was made head of the KGB in 1967 to restrain its leadership's resurgent political ambitions.

37. Aleksandr Shokhin in *NG,* Jan. 13, 2000.

38. Andrei Piontkovsky in *Russian Journal, JRL,* Feb. 13, 2000. For a favorable view of Putin's prospects as a leader, see Roi Medvedev, *Zagadka Putina* (Moscow, 2000). For Putin's presentation of himself, see Vladimir Putin, *First Person* (New York, 2000).

39. Pavel Valinov in *Current Digest of the Post-Soviet Press,* Dec. 29, 1999, p. 2. Similarly, see Igor Malashenko in *Newsweek International,* Dec. 20, 1999; Dmitrii Furman in *Obshchaia gazeta,* Feb. 10–16, 2000; and below, Part III, n. 26.

40. Andrei Piontkovsky in *Russian Journal, JRL,* Jan. 24, 2000. See, e.g., Chubais in *Current Digest of the Post-Soviet Press,* Jan. 12, 2000, pp. 10–11; and as reported by Elena Tokareva in *Obshchaia gazeta,* Jan. 20, 2000; and Nemtsov (with Ian Bremmer) in *NYT,* Jan. 5, 2000, and alone in *JRL,* March 1, 2000.

41. *NYT* editorial, Dec. 28, 1999; and, similarly, Lyudmila Telen in *Moscow News,* Dec. 22–28, 1999.

42. Boris Kagarlitsky in *JRL,* Feb. 17, 2000; and Andrei Piontkovsky in *Russian Journal, JRL,* March 12, 2000. Similarly, see Grigory Yavlinsky ibid., Feb. 13, 2000.

Part III

1. *NG,* Dec. 30, 1999.

2. Robert E. Rubin quoted in Reuters dispatch, *JRL,* March 19, 1999.

3. For the newspapers, see, respectively, Iraida Semenova and Aleksei Podymov in *Rossiiskaia gazeta,* Jan. 14, 2000; Svetlana Babaeva in *Izvestiia,* Feb. 29, 2000; and Margarita Vodianova and Konstantin Danov in *Obshchaia gazeta,* Dec. 23–29, 1999. For the survey, see the AFP dispatch in *CDI Russia Weekly,* Feb.18, 2000, in which seven of ten Russians said they were "poor." Two pro-reform papers put the level of actual poverty at about 50 to 55 percent. See *Argumenty i fakty,* cited in *RFE/RL Newsline,* March 10, 2000; and Sergei Karaganov in *Moscow News,* March 8–14, 2000. Astonishingly, over half the citizens of Moscow, Russia's most prosperous city by far, live below the poverty level. AFP dispatch, *JRL,* Feb. 29, 2000. On poverty more generally, see Bertram Silverman and Murray Yanowitch, *New Rich, New Poor, New Russia,* exp. ed. (Armonk, N.Y., 2000). For the shrinking population and "catastrophe," see Oksana Yablokova's report in *Moscow Times,* Jan. 26, 2000; and Valentin Pokrovsky quoted in AFP dispatch, *JRL,* Feb. 22, 2000.

4. Sergei Kovalev in *New York Review of Books,* Feb. 10, 2000, p. 7. For abuses, see the Human Rights Watch report *Confessions at Any Cost: Police Torture in Russia* (New York, 1999).

5. Even a longtime booster of Russia's "democratic transition" reported that the presidential election "is looking more like it is taken from a page in the history of the Soviet one-party state than from a pluralistic democracy." David Hoffman in *WP,* Jan. 14, 2000. For the media and elections, see the report by the European Institute for Media in *JRL,* Dec. 23, 1999; Boris Kagarlitsky, ibid., Jan. 14, 2000; Georgy Saratov, ibid., Jan. 24, 2000; above, Part I, n. 66, and Part II, nn. 30, 31; and Sarah Oates in *Problems of Post-Communism,* May–June 2000, pp. 3–14.

6. Sergei Markov quoted by Mikhail Delyagin and Delyagin himself in *JRL,* Jan. 29, 2000; Igor Oleinik in *Novaia gazeta,* Jan. 10–16, 2000; and Konstantin Titov quoted by Sophie Lambroschini in *JRL,* Jan. 18, 2000. For talk of a "police state" and "totalitarianism," see, e.g., Elena Bonner quoted by Paul Goble, ibid., Jan. 25, 2000; and Aleksandr Shokhin interviewed in *NG,* Jan. 13, 2000.

7. Pyotr Aven quoted by Ian Traynor in *Guardian* (UK), March 31, 2000. I have in mind, e.g., scores of books glorifying the national salvation role of the Soviet secret police and other intelligence agencies during World War II and the Cold War.

8. See Nikolai Popov in *JRL,* Dec. 10, 1999; Aleksandr Protsenko, ibid., Jan. 7, 2000; and for "fairness," the ROMIR survey, ibid., Jan. 25, 2000.

9. See the speech of Deputy Secretary of State Strobe Talbott at Oxford University on January 20, 2000, *JRL*, Jan. 25, 2000. Using similar language, a Russian state economist makes the same point. See Evgenii Gontmakher in *Trud*, Jan. 19, 2000.

10. For the surveys, see *JRL*, May 10, March 19, 2000; and *Obshchaia gazeta*, Dec. 16–22, 1999. For the toast, which was first noticed by Arnold Beichman in *Washington Times*, Jan. 10, 2000, see Akram Murtazaev in *Novaia gazeta*, Dec. 27, 1999–Jan. 2, 2000; and Grigorii Iavlinskii in *Obshchaia gazeta*, Dec. 30, 1999–Jan. 12, 2000.

11. For *Smuta* in history and today, see Robert C. Tucker, "What Time Is It in Russian History?," in Catherine Merridale and Chris Ward, eds., *Perestroika: The Historical Perspective* (London, 1991), pp. 34–45. Putin himself made the same analogy with 1917. See *NG*, Dec. 30, 1999. Oddly, assuming he knows what it means, the same U.S. architect of the crusade just cited (n. 9) also thinks the 1990s were a decade of *Smuta* in Russia, which is in nearly total conflict with his own claims for the "transition."

12. Thomas L. Friedman in *NYT*, July 25, 1998. To be exact, Friedman argues that the United States backed Yeltsin because he and his "team" were "on the right side of history."

13. Reports by Andrei Stepanov in *Izvestiia*, Jan. 15, 2000; Interfax in *JRL*, Jan. 15, 2000; and Sergei Pravosudov in *NG*, Jan. 15, 2000.

14. *Moscow Times*, Jan. 5, 2000, July 13, 1999; and, similarly, ibid., June 3, 2000.

15. Peter Reddaway (with Dmitri Glinski) in *Journal of Democracy*, April 1999, pp. 19–34; Arnold L. Horelick in Lilia Shevtsova, *Yeltsin's Russia* (Washington, D.C., 1999), p. ix. Similarly, see Reddaway and Glinski, *The Tragedy of Russia's Reforms: Market Bolshevism Against Democracy* (Washington, D.C., 2000). For the Russian scholars, see Shevtsova, *Yeltsin's Russia,* and Roi Medvedev in *Rossiiskaia gazeta*, Jan. 6, 2000. Nikita Khrushchev's son Sergei, now an American citizen, calls Yeltsin's policies "anti-reform." *Knizhnoe obozrenie*, May 26, 1998, p. 23.

16. Nikita Petrov quoted by Michel Wines in *NYT*, Jan. 20, 2000.

17. As suggested indirectly by Putin's first major programmatic statements just before and after Yeltsin's resignation. See *NG*, Dec. 30, 1999; and *Izvestiia*, Feb. 25, 2000. Putin's implied criticism of Yeltsin's reforms was quickly noted by the Russian press. See, e.g., Vitalii Golovachev in *Trud*, Jan. 19, 2000. And although Putin was created by Yeltsin's Kremlin, he was presented to the country as a

young, healthy, forceful ruler capable of cleaning up messes and imposing order—that is, as a kind of anti-Yeltsin.

18. Fritz Ermarth in *JRL,* Jan. 20, 2000. The former Polish dissident Adam Michnik calls it "bandit liberalism." *NG,* Jan. 13, 2000.

19. Nor can anti-Communism alone be a sufficient criterion for making Russia policy today. When a hero of the East European anti-Communist revolution declares to a chorus of American journalistic applause, "Better an ill Russia than a healthy Soviet Union," we understand the suffering and sentiment involved. But it could logically mean: Better a nuclear Russia in collapse or anarchy, or alternatively a despotic Russia, than a reforming Soviet Union. See Vaclav Havel quoted by William Safire in *NYT,* Sept. 17, 1998.

20. See above, Part I, n. 126.

21. *NG,* Jan. 14, April 26, 2000. The 1997 version stressed "partnership" with the West as the foundation of Russian security.

22. Russia's previous security doctrine mandated their use only if there was a threat to the "very existence" of Russia as a sovereign nation. The 2000 version mandates their use "to repel armed aggression" if other means have failed. Ibid.

23. When Russian troops unexpectedly took control of the airport, the American supreme commander of NATO ordered the British commander of NATO forces in Kosovo to evict them. The Briton, whose refusal was upheld at higher levels, replied, "No, I'm not going to do that. It's not worth starting World War III." As reported by Elizabeth Becker in *NYT,* Sept. 10, 1999. According to an unnamed Western diplomat, "It brought Russia within a millimeter of conflict with the U.S., an absolute 'nyet' in Soviet days." Quoted by Robert D. Novak and Rowland Evans in *WP,* Nov. 29, 1999.

24. For the doctrine, see *NG,* Jan. 14, April 26, 2000. An example of popular views is a survey finding that 72 percent of Russians believe the United States would cheat on any nuclear-related treaties, as reported by Yelena Boldyreva in *Current Digest of the Post-Soviet Press,* Dec. 22, 1999, p. 12.

25. Even usually pro-American Russian politicians blame the United States for the deteriorating relationship. See, e.g., the remarks of Aleksei Arbatov in *JRL,* Jan. 8, Feb. 4, 2000; and Andrei Kokoshin in *RFE/RL Newsline,* Feb. 4, 2000.

26. Pavel Valinov in *Current Digest of the Post-Soviet Press,* Dec. 29, 1999, p. 2; and on "anti-Western sentiments," Aleksandr Verkhovskii in *Obshchaia gazeta,* Dec. 30, 1999. Similarly, for commentary on the

behavior of these "liberals," see Sergei Rogov quoted by Sophie Lambroschini in *JRL,* Nov. 18, 1999; and Lyudmila Telen in *Moscow News,* Dec. 22–28, 1999. See also above, Part II, n. 39.

27. Both a British and a Russian journalist have so characterized the system. See John Lloyd in *NYT Magazine,* Aug. 15, 1999, p. 52; and Andrei Piontkovsky in *Russian Journal, JRL,* Feb. 8, 2000.

28. Nikolai Shmelyov in *Current Digest of the Post-Soviet Press,* April 19, 2000, p. 12; Shevtsova, *Yeltsin's Russia,* p. 4. Similarly, see Reddaway and Glinski cited above, n. 15. The dissidents are quoted by Lars-Erik Nelson in *JRL,* Feb. 23, 2000.

29. This judgment too has already been passed. See, e.g., Steven Munson in *WP,* Feb. 6, 2000; and Peter Bouckaert, ibid., Feb. 25, 2000. When the Russian flag was raised over the rubble of Grozny, Putin also used the word *liberate.* Quoted by Lyoma Turpalov in an AP dispatch dated Feb. 6, 2000.

30. George Tenet quoted by Susan Ellis in a USIA release, *JRL,* Feb. 3, 2000. Similarly, see FBI Director Louis J. Freeh quoted by Douglas Farah in *WP,* Oct. 2, 1997.

31. Fritz W. Ermarth in *JRL,* Jan. 20, 2000. For other commentary on the matter, see Janine R. Wedel's *Collision and Collusion* and her article in *Democratizatsiya,* Fall 1999, pp. 469–500; Holman W. Jenkins Jr. in *WSJ,* Sept. 2, 1998, Sept. 1, 1999; Zbigniew Brzezinski, ibid., Sept. 3, 1999; Raymond Bonner in *NYT,* Dec. 26, 1999; and David Ignatius in *WP,* Jan. 9, 2000. According to the House Banking Committee chairman, the bank case is "seminally significant because it represents a verifiable incident where the financial system has been corrupted." Representative Jim Leach quoted by Timothy L. O'Brien in *NYT,* Feb. 18, 2000. See also above, Part I, n. 14. Similarly, see O'Brien with Joseph Kahn, ibid., March 17, 2000; and David Ignatius in *WP,* April 12, 2000. Russians have also alleged corrupt financial activities by American insiders. See, e.g., the charges by Sergei Glazev reported by Matt Taibbi in *The Exile, JRL,* May 17, 2000.

32. High-level Russian corruption was known at the highest U.S. levels at least as early as 1995, when the CIA informed Vice President Gore of its suspicions that his diplomatic partner, then Prime Minister Viktor Chernomyrdin, was himself corrupt. Gore dismissed the allegation. See the reports by James Risen in *NYT,* Nov. 23, 25, 1998. In some Russian political circles it is believed that Chernomyrdin has a fortune stashed abroad safeguarded by U.S. agencies, which

explains his pro-American activities, particularly during NATO's war against Yugoslavia. For what may be an allusion to this possibility, see John Lloyd in *NYT Magazine,* Aug. 15, 1999, p. 52. For an ongoing Russian investigation of corruption that apparently involves Chernomyrdin, see the unsigned article in *Moscow News,* April 19–25, 2000. Chernomyrdin has also been accused of having authorized cocaine traffic through Russia to the West while he was prime minister. See Oleg Lure's report in *Novaia gazeta,* Dec. 27, 1999–Jan. 2, 2000. Regarding corruption more generally, a former State Department official tells us that "anyone involved with Russia . . . knew about it all along." Testimony of Wayne Merry to a U.S. Senate committee, *JRL,* Sept. 24, 1999.

33. One harsh critic, e.g., recommends a crusade informed by "a new doctrine of transition—a new Washington consensus," by which he means a new "template or set of standards." Another actually suggests that the United States support a "military coup" in Moscow that would put the right "political forces" in power. See, respectively, Fritz W. Ermarth and Jerry F. Hough in *JRL,* Jan. 20, 16, 2000.

34. Senator Joseph R. Biden quoted by Eric Schmitt in *NYT,* Sept. 26, 1999.

35. *NG,* Dec. 30, 1999.

36. Retired General William Odom paraphrased and quoted by Lars-Erik Nelson in *Daily News* (New York), Jan. 2, 2000. As cited by Nelson, Richard Perle, once an implacable cold warrior, takes the same position. According to an insider, "some in Washington are suggesting that maybe Russia didn't matter so much after all." Fred Hiatt in *WP,* March 7, 1999. Similarly, see the view of Fareed Zakaria in *NYT,* March 26, 1997.

37. Thomas E. Graham Jr., "A World Without Russia?," *JRL,* June 11, 1999; Jim Hoagland in *WP,* Nov. 21, 1999; John Lloyd in *NYT Magazine,* Aug. 15, 1999, p. 64. Similarly, see Nicholas Eberstadt, "Russia: Too Sick to Matter?," *Policy Review,* June–July 1999, pp. 3–24; George Soros cited on the IMF in AFP dispatch, *JRL,* Feb. 3, 2000.

38. Senate testimony of Deputy Secretary of State Strobe Talbott, *JRL,* Sept. 24, 1999; National Security Adviser Samuel R. Berger in *WP,* Sept. 15, 1999; David Remnick in *New York Review of Books,* Aug. 12, 1993, p. 20; John M. Broder in *NYT,* Sept. 27, 1999; Fareed Zakaria, ibid., May 9, 1995; and Michael McFaul, Pomars Policy Memo Series, no. 69, Oct. 1999, p. 10. Similarly, see McFaul in *Foreign Pol-*

icy, Winter 1999–2000, pp. 58–71; Richard Cohen in *WP,* Sept. 14, 1999; *LAT* editorial, Nov. 8, 1999; Jim Hoagland on *The NewsHour with Jim Lehrer,* PBS, Dec. 23, 1999; British Prime Minister Tony Blair quoted by William Douglas in *WP,* Jan. 1, 2000; and William Safire in *NYT,* April 27, 2000. For an early protest against this widespread view, see Stephen S. Rosenfeld in *WP,* Jan. 31, 1997, who concludes, "And you had thought the world was now a safer place."

39. Michael Krepon quoted by Eric Schmitt in *NYT,* Sept. 5, 1999; the report of the Committee on Nuclear Policy in *Arms Control Today,* Jan.–Feb. 1999, pp. 15–19. Similarly, see Graham T. Allison, *Avoiding Nuclear Anarchy* (Cambridge, Mass., 1996); Bruce G. Blair in *WP,* Sept. 29, 1996; the study by Physicians for Social Responsibility reported by Tim Weiner in *NYT,* April 30, 1998; Andrew and Leslie Cockburn, *One Point Safe* (New York, 1997); Michael Krepon in *WP,* May 25, 1999; Lloyd J. Dumas, *Lethal Arrogance* (New York, 1999); the opinion of arms control analysts reported by Judith Miller in *NYT,* Feb. 5, 2000; Paul R. Josephson, *Red Atom* (New York, 2000), pp. 272–96; and Jimmy Carter in *WP,* Feb. 23, 2000. For an overview and inventory of the dangers, see Jonathan Schell, "The Gift of Time," special issue of *The Nation,* Feb. 2–9, 1998.

40. So that readers do not have to rely solely on my perception, in the view of the *WP,* "Russia is in a state of gradual collapse"; in the view of a leading Russian political scientist, the regime is "highly unstable and fragile"; and in the view of a historian, the Russian Federation is "crumbling" as did the Ottoman Empire. See *WP* editorial, May 13, 1999; Shevtsova, *Yeltsin's Russia,* p. 289; and Michael Reynolds in *WSJ Europe,* Sept. 24–25, 1999. Shevtsova and Igor Klyamkin, another leading Russian political scientist, give us a minimal statement of the situation: "Even the most confirmed optimist would have a hard time these days denying that Russia is in the midst of a very deep systemic crisis encompassing all areas of Russian life—the economy, the polity, the social sphere." *JRL,* Aug. 22, 1999.

41. Matthew Bunn and former Senator Sam Nunn quoted by H. Joseph Herbert, AP dispatch, *JRL,* Feb. 6, 2000; Graham T. Allison and Sam Nunn in *WP,* April 24, 2000. For secure materials and the lack of an inventory, see Bunn's *The Next Wave: Urgently Needed New Steps to Control Warheads and Fissile Material* (Washington, D.C., 2000); and on safeguarding stockpiles, Dumas, *Lethal Arrogance,* pp. 74–81. Similarly, on the need for an inventory, see the remarks of Governor

George W. Bush in *JRL*, Nov. 20, 1999. For tactical weapons, see Thomas W. Lippman in *WP*, Sept. 29, 1994; and William C. Potter and Nikolai Sokov in *International Herald Tribune*, May 31, 2000. In 1997, the issue of a tactical-weapons inventory was raised anew by General Aleksandr Lebed, who, having served as Kremlin national security chief, announced that forty-eight suitcase-size nuclear bombs were missing. His allegation was hotly denied in both Moscow and Washington, but supported by other testimony, leaving us without a definitive answer.

42. Thomas Halverson in *Bulletin of Atomic Scientists*, July–Aug. 1993, p. 43; statement of Senator Richard G. Lugar in *JRL*, Oct. 3, 1999; and the report summarized in *Izvestiia*, May 11, 2000

43. Michael Dobbs's report in *WP*, Feb. 13, 2000; and *RFE/RL Newsline*, March 29, 2000. Similarly, see James Rupert, ibid., April 19, 1996; Alan Cooperman, "The Next Chernobyl?," *U.S. News and World Report*, April 29, 1996, pp. 46–48; Rupert Cornwell in *Independent* (UK), Oct. 20, 1998; and Rod Nordland, "Where Is the Next Chernobyl?," *Newsweek*, Oct. 18, 1999, pp. 34–40. More than 16,000 safety standard violations were reported in Russia's nuclear energy sector in 1999. Itar-Tass dispatch, *JRL*, March 29, 2000.

44. Alan Cooperman in *U.S. News and World Report*, April 19, 1996, p. 47. Similarly, see Nordland, "Where Is the Next Chernobyl?"

45. Rupert Cornwell in *Independent* (UK), Oct. 20, 1998. Similarly, see Fred Barbash in *WP*, Oct. 11, 1996; Aleksandr Kurchatov, "New Chernobyl at Sea," *Moscow Times*, March 2, 1996; Greg Neale in *Electronic Telegraph* (UK), May 23, 1999; and Dmitri Litovkin, "100 Floating Chernobyls," *Moscow News*, Sept. 29–Oct. 5, 1999.

46. Yuri Balashov quoted by David Hoffman in *WP*, May 14, 1998. According to another Russian expert, "our missiles are old and no longer safe." Quoted in *RFE/RL Newsline*, Aug. 10, 1999.

47. Pavel Felgenhauer in *St. Petersburg Times*, Jan. 21, 2000.

48. See the study reported by Tim Weiner in *NYT*, April 30, 1998; and Philipp C. Bleek and Frank N. von Hippel in *WP*, Dec. 12, 1999. Similarly, see Judith Miller in *NYT*, Feb. 5, 2000, who reports that "some arms control analysts say that the threat of nuclear war is actually greater now"; the warning by former CIA Director James Woolsey on Military Newswire Service, June 18, 1996; the German study cited by Reuters, *JRL*, Aug. 12, 1997; Michael Krepon in *WP*, May 25, 1999; the information reported by Greg Schneider in *Baltimore Sun*, Aug. 27, 1999; Dumas, *Lethal Arrogance;* the experts cited

by Jonathan S. Landay in *Miami Herald,* Jan. 9, 2000; the scientists cited by William J. Broad in *NYT,* May 1, 2000; Russian experts themselves cited by James T. Hackett in *WSJ,* March 28, 1997; and Frank von Hippel and Bruce Blair in *WP,* June 6, 2000. For a failing component of Russia's early-warning system, see the report by David Hoffman, ibid., June 1, 2000.

49. See the examples cited by Andrei Piontkovsky and Brian Whitmore in *Moscow Times,* Sept. 23, Oct. 15, 1999; and by Robert Chandler in *Times Literary Supplement,* Dec. 3, 1999. Similarly, see the military officer quoted by David Filipov in *Boston Globe,* Oct. 6, 1999; Vladimir Zhirinovsky cited by Dmitri Glinski Vassiliev in *JRL,* Dec. 17, 1999; and Kursk Governor Aleksandr Rutskoi quoted by Marcus Warren in *Electronic Telegraph* (UK), Jan. 18, 2000.

50. See Pavel Felgenhauer in *Moscow Times,* Feb. 10, 2000, and, similarly, David Hoffman in *WP,* Aug. 31, 1999; Pavel Baev in *JRL,* May 21, 2000; and, on the use of tactical nuclear weapons, Potter and Sokov cited above, n. 41.

51. On such reports, see, e.g., General Aleksandr Lebed cited in *RFE/RL Caucasus Report,* Sept. 30, 1999; and Brian Whitmore in *Moscow Times,* Oct. 15, 1999. For security and public fear, see the AFP report, *JRL,* Sept. 10, 1999; Michael Evans in *Times* (UK), Oct. 1, 1999; and the survey poll reported in *Current Digest of the Post-Soviet Press,* Dec. 22, 1999, p. 12. In the first war, in 1994–96, there was considerable speculation in the Moscow press whether or not the Chechens might possess leftover Soviet nuclear devices. See, e.g., Aleksandr Pogonchenkov in *Moskovskii komsomolets,* Aug. 22, 1995; and Boris Vishnevskii in *Komsomolskaia pravda,* Dec. 1–8, 1995.

52. Strobe Talbott as cited above, n. 9. I borrow "happy talk" from James T. Hackett in *WSJ,* March 28, 1997.

53. According to a majority of foreign editorialists and analysts commenting on the tenth anniversary of the end of the Soviet bloc in Eastern Europe, the result "did not yield a safer and more stable order" but "more conflicts" and "chaos." See the U.S. State Department survey in *CDI Russia Weekly,* Nov. 12, 1999. For the possibility of officially sanctioned cocaine traffic, see above, n. 32.

54. I borrow the "archive" expression from the Italian journalist Giulietto Chiesa in *Moskva,* no. 5, 1999, p. 3, who also criticizes it.

55. On the "warping of intelligence analysis to fit official political agendas" in the Clinton administration, see Fritz W. Ermarth in *National Interest,* Spring 1999, pp. 11–13; and for a similar practice in

reporting by the U.S. embassy in Moscow, Donald Jensen interviewed in "Return of the Czar," PBS, May 9, 2000. For an example of revived Cold War thinking even among moderates in the political elite, see Representative James A. Leach, "The New Russian Menace," *NYT,* Sept. 10, 1999. As for popular attitudes, a 1999 survey found that 54 percent of Americans saw Russia as an enemy of the United States second only to China. Bloomberg dispatch, *JRL,* Sept. 1, 1999.

56. Russian analysts often commented on these incongruities. On the ratification of START II, see, e.g., Sergei Rogov in *NG,* Feb. 8, 2000; and on the relationship between Kosovo and Chechnya, Tatiana Matsuk in *JRL,* Feb. 19, 2000.

57. A Russian journalist observed, "The West, after all, was far more considerate toward the hostile Soviet Union than toward the more loyal Russia." Aleksandr Golts in *CDI Russia Weekly,* Oct. 22, 1999.

58. Grigory Yavlinsky quoted in Bloomberg dispatch, *JRL,* Oct. 6, 1999. Without changing the meaning, I have edited the English translation a bit.

59. Igor Volgin in *NG,* Sept. 7, 1999; Sergei Khrushchev quoted by Genine Babakian in *Moscow Times,* Jan. 15, 2000, who mentions Primakov in this connection. Similarly, see the popular hope for an "honorable" leader in the survey reported by APN in *JRL,* Jan. 20, 2000.

60. See, e.g., Sergei Markov, a pro-democracy analyst, in *JRL,* Jan. 29, 2000; and Anatolii Utkin in *NG,* April 12, 2000.

61. For the axis during the Cold War, see my *Rethinking the Soviet Experience: Politics and History Since 1917* (New York, 1985), p. 157; and my *Sovieticus: American Perceptions and Soviet Realities,* exp. ed. (New York, 1986), pt. 4. For a Russian comment on the revived, present-day axis, see Maksim Iusin in *Izvestiia,* June 4, 1999.

62. Michael McFaul in *WP,* March 3, 2000. Similarly, see Sarah E. Mendelson, Program on New Approaches to Russian Security (Harvard Davis Center), Policy Memo no. 144, April 2000. For the opposing and necessary view that "the nuclear threat must take precedent over . . . our desire to see democratic and economic reforms institutionalized in Russia," see Richard H. Haass in *Newsday,* Jan. 3, 2000.

63. See Jim Hoagland's critical characterization of the approach of Madeleine Albright in *WP,* Jan. 6, 2000; and Thomas L. Friedman in *NYT,* April 16, 1999.

64. See, e.g., Putin's pointed emphasis on different Russian and Anglo-

American attitudes about the role of the state, in *NG,* Dec. 30, 1999. For the preferences of the Russian people, see Shlapentokh cited below, n. 86.

65. See, for example, Gennadii Ziuganov's presidential campaign statement in *Rossiiskaia gazeta,* March 14, 2000; and the programs cited below, n. 80.

66. Martin Malia, *Russia under Western Eyes* (Cambridge, Mass., 1999), p. 411.

67. Charles William Maynes quoted by Tyler Marshall in *LAT,* Sept. 27, 1999. Similarly, see Anatol Lieven in *NYT,* March 17, 1999. For a benign Russian statement of this strategy, see the interview with Sergei Glazev in *Executive Intelligence Review,* July 23, 1999, p. 12.

68. Quoted by Michael R. Gordon in *NYT,* Nov. 10, 1999.

69. Andrei Piontkovsky, a Westernizer, quoting the poet Aleksandr Blok, in *Russian Journal, JRL,* Dec. 23, 1999.

70. See the report by Craig S. Smith in *NYT,* Feb. 9, 2000. For sales to China and India, see Nikolai Novichkov in *Moscow News,* May 10–16, 2000.

71. George F. Kennan, *American Diplomacy* (New York, 1952), p. 112. The article quoted here first appeared in *Foreign Affairs,* April 1951. Oddly enough, a primary architect of the American crusade received a more contemporary and intimate warning from the philosopher Isaiah Berlin, under whom he had once studied at Oxford and whom he revered. Upon hearing his former student's plan for Russia, Berlin replied, *"Surtout pas trop de zele."* U.S. Deputy Secretary of State Strobe Talbott in *JRL,* Jan. 25, 2000. For an opposing view— "Letting Russia be Russia . . . cannot be a sound policy"—see William G. Hyland, *Foreign Affairs,* no. 1, 1992, p. 48.

72. David Ignatius in *WP,* Sept. 9, 1999; Michael McFaul, "Getting Russia Right," *Foreign Policy,* Winter 1999–2000, pp. 65–67. Similarly, see McFaul's article in *WP,* March 3, 2000; and his Senate testimony, *JRL,* April 14, 2000.

73. Thomas Carothers, "Think Again: Civil Society," *Foreign Policy,* Winter 1999–2000, pp. 18–25. For another critique, see David Rieff, "The False Dawn of Civil Society," *The Nation,* Feb. 22, 1999, pp. 11–16. See also above, Part I, n. 63.

74. *NYT,* Nov. 14, 1999. For an entrepreneurial Columbia University institute, on the other hand, it happens to include environmental groups in the oil-rich Caspian Sea region. (*News from the Harriman Institute,* Feb. 2000, p. 9.) It might also mean the Russian Mafia.

(For a discussion, see V. G. Khoros, ed., *Grazhdanskoe obshchestvo.* [Moscow, 1998], pp. 228–56.) In the former Soviet Union, as in the West, a Belarus scholar tells us, "The notion of civil society is polemic and closely tied to the individual context." Larissa G. Titarenko in *Democratizatsiya,* Summer 1999, p. 415. Similarly, see John Ehrenberg, *Civil Society* (New York, 1999), p. 234, where we learn that "civil society is an unavoidably nebulous and elastic conception."

75. For an example of advocating funds "aimed at deepening Russian democracy" but none for the economy or impoverished people, see the editorial in *WP,* Dec. 1, 1998; and, similarly, for favoring budgetary austerity over poverty, *NYT* editorial, March 27, 1999.

76. See above, Part I, n. 102.

77. Even the leader of a minority democratic reform party tells us, "The Russian Parliament mirrors Russian society." Grigory A. Yavlinsky in *NYT,* Sept. 14, 1995.

78. As early as 1995, a Russian observer pointed out that the concept "economic reforms," like previous Marxist-Leninist ideas, was being officially defined in various and even contradictory ways. See Iurii Kozlov in *Rossiia,* Jan. 25–31, 1995.

79. A group including five Nobel laureates published its statement jointly with several Russian economists in *NG,* July 1, 1996. An abridged English-language version appeared in *JRL,* Jan. 11, 1999. Similarly, see David M. Kotz in *Central Europe Review,* Oct. 25, 1999, Internet publication; and Lawrence R. Klein and Marshall Pomer, eds., *The New Russia: Transition Gone Awry* (Stanford, 2000), esp. pt. 3.

80. For a range of critical and programmatic views, see, e.g., Grigory Yavlinsky quoted in RIA Novosti dispatch, *JRL,* Jan. 31, 2000; N. Shmelov in *Voprosy ekonomiki,* no. 8, 1999, pp. 49–63; L. I. Abalkin, *Vybor za Rossiei* (Moscow, 1998) and *Spasti Rossiiu* (Moscow, 1999); N. Petrakov and V. Perlamutrov in *Voprosy ekonomiki,* no. 3, 1997, pp. 74–83; N. Ia. Petrakov, *Russkaia ruletka* (Moscow, 1999) and his articles in *Rossiiskaia gazeta,* Dec. 17, 1999, and *Obshchaia gazeta,* Jan. 13, 2000; Stanislav Menshikov in *Moscow Tribune,* Feb. 15, 2000; Sergei Glazev interviewed in *NG,* Sept. 24, 1999, and his *Genotsid* (Moscow, 1997); Aleksandr Potapov in *Rossiiskaia gazeta,* Nov. 16, 1999; the press conference by Gennady Zyuganov, Pyotr Romanov, Sergei Glazev, and Viktor Vedmanov in *JRL,* Feb. 18, 2000; and O. T. Bogomolov, *Moia letopis perekhodnogo vremeni* (Moscow, 2000). Implicitly, Putin expressed a similar view in *NG,* Dec. 30, 1999.

According to Petrakov, "it has become fashionable to speak about the country's economic security." *Obshchaia gazeta,* March 2–8, 2000. See also above, Part I, n. 51.

81. For this point, I am indebted to Professor James R. Millar, the eminent specialist on the Russian economy. Similarly, see Paul Starobin, "What Went Wrong," *National Journal,* Dec. 4, 1999, pp. 3450–57; and David M. Kotz in *JRL,* Oct. 27, 1999. According to a 1993 report, a senior IMF director argued for a Marshall Plan–like approach to Russia but was ignored. See the appeal submitted by W. George Krasnow in *JRL,* Feb. 23, 1999.

82. For the New Deal and FDR, see, e.g., N. Petrakov and V. Perlamutrov in *Voprosy ekonomiki,* no. 3, 1997, pp. 77–78, 82; Anatoly Sobchak quoted by Michael Wines in *NYT,* Jan. 2, 2000; Gennady Zyuganov in *JRL,* Feb. 15, 2000; and Anatolii Utkin in *NG,* April 12, 2000. For Keynes, see N. Shmelov in *Voprosy ekonomiki,* no. 8, 1999, p. 62, whose title is "On Consensus in Russian Economic and Social Policy"; Iraida Semenova and Aleksei Podymov in *Rossiiskaia gazeta,* Jan. 14, 2000; and Aleksandr Potapov, ibid., Nov. 3, 1999, who comments also on "Putin's Third Way" and Russia's Truth." See also Putin himself cited below, n. 84. For a similar perception of a "Moscow Consensus," see Clifford G. Gaddy and Barry W. Ickes in *Brookings Review,* Winter 1999, pp. 44–48.

83. N. Petrakov and V. Perlamutrov in *Voprosy ekonomiki,* no. 3, 1997, p. 82.

84. See, e.g., Putin's comments on the state, as cited above, n. 64, and in *Izvestiia,* Feb. 25, 2000. A much admired Russian economist put it this way: "In Russia today, there is no real force other than the state capable of solving these problems, and there will not be one for a long time." Nikolai Shmelov in *Voprosy ekonomiki,* no. 8, 1999, p. 54.

85. Charles Krauthammer in *WP,* Feb. 9, 1996; similarly, the opinion of London's International Institute for Strategic Studies as reported in a Reuters dispatch by David Ljunggren, *JRL,* May 4, 1999.

86. On official contempt for the poor and the preferences of the Russian people, see the polling data presented by Vladimir Shlapentokh in *Europe-Asia Studies,* Nov. 1999, pp. 1167–81, and in *Communist and Post-Communist Studies,* Dec. 1999, pp. 453–60. In the former article (p. 1168), the onetime "young-reformer" privatizer Alfred Kokh is quoted as saying that "the Russians deserved their miserable fate." For popular preferences, see also the poll results reported by Anna

Zakatnova in *Current Digest of the Post-Soviet Press,* May 24, 2000, p. 12. For Putin, see above, n. 84.

87. Nikolai Shmelov in *Voprosy ekonomiki,* no. 8, 1999, p. 52.

88. For examples of these proposals, see above, n. 80.

89. N. Petrakov and V. Perlamutrov in *Voprosy ekonomiki,* no. 3, 1997, p. 79; Ekaterina Borisova and Tatiana Degtiareva in *Rossiiskaia gazeta,* June 9, 1999; Pavel Bunich quoted by Yevgenia Borisova in *Moscow Times,* Dec. 2, 1999. Another source gives an even greater discrepancy between the value and the price—$1 trillion of state property sold for $5 billion. *Ekonomika i zhizn,* no. 10, 1999, *JRL,* March 13, 2000. The Russian Communist Party is, of course, the main advocate of some renationalization, but even the former U.S. chief economist of the World Bank thinks it is necessary. See Joseph E. Stiglitz quoted by Louis Uchitelle in *NYT,* Dec. 3, 1999. During his rise to the presidency, Putin adamantly opposed any "deprivatization," but it may not remain his position. See *Current Digest of the Post-Soviet Press,* Dec. 22, 1999, pp. 12–13.

90. Some Russian economists estimate that the government could muster about three-fourths of what is needed. See *Ekonomika i zhizn* cited in the preceding note. For "genetic code," see Vladimir Putin, *First Person* (New York, 2000), p. 186.

91. Pension and state wage arrears, which seem to have totaled about $2 billion to $3 billion in late 1999 and then declined to about $1.5 billion in early 2000, are difficult to estimate because the government rarely reveals their full dimensions. Putin has promised to pay them in full very soon, but even if he does, arrears will almost certainly grow again when world oil prices, which helped Moscow reduce them, fall.

92. Mortgage lending programs have been proposed by U.S. Representative Curt Weldon and former Senators Gary Hart and Gordon Humphrey, and a modest one (in dollars) announced by the U.S. Russia Investment Fund in March 2000. See, respectively, *JRL,* Sept. 17, 1999; the Hart-Humphrey letter in *WP,* Feb. 11, 1999; and the Reuters report, *JRL,* March 15, 2000.

93. Though it seems implausible, and excludes Grozny, the Russian government puts the cost of damage done in Chechnya at 7 to 10 billion rubles, considerably less than $1 billion. See the MN File in *Moscow News,* April 12–18, 2000; and Yevgenia Pismennaya, ibid., May 3–9, 2000.

94. Estimates of Russia's total external debt vary, ranging as high as

$195 billion. I have taken the 1999 estimate of the International Institute of Finance.

95. William Safire in *NYT,* Sept. 9, 1999. Most Russian proponents of the new Moscow consensus count on retrieving some of these funds. See, e.g., Nikolai Petrakov in *Obshchaia gazeta,* Jan. 13–19, 2000; and Sergei Glazev in *NG,* Sept. 24, 1999.

96. Michael Hudson in *JRL,* Nov. 24, 1999; Louise I. Shelley in *NYT,* Feb. 26, 1999.

97. Louise I. Shelley in *NYT,* Feb. 26, 1999.

98. Many experts blame the administration for failing to lead in this area. See, e.g., Thomas B. Graham quoted by David Hoffman in *WP,* April 17, 1996; Bruce G. Blair, ibid., Sept. 29, 1996; John Mearsheimer quoted by Steve Chapman in *Chicago Tribune,* Dec. 12, 1999; the report cited by H. Joseph Hebert in an AP dispatch, *JRL,* Feb. 2, 2000; and Jimmy Carter in *WP,* Feb. 23, 2000. Similarly, see the other experts cited above, n. 39.

99. Jon B. Wolfsthal quoted by John Donnelly and David Beard in *Boston Globe,* Feb. 26, 2000.

100. A number of experts have made these or similar proposals. See, e.g., Bruce G. Blair in *WP,* Sept. 29, 1996; Bruce Blair, Harold Feiveson, and Frank von Hippel, ibid., Nov. 12, 1997; Stansfield Turner, ibid., Nov. 1, 1999; the Committee on Nuclear Policy in *Arms Control Today,* Jan.–Feb. 1999, pp. 15–19; the proposals reported in *NYT,* Dec. 10, 1999; Stephen S. Rosenfeld in *WP,* March 6, 2000; and von Hippel and Blair, ibid., June 6, 2000. In early 2000, Russia proposed cutting warheads to 1,500, but the American side refused, insisting the United States needed at least 2,000 to 2,500. See Steven Mufson's report, ibid., Jan. 28, 2000. During the 2000 presidential campaign, Governor George W. Bush suggested that, if elected, he might adopt some of these proposals, at least in part. See below, n. 121.

101. Even its proponents acknowledge that "the Russians could clearly overwhelm the system." Bill Carpenter quoted by Bradley Graham in *WP,* Jan. 17, 2000. Similarly, see the findings of scientists reported by Vernon Loeb, ibid., April 12, 2000. Indeed, the U.S. government gave the same assurance to the Russian side, as reported by Steven Lee Myers and Jane Perlez in *NYT,* April 28, 2000.

102. E.g., in early 2000, Russian and foreign scientists completed a comprehensive database of dangerous sources of nuclear contamination on former Soviet territory. RIA Novosti report, *JRL,* March 31, 2000.

103. For this proposal, see the reports by Greg Schneider in *Baltimore Sun*, Aug. 27, 1999; and Jonathan S. Landay in *Miami Herald*, Jan. 9, 2000. For the Russian ministry's plan, see Michael Dobbs in *WP*, March 11, 2000.

104. Matthew Bunn cited by John Donnelly and David Beard in *Boston Globe*, Feb. 26, 2000. Funding for some programs has actually been reduced. See, e.g., the report by Walter Pincus in *WP*, Nov. 12, 1999. For the $10 million announced by Secretary of State Albright in Moscow, see Reuters dispatch, Jan. 25, 1999.

105. Matthew Bunn quoted by H. Josef Hebert, AP dispatch, *JRL*, Feb. 7, 2000.

106. Steve Chapman in *Chicago Tribune*, Dec. 12, 1999.

107. Aleksei Arbatov quoted by Paul Tooher in *JRL*, Feb. 4, 2000. Arbatov is a democratic, pro-Western politician.

108. Aleksandr Golts quoted in AFP dispatch, ibid., March 22, 2000. Accordingly, on March 31, Putin restated the Kremlin's intention to modernize its nuclear arsenals.

109. For an early effort to turn this presumption into a strategic doctrine, see Zbigniew Brzezinski in *Foreign Affairs*, March–April 1994, pp. 67–82.

110. For a similar argument, see Jonathan Power in *Boston Globe*, Dec. 6, 1999.

111. Energy Secretary Bill Richardson quoted by David Ignatius in *WP*, Jan. 26, 2000.

112. For U.S. relations with these regimes, see Wayne Merry, "Coddling Dictators," *The Nation*, Jan. 31, 2000, pp. 5–6.

113. U.S. politicians sometimes imply that a fulsome relationship with the UN is impossible because the organization is unpopular. In fact, some 80 percent of Americans favor strengthening the UN. See Steven Kull and I. M. Destler in *Chronicle of Higher Education*, Sept. 3, 1999, p. B8.

114. For reports on this development, see Roger Cohen in *NYT*, Jan. 14, Feb. 2, 2000; and Suzanne Daley, ibid., April 9, 2000. While anti-Americanism is growing, half the Russians surveyed favored strengthened ties with Europe. ROMIR report in *JRL*, May 16, 2000.

115. Quoted, respectively, by Will Englund in *Baltimore Sun*, April 9, 2000; and Ian Traynor and Ewen MacAskill in *Guardian* (UK), April 11, 2000. Similarly, see Vladimir Putin, *First Person*, p. 169, where the new Russian president says, "We are Europeans"; and proposals

for a new European Union relationship with Russia in *Financial Times,* April 25, 2000.

116. Bill Keller's review of Leon Aron's *Yeltsin* in *NYT Book Review,* March 19, 2000, pp. 1, 6; Fred Hiatt in *WP,* March 23, 2000; Jack F. Matlock Jr. in *NYT,* March 26, 2000; Martin Malia's review of Aron in *WSJ,* March 15, 2000; Jeffrey Sachs in *Washington Monthly,* March 2000, p. 37; Nicolai N. Petro (with Robert Bruce Ware) in *JRL,* April 10, 2000. For Matlock, see also his review of Aron's book in *LAT Book Review,* May 14, 2000.

117. For this paragraph and the preceding one, see, respectively, the smi.ru commentary in *JRL,* May 24, 2000; Robert Legvold quoted by Eric Schmitt in *NYT,* Sept. 26, 1999; Rose Brady in *Business Week,* March 13, 2000; Michael Wines in *NYT,* May 11, 2000, and David Hoffman quoting Al Breach in *WP,* May 11, 2000; Graham Allison cited and summarized by David Nyhan in the *Boston Globe,* March 26, 2000; Johanna Granville in *Demokratizatsiya,* Winter 2000, p. 39; George Soros in the *New York Review of Books,* April 13, 2000, p. 12; Michael McFaul in *JRL,* April 14, 2000; and *WP,* June 1, 2000. Similarly, see the *NYT* editorial, June 3, 2000.

118. Thomas E. Graham Jr. and Michael McFaul, in *JRL,* April 13, 14, 2000; Harley Balzer, in *JRL,* Feb. 29, 2000; John Lancaster, in *WP,* March 28, 2000; Thomas L. Friedman in *NYT,* March 10, 2000. Similarly, on NATO and a failure to see Russia's nuclear threats, see Robert Kagan in *WP,* April 10, 2000. Earlier, Kagan told readers that there is only one "present danger" in the world—an underfunded U.S. military budget. Ibid., March 19, 2000. For the silence of expert Russia-watchers, see also those interviewed in the PBS documentary film *Return of the Czar,* broadcast on May 9, 2000.

119. AP dispatches by Walter R. Mears, June 5 and 6, 2000. For Clinton's speech, see *JRL,* June 6, 2000. For the preceding paragraph, see, respectively, Strobe Talbott's testimony to a Senate committee, *JRL,* April 5, 2000; Madeleine Albright quoted by Charles A. Radin in *Boston Globe,* April 8, 2000. Similarly, see Thomas R. Pickering's dismissal of "Putinology" in *JRL,* April 2, 2000.

120. See, e.g., the speech in Moscow by the IMF's acting director Stanley Fischer, *JRL,* April 12, 2000. For "work in progress," see Talbott and Pickering cited in the preceding note.

121. Daryl G. Kimball quoted by Sharon LaFraniere in *WP,* April 22, 2000. For the UN conference, see the report by Colum Lynch, ibid., April 25, 2000; and, for Bush's proposals, the text of his remarks in

NYT, May 24, 2000. According to a U.S. participant in an American-Russian study cosponsored by the Carnegie Endowment for International Peace, the "enormous power of the United States is creating what many in Russia would call a rogue hegemon." Robert Legvold, *JRL,* Jan. 25, 2000. For more general skepticism about the U.S. commitment to arms control, see William Drozdiak in *WP,* June 15, 2000.

122. Condoleezza Rice quoted by John Simpson in *Electronic Telegraph* (UK), Jan. 16, 2000. It should be recorded that in a speech at Brown University on March 3, 2000, the losing candidate in the Democratic primaries, former Senator Bill Bradley, criticized the Clinton administration's Russia policy as "perilously counterproductive." See also Bradley's post-campaign book, *The Journey From Here* (New York, 2000), chap. 8. A third-party candidate, Patrick J. Buchanan, also criticized the administration for "treating Russia as a defeated nation." See the excerpt from his speech, *JRL,* Nov. 23, 1999. In a major foreign policy statement, Rice did not include Russian nuclear threats among her candidate's "key priorities." *Foreign Affairs,* Jan.–Feb. 2000, pp. 46–47.

123. See, e.g., the interview with Aleksei Arbatov, *JRL,* Feb. 3, 2000; and the remarks of Vladimir Lukin, ibid., Jan. 25, 2000.

124. Anatolii Utkin in *Svobodnaia mysl,* no. 6, 1999, p. 35.

125. For this remarkable development, see Robert English, *Russia and the Idea of the West: Gorbachev, Intellectuals, and the End of the Cold War* (New York, 2000).

INDEX

About the Author

Stephen F. Cohen is Professor of Russian Studies and History at New York University and Professor of Politics Emeritus at Princeton University, where for many years he was also director of the Russian Studies Program. Cohen grew up in Owensboro, Kentucky. He earned his undergraduate and master's degrees at Indiana University and his Ph.D. at Columbia University. He has received several honors, including nomination for a National Book Award and two Guggenheim Fellowships. Cohen's other books include *Bukharin and the Bolshevik Revolution: A Political Biography*; *Rethinking the Soviet Experience: Politics and History Since 1917*; and *Sovieticus: American Perceptions and Soviet Realities*. In addition to his articles for newspapers and magazines—his "Sovieticus" column in *The Nation* won a 1985 Newspaper Guild Page One Award—Cohen is a frequent commentator on television and consultant on Russian affairs for CBS News. With the producer Rosemarie Reed, he has also been project adviser and correspondent for three documentary films about Russia: *Conversations with Gorbachev*; *Russia Betrayed?*; and *Widow of the Revolution*. Cohen has visited and lived in Soviet and post-Soviet Russia regularly for twenty-five years.